THE HORSEMAN'S GUIDE

THE HORSEMAN'S GUIDE

E. HARTLEY EDWARDS

With a foreword by Raymond Brooks-Ward

COUNTRY LIFE BOOKS

© Copyright E. Hartley Edwards 1969

ISBN 0 600 43176 2

Reprinted in 1970, 1973, 1974, 1976

Published for Country Life Books by
THE HAMLYN PUBLISHING GROUP LIMITED
LONDON · NEW YORK · SYDNEY · TORONTO
Astronaut House, Feltham, Middlesex, England

Printed in Great Britain by
Hazell Watson & Viney Ltd
Aylesbury, Bucks

*To Michael of Kishmul (Poochie), our Dachshund,
who kept me company during the many hours
involved in writing this book, and who died on his
third birthday, just as it neared completion*

Contents

Foreword

Before the last war riding was very much a rich man's sport, but with greater leisure time and more money to spend the increase in the popularity of riding has been enormous, and the Government now regards it as a growth sport. The fundamental difference to the pre-war years is, however, that few people can afford their own grooms. Most people who have taken up riding themselves or encouraged their children to do so have had no previous background with horses, and cannot just turn the animal over to a groom after a day's hunting or riding. This is where Captain Hartley Edwards comes in, for he is essentially a do-it-yourself man, fully aware of the problems facing a family about to embark on its first horse or pony.

In this book can be found most of the answers to anxious questions. He takes us patiently through the various steps from how to buy a horse, to keeping it, feeding it, developing an understanding of its ailments, and finally to riding it.

Hartley Edwards is the first to admit that many books have been devoted to the Horse and that many views expressed are the exact opposites to each other. The great difference here is the underlying certainty running through the book that this is a man who has had to do it all himself on a limited budget. He states clearly and concisely what he feels is the right method, but is not afraid to give other people's opinions however opposite they may be. Having read the book, I can't help feeling that Mrs. Hartley Edwards is sometimes the long-suffering groom, but at least the horse is shared by the family!

The author, the Editor of *Riding*, is a keen foxhunter and a dedicated and tireless worker for the Riding Club movement. No mother with a small child and a new pony should be without the book—and this goes for father too.

Raymond Brooks-Ward, The British Horse Society,
35 Belgrave Square, London, SW1.

Preface

There are many, very many, books on horses and it is probable that no other animal has attracted so great a wealth of literature. But then probably no other animal attracts so much devotion, and often controversy, too, or exerts so great an influence on the lives of his admirers.

More and more people each year seem to fall under the strange influence that the horse is able to exert, and more and more of them are fixed with an ardent desire to become his 'faithful servant'. There are many reasons advanced as to why this should be so.

Some see it as an urgent human need to maintain a relationship with a living creature of another species, before the ability to do so is lost for ever. They see it as a reaction against the advance of automation and urbanisation, and as an escape from a world which accepts the necessity of the Bomb. The more materially minded regard it as an inevitable result of an affluent society with leisure on its hands and money in its pocket. There are, I believe, people who hold that the ownership of a horse or pony is a form of social snobbery or one-upmanship. And, of course, in 1968, there are bound to be some who relate horse-ownership, horse-riding and even horse-admiration with a form of sexual motivation.

Whatever the truth may be (for myself I just enjoy horses without indulging in an analysis of my reasons for doing so) the cult of the horse goes on increasing and as a result the literature of the horse is enlarged correspondingly.

It is not possible, in my view, to learn to ride or to care for horses from books alone, and certainly not from this one.

Nevertheless, the written word is an important, and even an essential, factor in an equestrian education. However bad the book, there is always something to be learned from it—even if it is only what not to do. This is, perhaps, part of the fascination of the horse, for even the greatest of horsemen will admit that they are always able to learn something new. For myself the more I know, the more clear it becomes to me how much I have to learn.

Book learning is no substitute for practical experience acquired under a skilled instructor, but once this latter has been established it is a valuable means of enlarging and deepening our understanding and our knowledge.

It is as well, however, for the newcomer in the horse-world to remember that while there are plenty of books (a list of suggested reading appears at the end of this one) they do not, as might be supposed, say much the same thing in slightly different ways. Some of them, in fact, present diametrically opposed views, the mental consumption of which can be reckoned to cause confusion and even dismay in the strongest and most stable of minds.

It is, indeed, more than possible that certain aspects of this book will disagree with statements appearing in others of similar subject matter and, in all probability, written by authors of far greater distinction than myself.

Although more than ready to admit fallability, such a situation does not necessarily mean that I am wrong and they are right, or vice versa. Providing that a statement or practice is backed by sufficient logic it merely proves that 'there are many paths to the top of the hill'. The fact that there are a number of ends which can be achieved by varying means is just one more delightful facet in the study of the horse.

What we all have to do, having acquired a basic knowledge of horsemastership and a seat of some security, is to recognise this fact and, while regarding the other fellow's approach with tolerance, decide how far up the hill we wish to go (you don't always get the best view from the top), then choose the path which seems to be most suited to us.

The motives that drive people to commit their thoughts, theories and advice to print are as diverse, and as arguable, as those that prompt people to share their lives with horses.

It would be presumptuous of me to say that this book came into being because I wished to share the happiness and enjoyment I have received from horses with other people, or because I wished to improve the lot of horses and ponies and to help their owners to get more enjoyment from their association. And yet if this book does any one of these things for some horse or some rider, even to the smallest degree, its existence will be amply justified.

I have tried to cover the main aspects of horse management and training in an elementary fashion in the hope that it will be useful to those individuals and families who are just embarking, or have recently embarked, on horse and pony ownership.

There are, therefore, chapters and passages devoted to the handling and training of ponies and the part that grown-ups can play to ensure that the children get the maximum enjoyment from their mount, while the parents enjoy peace of mind in similar proportions.

To enjoy a happy family life is one of the most precious gifts man can receive. When horses and ponies can be brought into that circle then, surely, the cup overflows.

If we establish a proper relationship with the horse we attain something that is both satisfying and rewarding. Through him, who is neither wholly saint nor wholly sinner, we and our children learn patience, tolerance, the exercise of kindness combined with firmness, self-control and unselfishness—even, perhaps, a little harmless guile. There is no room for force, harsh words or actions, temper or anger. These may be somewhat old-fashioned qualities, but then I am old-fashioned enough to think them worthwhile.

Raydon, 1968   E.H.E.

First Find Your Horse

Every year, every day, and for all I know every hour, there are a number of people who experience disappointment, sometimes even heartbreak, and certainly financial loss over the purchase of a horse.

This is regrettable and one has every sympathy with the person who has clearly been sold a pup. There are, however, many more cases where the purchaser, through ignorance, has bought a horse or pony quite unsuitable for his or her purpose and suffered in consequence.

Buying an animal is always likely to be something of a gamble, but the odds against one buying a real pig in a poke can be greatly reduced if one sets about the operation with forethought and is armed with a certain elementary knowledge.

Relevant Factors

The first thing to decide is the type of horse you want, and this choice should be governed by factors other than those of personal preference.

Logically your choice must be influenced by the purpose for which the animal is intended, the facilities you have for keeping him and the amount of time you can devote to him, your own equestrian ability and personal conformation, and of the utmost importance, how much you can afford to pay.

If you keep a competent groom, or are able to devote most of your time to a horse, the matter is obviously simplified and your choice, all other things being equal, is less restricted.

If, on the other hand, you intend to ride and care for the horse yourself, with the help of co-operating members of the family, and earn a living as well, it is wise to consider all these factors very carefully.

Much will depend on your circumstances and the facilities you possess. People of average means with jobs to do may find it difficult, if not impossible, to keep a horse stabled in the winter. Stabled horses need a great deal of attention and, of course, considerable exercise. It is more likely, and certainly more advisable, for a person in this situation to decide on either keeping the horse out at grass entirely, leaving him unclipped, but with a shelter against prevailing winds, or possibly going in for the so-called *combined method*, entailing stabling the horse at night and turning him out in a New Zealand rug during the day.

Types and Breeds
Either of these two methods precludes the majority of Thoroughbred horses, who rarely winter out well. It is possible to use the combined method with some Thoroughbreds but, in general, a three-quarter or half-bred horse would be a better choice.

The ideal horse to live out would be one of the larger native breeds, the Fell, the Highland or the excellent Welsh cob, or at any rate, something containing a large percentage of mountain and moorland blood. These animals inherit qualities of unsurpassed hardiness and have remarkably robust constitutions. All of them, of course, can be hunter clipped and kept on the combined method if one wishes to hunt regularly. The three breeds mentioned, particularly the Welsh cob, make ideal hunters in anything but real galloping country and are all well up to the weight of the average adult. As an all-round family horse which can be ridden by parents and older children they are probably unsurpassed. They also go well in harness.

If, however, you are more ambitious and wish to hunt more seriously and perhaps to enter into competitive events, you will need an animal possessing greater scope. You will also, of course, need the time and facilities to care for him properly. If you have these requirements you may consider the Thoroughbred, for whom I confess to having a personal preference. He is the Rolls-Royce of horses, being extremely responsive and having natural balance, good paces and great courage.

There are, however, drawbacks to high breeding when used other than for racing. The Thoroughbred is not always the easiest of rides and it is rare that you will find one who has the necessary temperament for either show-jumping or dressage. To enjoy him to the full you need to be an experienced horseman and horsemaster and you must have a secure seat, light hands and an abundance of equestrian tact. His constitution, too, is more delicate and he needs far more care and attention than his humbler brethren. Most people, and certainly those of average ability, will be better suited to the half or three-quarter bred animal. The majority of them, indeed, would be sadly at sea if put on a fit Thoroughbred.

14

I have little experience of Arabs in this country. They certainly have outstanding qualities of stamina and they are delightful and intelligent rides, but they are rarely seen in competitive events or in the hunting field. In this latter respect their size is somewhat against them—a four-foot fence looks very much more formidable from the back of a 14 h.h. Arab than from a larger hunter.

Anglo-Arabs are, however, bigger and exceptionally good. Indeed, a percentage of Arab blood in any horse is no bad thing.

Assessing Physique and Ability

At this stage it is as well to make an honest assessment of one's own ability. Very few of us are first-class horsemen and some of us will never become anything more than average. In buying a horse, or in dealing with one, nothing is more important than to be able to recognise one's limitations.

There is no more pitiful a sight than a rider obviously over-horsed. You may secretly dream of amazing your friends by appearing on a magnificent Thoroughbred, prancing and cavorting 'to witch the world with noble horsemanship'. Unless, however, you are sufficiently competent, buy something more suited to your capabilities and let the dream remain but a dream. You will be far happier, safer, and less likely to die of fright, or a broken neck, on something not so spectacular, but more suited to your standard of riding.

It is just as important to recognise the failings of your own temperament. So often a horse is said to have a bad temperament, he is nervy or impetuous, or just down-right bad tempered. There are, of course, horses that are more difficult than others, but nine times out of ten it is man who has made them so. The demeanour and behaviour of a horse, a dog or a child is, I believe, a reflection of the master's or parents' character. The highly strung horse is certainly made more so if his rider is cast in the same mould, and conversely the idle animal becomes increasingly dull under a lethargic rider. If, therefore, you are of a hasty, impatient, hot-headed nature, all of which faults you should seek to eradicate if you want to succeed with horses, it is hardly sensible to choose a tearaway sort of animal as a companion. In general, the rule of contrasting opposites, often so successful in human relationships, is a good one to follow in the choice of a horse.

Jorrocks said that as he didn't ride steeplechases his weight was a matter between himself and the horse. Weight, and shape too, is, however, a consideration when looking for an equine partner.

Capacity to Carry Weight

The weight carrying capacity of a horse is not determined by his height but by the size and density of his bone (measured below the knee) and his general proportions. Welsh cobs and our other native breeds are usually up to very much more weight than the beginner might think, and display wonderful bone and excellent limbs. As a rough guide a horse having 8 inches of bone below the knee should be up to 11–12 stone, 9–10 inches up to 13–14 stone, and 10–11 inches up to 15 stone and over.

Much, however, depends on his proportions and, in fact, the bone of the Thoroughbred, being of greater density, will carry a greater weight inch for inch than that of a common bred horse, where the bone structure is coarser and more open. Bone is in fact constructed like a tube and has a hollow centre, or rather a centre that *would* be hollow if it were not filled with marrow. The strength of the bone depends on the thickness and density of the substances surrounding this central core. The best and strongest structure is obviously that with the smallest core and the greater surrounding area of bone. However large the bone measurement, it is of little value if the central core is wide and encompassed by only a thin wall.

There is, of course, no way of discovering the type of bone structure by external examination, but it is as well to remember that 10 inches of common bone may be a weaker structure than 8 inches in a better bred horse.

Now horses with the ability to carry a heavy weight, particularly when that ability is accompanied by scope and quality, are hard to come by and correspondingly more expensive than the lighter type of horse. It follows, therefore, that it is just as stupid for a person of 11 stone to buy a horse up to 15 stone, as it is for a heavyweight to risk breaking down a horse well below his weight.

The height of a horse in relation to the height of the rider must also be taken into account and so must the rider's physical shape. Big horses, by which I mean the 17 h.h. gargantuan, may make fences look small and their riders feel big sitting on the top of them, but they have disadvantages. Apart from the difficulty of getting on to the animal without a pair of stepladders, his limbs have a greater body mass to carry and, in the case of jumping, to lift over an obstacle. It is true that he may have greater physical strength in proportion, but there are many cases when the weight factor is in excess of the physical effort that can be applied.

Big horses, too, are more liable to go in the wind and seem to be more prone to the throat formation which predisposes this failing. They are rarely clever horses, able to get themselves out of trouble, although there are exceptions, and they are usually less intelligent, less responsive and slower on the uptake. Much of this may be attributed to the admixture of cart-blood in their breeding, which may also account for their size.

A smaller horse, closer to the ground, is usually better balanced. He is handier and more responsive, and to my mind always the more receptive.

People with short, round legs will find a broad, roly-backed animal difficult to encompass. I am myself of the short-legged variety and I can testify to the discomfort of sitting on an enormous broad-backed horse which spreads my short legs out, almost at right angles, and makes me feel as secure as the proverbial pea on a drum. A narrow horse is infinitely easier to sit into for those of this conformation.

Incidentally, while long legs and flat thighs look pleasing on a horse, they are no more effective than the short, thick ones. Both Brigadier Lyndon Bolton (*Training the Horse*) and myself are agreed on this point. Both of us, of course, have short legs!

The Price to Pay
Always with us, like the poor, is the problem of cash.

If one has plenty of it there is no problem, and if one requires a potential eventer or show-jumper the fact that money is of little object makes the way easier. There are, however, good workmanlike horses, not of top quality, perhaps, but useful animals, to be obtained at prices between £150 and £300. The price of a horse depends upon his conformation and appearance, his capacity to carry weight, his age, his soundness, his stage of training and his manners. A well-bred horse will always command a higher price than a common one.

So if you want a five-year-old horse up to 15 stone, well bred, and good looking, who has been trained by an experienced trainer and is completely sound, you will pay a large sum of money for him, after you have spent a very long time looking for him. It follows that those whose pockets are not so deep will have to accept a horse lacking in one or more of these qualities to some degree.

Importance of Conformation
Good conformation is desirable because a well-made horse should, in

theory, be able to work better, with less effort and less wear and tear, than one of poor conformation. Nevertheless, I have had horses whose conformation left much to be desired, but who have proved themselves exceptional performers. Very often, in fact, a horse that is deficient in one aspect may be compensated by having particularly good points elsewhere. I believe there is a theory, dependent on related triangles, which proves this point, but I must confess that my mathemetical prowess has never permitted me to understand it.

It is certainly true that although one is unlikely to produce a silk purse from a sow's ear, correct training and management can improve the appearance of any horse and defects, while they cannot be eradicated, can be made much less noticeable.

Lack of conformation, in certain respects and within reason, must, therefore, be acceptable in the cheaper horse and the subject is dealt with more fully later in this section.

Breeding and weight carrying ability have already been discussed and will affect the choice of the individual according to his own make and shape and his circumstances.

The Effect of Age Upon Price

Age has a definite effect upon price and the value of the horse increases up to about seven years. It then decreases slightly until the animal is around twelve years, after which the price falls more rapidly.

At the present time there is a distressing tendency for horses to be broken, sold and ridden at too early an age. It is nonsense to buy a three-year-old with the idea that he will 'grow up with the family' or to fall for the dealer's patter, 'Well, of course he's got all his life in front of him'. He may have, but because he has been used when his bones are unformed and his muscles and organs immature his useful working life has already been shortened.

I used to think that a horse was best broken at three, put away for a year until he was four and then put into work quietly, but now I am not so sure. Colonel V. D. S. Williams, for whom I have the highest regard, recommends breaking at four, putting into quiet work at five and hunting at six, and I believe him to be right.

Any young thing should be allowed to develop physically and mentally before being asked to do a serious job of work. In the case of the horse he is immature at three, is still growing at four and even five, and does not reach maturity until six or seven. If he is used too early we run the risk of doing him permanent damage and shortening his working life. Given time to develop, and being properly trained thereafter, he may continue to be active well into his twenties. The Lippizanners of the Spanish Riding School, for instance, perform the most demanding exercises at an advanced age. Although the breed is famed for its longevity much of this ability is due to their systematic and unhurried training.

Thoroughbreds, as we all know, are raced as two-year-olds, but few thinking horsemen could accept this practice as anything but a necessary evil dictated by economics. The wastage from unsoundness in horses raced at this age is high and, indeed, one has only to visit the Natural History Museum to see the effects of weight having been carried on an immature bone structure. The racehorse is not meant to last and is unlikely to do so while he is worked at so early an age, on the other hand the type of horse I am discussing should have a working life spread over a fairly large number of years.

A good age to buy a horse ready for work is between six and nine, but don't disregard the older horse if price is to be considered and if he is sound. There is many a good tune to be played on an old fiddle, but you must not be surprised if he has developed habits which prove difficult or impossible to correct. If you have the time and the necessary experience an unbroken three-year-old will be less money and is probably the most satisfying horse of all. Unfortunately, people with time and experience to make a horse are rare birds and most of us have to buy horses which may have had a number of owners.

Unsoundnesses and Blemishes
The one essential I would always insist on is that the horse be sound. An unsound horse will be cheap to buy, but may prove to be an expensive purchase in the long run.

There are minor unsoundnesses which could be overlooked, a horse for example who has suffered a sprain of the back tendon and check ligament is quite likely to continue to give good service, but one that has suffered a rupture of the suspensory ligament (the term used to describe this injury is 'broken down') will seldom be of much use.

A horse that has been 'tubed', or Hobdayed (an operation performed on the larynx for roaring, which is an affection of that organ), is probably a good one, otherwise the operation would not have been carried out, but his price will be lower. Otherwise steer clear of any suspicion of unsoundness.

Blemishes are a different matter, for although they are disfiguring

19

they do not affect either soundness or performance. If one does not wish to show the animal they are of no significance, except in regard to price.

Manners and Temperament

Manners and temperament are important in a horse and must have a bearing on the price. The stage of training is not so essential if one can do a little for oneself, but if you want to buy a nicely schooled horse you must expect to pay for the time and knowledge an expert has expended. One should, however, bear in mind that one's own stage of training and competence must be equal to that of the horse, otherwise the result is likely to end in a confused and spoilt animal and a discouraged rider. In any case it is really much more fun to school your own horse and not really all that difficult if you have taken the trouble to acquire a proper seat and some fundamental knowledge.

If a horse is said to have good manners under saddle and in the box one should be able to take it for granted that he is a safe ride, quiet to handle, and free from all the common vices.

A strong, not a rough, horseman might safely buy at a lower figure a horse known to be nappy, but I would never advise buying a horse that bucks with the determined intention of getting rid of his rider, nor would I touch one that reared persistently. Twenty years ago I quite enjoyed horses of this type and as a result bought some very cheap ones, but they are not to be recommended once the nerve, or foolishness, of youth has passed. Likewise horses that quite suddenly seem to go berserk and take-off for no apparent reason should on no account be considered, even as a gift. Usually the poor animal is suffering from some damage to the brain and it is kinder to put him down before he kills someone.

Of the other vices I would be prepared to cope with a crib-biter if he was otherwise a good horse and the price was commensurate, and I might stretch a point concerning an animal who was not over friendly in the box. This latter failing can usually be eradicated by judicious and firm handling, but, again, if one has any doubts about one's ability the horse is better left alone.

The one failing I would not accept, unless I lived on a moor and was never likely to ride on a road, is a horse that is traffic shy. It is possible to effect a cure, but it requires experience and, as always, much time. Even then under present day conditions the element of danger, not only to oneself but to other road-users, is too great.

20

There are, in any case, so many perfectly genuine horses to buy that unless price is a real problem it is just not worth burdening oneself with an animal who is hardly a pleasure to keep.

Having said that I must admit to still retaining a personal sympathy for some of these fallen angels. When I see a horse that is difficult my first reaction is one of anger. Not for the horse, but for the men who reduced him to his unhappy state. More often than not he *is* unhappy. Very few horses are born difficult and the great majority are happiest when they can place their trust in man and lead a useful organised life. If they have been abused and ill-treated is it surprising that they should become first bewildered and eventually driven into making resistances which brand them as equine delinquents? Nothing is more satisfying than to be able to regain their trust and it can usually be done if one is prepared to be very patient and to proceed very slowly.

This digression has, however, little to do with the subject in hand and I am not suggesting, for a moment, that my readers should think of purchasing a horse of this type.

Colour and Sex

One last word before considering where and how to buy a horse. This concerns sex and colour, both of which are personal preferences. The female of any species, can be, if not more deadly, certainly less predictable than the male. If one buys a mare it is possible that one has at the back of one's mind the idea that one day she might breed a foal and so her value need never be entirely lost. A mare, however, can be more temperamental than a gelding, and may be touchy when in season. This natural occurrence can take place every three weeks, approximately, between February and June and in some cases the mare will appear a little off-colour and will lose concentration when at work. She may also be inclined to kick in the stable and be generally irritable. This is not so in all cases and in some mares the cycle is hardly noticeable. A gelding, on the other hand, being unaffected sexually, is likely to have a more equable disposition.

As far as colour goes a good horse is never a bad one, but certain skin pigmentations are significant. Washy, ill-defined colours are supposed to denote a weak constitution, strong colours, of whatever sort, denote the opposite quality. Chestnuts, particularly mares, have a reputation for excitability, while greys are sometimes termed 'rich mens' horses' because of the labour involved in keeping them clean. Where the horn of the foot is white it is often supposed to indicate softness and a poor quality, but while many experts accept this as true there are others who do not hold this opinion. There is also the old adage about 'one white sock buy him, two white socks try him . . .' and so on, but there does not appear to be any sound foundation to justify this one.

Writers of the 16th and 17th centuries, and even before, did, however, lay great stress on colouring, but I wonder whether this might not have been the result of some personal prejudice which, as it was handed down, gained credence and acceptance. I am sure that if one did happen to have particularly unpleasant experiences with a horse or horses of a certain colouring it would not be difficult to form a prejudice against similarly coloured animals.

Where to Buy
There are three principal methods of buying horses. They can be bought from a reputable dealer, from private owners or at public sales. Reputable dealers do still exist, running horse businesses which are their main source of income. Unfortunately there are also a great number of back-yard dealers who attract the unwary by a mixture of patter and the prospect (a quite impossible one) of obtaining a good horse for very little money.

With very little justification the term horse-dealer is synonymous, in the minds of many people, with roguery and skullduggery. There may still be horse-dealers of the type described by Surtees in his novels, but I have, fortunately, never made their acquaintance. This is not to say that all horse-dealers are knights in shining armour, but the vast majority are honest business men and it is not in their interest to sell bad horses and lose goodwill by doing so.

Don't, however, confuse these people, whose wares will in any case be realistically priced, with the back-yard dealer I have mentioned. In spite of the Riding Establishments Act, which makes it illegal to operate a riding school without it being passed as satisfactory and registered with a local council, there are still wretched establishments, claiming to teach riding, run by incompetents who are only too willing to sell their under-fed and possibly unreliable animals.

If you do not know of a good dealer in your area ask around until you find one. If children belong to the Pony Club the District Commissioner is likely to be helpful and, of course, for adults membership of a riding club brings plenty of horse-minded contacts.

Many good riding schools, besides teaching riding, may also operate a dealing side where the beginner, particularly if he is already a client, may obtain a reliable animal. There is an advantage in this method of purchase in that the proprietor or manager will have first-hand knowledge of your capabilities and should be able to find a horse to suit you and them.

A word of warning, however, don't buy a riding school plug for whom, in an ecstasy of enthusiasm for all things equine, you may have formed a strong attachment. In the school, properly fed and receiving an abundance of work, he may plod round as quietly as a lamb. He has become accustomed to the work and to the presence of his companions. Removed from this environment and divorced from his particular herd he can, in combination with an insufficiency of exercise, become a different and even a difficult animal. The quiet hack, who followed dutifully the tails of his preceding brethren at the school, is quite likely to view his new world with some trepidation and to refuse to put one foot in front of the other.

If you have set your heart on a particular breed, an Arab, a Welsh cob or perhaps a Fell, Highland or Dales pony, it is as well to write to the secretary of the breed society concerned asking for advice as to whom you may approach. A list of their addresses appears at the end of this section.

Incidentally, should you decide to buy from a riding school make quite sure it is a properly run one, preferably one approved by the British Horse Society and where qualified instruction is obtainable. If you are in any doubt buy the B.H.S. Supplement of British Riding Schools, price 5/-, which gives a complete list of registered schools together with the facilities and standards of instruction available.

If you decide on going to a dealer you will expect him to be honest with you. Meet him halfway and be honest with him in return. Tell him what you want the horse for, how good you are and how much, exactly how much, you want to pay. It is no use to make out that you are an experienced horseman, capable of riding anything, if you are really something of a rabbit. Nor is it sensible, or even reasonable, to suggest that you might consider paying a higher price than you can afford. It may seem rather silly when seen in print, but this is exactly what people do. If they then get an unsuitable horse they will blame the dealer when the fault is really their own.

You may, of course, prefer to buy privately, in which case it is no bad plan to confine your activities to the area in which you live. In this way you will be able to make local enquiries about the horse and there is the additional point that few people are so thick skinned as to sell a bad one on their own doorstep.

Hundreds of horses, most of them perfectly genuine, are sold each week through the columns of *Horse and Hound,* but again, if only for reasons of economy, it is as well to keep within reasonable distance of home, unless the horse is one you know.

Advertisements for horses are rather like those inserted by house agents—they can be a tribute to the power of the pen. Most people have suffered disappointment, if nothing worse, from taking the effusions of house agents too literally. The same can apply where horses are concerned.

A further point to remember when buying privately is that all of us tend to regard our geese as swans to some degree, and that many of us, unaware, possibly, of general price levels, see our horses as being of greater value than they really are.

Lastly, you may try your hand at a public sale, but there is a very definite chance of your paying dearly for the experience. At some sales you will be able to try the animal, but at many more you will not, although where horses are advertised previously as being entered for a particular sale there may appear a line or two saying 'these horses may be ridden at Blank Stables by appointment'. In general, however, you will be confined to looking at him in his box or at best having him run up outside for you.

If he is a good and well-known horse other people will have noticed him too and bidding is likely to be brisk. On the other hand it is by no means the crocks who fill a sale catalogue. Many people prefer to sell this way and a number of Hunt establishments sell their horses regularly each year at places like Leicester. Every so often, in fact, it is possible to pick up a bargain, but you must remember that you are taking a gamble on an untried and very much unknown quantity.

Descriptions and Warranties
The principal auction sales are well conducted and respectable affairs and the buyer, by reading the conditions of sale which the auctioneers print on their catalogues (and these may vary from one to another), will find that he is well protected against any outright dishonesty. In addition a number of words or phrases will appear in the descriptions accorded to individual entries, some of which, in law, are a good deal more binding than, for instance, the so-called guarantees one gets with a motor car. One does, however, need to understand the implications

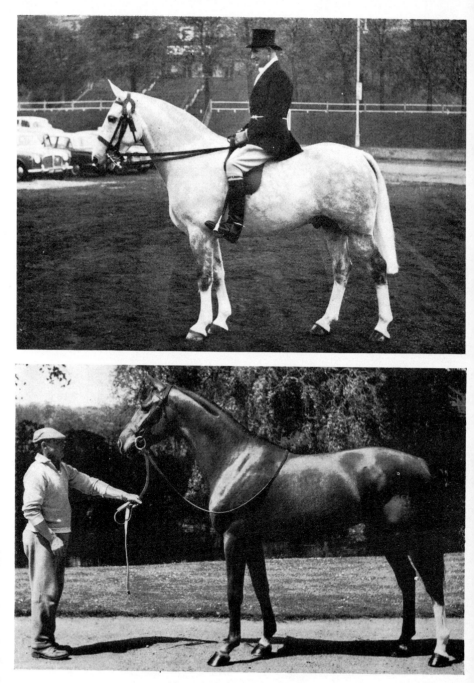

1 ABOVE: *Mr. and Mrs. Clark's champion cob,* Sport
2 BELOW: *A Russian horse of the Donsky breed*

3 A delightful Thoroughbred hack

4 An Anglo Arab

5 A pure-bred Arabian under saddle

6 Mr. Hugh Haldin's Marksman

7 ABOVE: *Mrs. Warren Wofford (née Palethorpe) and* Earlsrath Rambler
8 BELOW: *A useful half-bred horse*

of some of these expressions and what constitutes a complete warranty and what does not.

Among the most common descriptions is 'Good Hunter'. This is a complete warranty that the horse is sound in every respect, is quiet to ride and is capable of hunting. A horse described as a 'Hunter' must be quiet to ride and capable of being hunted, he must also be sound in wind and eye. But you will notice there is no mention of the last member of the trio, action. This does not, therefore, constitute so complete a warranty and some inherent weakness may be suspected. When the description 'Hack' is applied to a horse it may be taken to mean that the animal is sound in action and quiet to ride—again an incomplete warranty if unsupported by any other statement.

The phrase 'a Good Performer' is almost as complete as 'a Good Hunter', but not quite. It only means that the horse is sound in action at the time of sale and admits, therefore, to there being some doubt as to how long he remains so. The words 'Believed Sound' are a warranty of soundness in all respects. A veterinary surgeon's certificate is usually 'lodged in the office' and can, or should be, inspected by the intending purchaser. Even so such a certificate is subsidiary to any warranty of soundness as it appears in the catalogue.

Certain faults must accompany the description of any entry suffering from them, and are three in number. They are crib-biting, wind-sucking and any operation for unsoundness of the wind that the horse may have undergone.

Despite these safeguards should you buy a horse which does not fulfil his warranty you are at liberty to return him providing you adhere to the ruling laid down by the auctioneers in this respect and which is printed on the catalogue.

For anyone with a legal turn of mind who wishes to study the intricacies of the law of warranty I would recommend the purchase of T. J. Sophian's *A Guide to the Law Relating to Horses, Riders and Riding Establishments* (J. A. Allen and Co.). It is really quite enlightening to see how much legislation there is concerning the horse.

As a last word on warranties I will quote a very relevant passage from Mr. Sophian's book. It does not, of course, apply to horses purchased at a sale where the warranty is implicit in the description given, but rather to buying a horse from a private person.

'The General rule of Common Law is *caveat emptor*, let the buyer beware. There will be no implied warranty or condition on the sale of a horse, and it is up to the purchaser to protect himself by taking adequate warranties and the like. Unless he does so he must accept the animal as he finds it, and he cannot be heard to complain afterwards if the animal happens to be unsound or vicious, or unsatisfactory in any other way.'

Nevertheless, we may still take heart, for the law says also, and again I quote Mr. Sophian:

'Certain warranties and conditions are implied and read into every contract for the sale of goods (and therefore of horses) by the Sales of Goods Act 1893, unless such warranties are expressly, or by necessary implication, excluded or modified.' Mr. Sophian then quotes sections of the Act among which, under Section 14, the law states, 'where the buyer makes known to the seller the particular purpose for which he requires the goods, so as to show that he relies on the seller's skill or judgment, and the goods are of a description which it is in the course of the seller's business to supply, then there is an implied condition that the goods are reasonably fit for the purpose.'

In other words, if you asked Mr. A, the dealer, to supply you with a show jumper and that animal refused outright to enter the ring, let alone participate, then you have a case against Mr. A who did not supply you goods 'reasonably fit for the purpose.'

As the man said, '*Caveat emptor*'. You may think it advisable to beware of the law, too!

One last word of warning. When I talk of sales I mean those such as are held at Leicester, Ascot or Hereford and run by properly established auctioneers with experience in this field. Affairs held in the market square of your local town or behind the pub are best avoided. Prices are undoubtedly lower, but so is the quality of the animals brought there. Nothing makes me so angry, and at the same time so sad, as to see a fond parent, with a shining-eyed daughter, buying some virtually unbroken youngster, too weak to display any spirit, in the mistaken belief that they have acquired an ideal pony (young too) for £15 or £20.

There is more abuse of young, immature animals in this way than in any other and I know only too well how much trouble can be caused, not only to the pony or horse, but to the buyer as well.

Now for a few general remarks before we consider what you should look for in a horse when you have decided on the type and from what source you intend to buy.

Strangely enough, in view of the preceding paragraphs, you need not take your lawyer with you when you go to look at a horse. You can take your vet., but you must not expect him, unless he is a personal friend, to make your mind up for you. He will rightly confine himself to giving his opinion on the conformation of the horse, his age, and his soundness or otherwise.

If you do not have your own vet. with you *insist* upon having a veterinary certificate of soundness from the owner. Anyone who is not prepared to have their animal vetted must expect to be suspected of having something to hide.

If you have a really knowledgeable friend who will accompany you by all means take him or her along. But do make sure that the friend is, in fact, knowledgeable and experienced, otherwise it will be a case of the blind leading the blind. Some 'young girl' who has 'ridden all her life' (she may be twenty or fifty) is not necessarily an experienced person. Even young ladies with letters after their name, beautifully though they may ride, are not always so skilled when it comes to deciding what is, or is not, a suitable horse. Try to find someone who is properly qualified to advise you—if you can't you are probably better on your own, having spent the preceding evening reading this chapter over and over again.

The Hunt Horse

Many people on seeing that a hunt horse is for sale take it for granted that he must be a good one and off they go to see him with their minds full of images of well-mannered horses standing quietly at covert-side, and performing thereafter with urbane and almost supercilious expertise. It is true that he probably is a good horse and he may well be nicely mannered, considering the amount of work he gets through in a season. He will, however, have done a great deal of work and may be quite uncontrollable when asked to wait his turn instead of going in front as was his wont. This is not to say that you should not under any circumstances buy a hunt horse, although some of them, particularly those habitually relegated to carrying the whipper-in, can be very rough customers, but you should do so with your eyes wide open.

Remember, too, that a weak, under-conditioned horse may ride quietly enough in the dealer's yard, but may turn out to be a very different gentleman when he has been fed and is fitter and stronger.

If you can get a horse on a week's trial, or if you are offered a day's hunting on him, accept with alacrity. You will have an opportunity of finding out something about him before committing yourself. Don't, however, *expect* such offers. They are occasionally made, but it is by no means a regular rule, and there are not many people who will entrust a horse to a stranger for a week or for a day's hunting.

Whatever else you do you must ride the horse, for you cannot come to a decision without sitting on him. No private seller or a dealer will refuse you this right.

What to Look For

Having got as far as the box of your intended purchase you should have in your mind what points you are particularly going to look for and also those which need not weigh so heavily. The ability to size up a horse, or as it is known 'having an eye for a horse', is not acquired from books nor is it gained overnight. Some people have an instinctive ability to sum up a horse's points, but you may rest assured that they have spent many years developing their gift.

Nonetheless, most of us can improve ourselves in this respect if we are prepared to learn what to look for and then to spend as much time as we can watching the well-known judges dealing with a top flight show class.

It is possible that you may at first be puzzled by the selections made, but gradually you will begin to see what the judge is looking for as to type, conformation and action, and in time you may even find yourself disagreeing with their decisions on occasions. When this happens, providing your disagreement can be based on a sound argument, you are *beginning* to develop an eye for a horse.

Long before this happens, however, you should have been able to fix in your mind's eye a picture of a well-made horse; it is this picture you must hold onto when your intending purchase comes out of his box.

Conformation

Compare his make and shape and his general appearance with that perfect model in your head and make a mental note of points which do not measure up to the ideal. Now stand back and take a really good look at him. At this point the seller will usually begin to enumerate the animal's good points, studiously avoiding those that are not so good. Do not allow yourself to be distracted. My own defence in this instance is to interrupt the eulogistic flow with a request to 'stand him up, will you please' and pretend that I am so lost in contemplation that I haven't heard.

Good conformation is a matter of proportion, no one aspect of the horse impressing itself more than, or to the exclusion, of another. If the head is too large or the limbs too long they are immediately noticeable because they are disproportionate to the rest of the body. The horse of perfect conformation is perfectly proportioned, and is yet to be foaled, while those of near perfect conformation do not come within the range of anything but the deepest pocket.

Nevertheless, we must try to buy a horse whose deficiencies in conformation are not over exaggerated and one of as good a make and shape as our resources allow. All things being equal, as I have mentioned before, good conformation should mean greater, and longer lasting, working efficiency (*Figs 1 and 2*).

The Head

Having taken your good, long look now concentrate on the individual points of the animal and I suggest you start with the HEAD.

The head and eye by their shape, size and general appearance can tell us a great deal (*Plates 20, 23, 24 and 25*).

It is not very difficult to make an assessment of the character and intelligence in the extremes of the human head, although the intermediate appearances may present more of a problem. In a general way if we see an unattractive, course-featured individual, low browed with close set, piggy eyes and a generally dull look about him we are likely to hazard a guess that he is unlikely to be of a high level of intelligence. We may also think that he is not a very pleasant individual. It is possible that we may be maligning a perfectly good citizen, but without knowing him intimately this is the only way open to us to make an assessment of his character. Conversely, we associate a man with refined, clearly cut features and the alert look with intelligence. Again we may not be correct in the assumption, but this is the impression we receive. It is, also, not too difficult to recognise the genial, jolly, honest sort of fellow by his face, or by the same means the miserable, perpetually disgruntled one. I am sure that human characters, although more complicated than those of animals, are portrayed in the face, particularly when the character of the individual contains the extremes of human failings and virtues.

In the same way as we do not have a close acquaintance with the horse we are thinking of buying, it is only by an examination of his head and the general impression it creates that we can make a judgment of his character and temperament. We may be able to add to our impression later by noting his reactions to our handling of him, but initially we shall have to form our opinion by studying that part of him which is most capable of expression.

Fig 1 Points of the Horse

The Eye

The impression one should gain is of alertness, interest and kindness. The eyes should be calm and large and placed well to the front, with the intervening space of the forehead wide, but not *too* much so. On the width of the forehead depends the ability to see objects directly in front more or less accurately. Horses with a high percentage of blood have narrower foreheads than the more common bred ones who, like the cart-horse, have their eyes placed more to the side; a position which gives greater facility of lateral vision, but entails making more exaggerated movements of the head when the eyes wish to focus on objects in front of them.

30

1 Ear
2 Forelock
3 Forehead
4 Temple
5 Haw
6 Eye
7 Face
8 Cheek bone (zygomatic ridge)
9 Nasal bones
10 Lower jaw
11 Nasal peak
12 Nostril
13 Muzzle
14 Upper lip
15 Lower lip
16 Chin
17 Chin groove (or curb groove)
18 Bars of jaw
19 Sub-maxillary groove
20 Cheek (overlying masseter muscle)
21 Throat (gullet)
22 Trachea (windpipe)
23 Jugular groove
24 Point of shoulder
25 Breast
26 Pectoral muscle
27 Forearm
28 Elbow
29 Knee
30 Cannon bone
31 Fetlock joint
32 Pastern
33 Back of knee (pisiform bone)
34 Tendons
35 Brisket
36 Spur vein
37 Girth
38 Base of neck
39 Spine of scapula (or shoulder)
40 Ribs
41 Belly
42 Groove formed by rib cartilages
43 Barrel
44 Triceps muscle
45 Sheath
46 Stifle
47 Shin
48 Chestnut
49 Coronet
50 Hoof (wall of foot)
51 Heel
52 Hollow of heel
53 Ergot
54 Fetlock
55 Back tendons
56 Shank
57 Seat of curb
58 Hock
59 Point of hock
60 Gastrocnernius tendon (hamstring)
61 Gaskin (second thigh)
62 Tail
63 Patella
64 Buttocks
65 Point of buttocks (tuberischii, seat-bone)
66 Dock
67 Root of tail
68 Hip joint
69 Thigh
70 Quarter
71 'Poverty' mark
72 Croup
73 Point of croup
74 Point of hip (haunch bone or angle of haunch)
75 Flank
76 Back (saddle)
77 Withers
78 Mane
79 Crest
80 Axis
81 Wing of atlas
82 Supra-orbital fossa
83 Poll
84 Loins

The theory is often held that great width between the eyes allows room for a larger brain. This, however, is a fallacy.

The brain of the horse, which is not very large, is contained within the cranium which is placed beneath the temporal muscles and between the ears. The width between the *eyes* can, therefore, have little effect upon either the size or capabilities of the brain.

The Arab horse often shows considerable width between the eyes, but somehow manages to avoid having the exaggerated lateral type of vision associated with cart-breeds.

Sunken, pig eyes seem to go with sulky dispositions and a mean temper and most people avoid horses who do not have a good eye. A

Fig 2 Skeleton of the Horse

pit above the eye, almost a hole, is a sign of advanced age or poor condition.

A clean-cut, chiselled head, lean and fine with a thin skin covering is indicative of breeding, a heavy, coarse head shows common blood. A bump between the eyes is generally taken to be a sign of a stubborn disposition and a surly, mean nature. Nearly every horseman will tell you this, although there is no real explanation or foundàtion for the assumption. It does, nevertheless, give a rather unpleasant look to the head and I would not wish to argue the significance of a point that so many eminent horsemen have made.

A dished, concave face is a characteristic of the Arab and much

1 Parietal	} skull	32 Femur
2 Eye socket		33 Ilium
3 Nasal bone		34 Trochanter } Pelvic girdle
4 Lower jaw		35 Ischium

1 Parietal ⎫
2 Eye socket ⎪ skull
3 Nasal bone ⎬
4 Lower jaw ⎭
5 Supra-scapula cartilage
6 Spine of scapula
7 Scapula
8 Shoulder joint (point of shoulder)
9 Humerus
10 Ulna
11 Radius (forearm)
12 Pisiform
13 Knee joint (or carpus)
14 Cannon or metatarsal bone
15 Fetlock joint
16 Suffraginis (long pastern)
17 Short pastern
18 Os pedis (coffin bone)
19 Navicular
20 Trapezium
21 Rib cartilages (or costal cartilages)
22 Ribs (23 – last rib)
24 Patella
25 Inner splint bone
26 Os coronae
27 Heel
28 Sesamoid bones
29 Outer splint bone
30 Os calcis (point of hock)
31 Tibia and fibula

32 Femur
33 Ilium
34 Trochanter ⎫
35 Ischium ⎬ Pelvic girdle
36 Caudal (tail or coccygeal vertebrae)
37 Lumbar vertebrae
38 Dorsal vertebrae
39 Anterior vertebrae
40 Cervical vertebrae
41 Axis
42 Atlas
43 Occipital
44 Malar bone
45 Sacral vertebrae (or sacrum)
46 Molars
47 The bars
48 Canines
49 Incisors
50 Elbow joint

prized by his admirers. A Roman nose belongs to more plebeian stock, but is ideally formed for looking down.

Looking at the head in detail the formation and action of the ears is also worth a glance, they should be responsive and mobile. They will be neat, not unduly large or hairy in the better class of horse and easily and frequently pricked. The movements of the ears in a commoner are less active, and the ears themselves coarser. Ears laid back, accompanied with a wild eye showing the white are a means of expressing temper.

Lop ears are unsightly, but many good horses have them and they are thought to be found in horses of stamina. Their disadvantage is that they are unable to give the rider any signal of the horse's intention.

The nostrils in a horse (who does *all* his breathing through them) should be wide and well developed if he is to be able to breathe effectively, particularly in moments of physical stress.

Probably the most important thing about the head is that it should be proportionate to the shape and size of the neck and be properly connected ('set-on' is the horsy term) to that part of the horse.

This really is important because the head and neck is the agency by which the horse balances himself. His neck is used like a pendulum with the head as a weight on the end of it. A heavy head on a weak neck throws his balance on the forehand and is bound to make the horse heavy on the hand. Where the head is heavy, and it is in many weight carriers, it must have a correspondingly strong neck, even though it be rather shorter than a judge would think ideal. In perfection we shall have a fairly fine, small head on a graceful, muscled neck forming an elegant curve from the withers to the head.

The angle at which head and neck should meet is between 90 and 100 degrees, a more acute angle than this makes the horse more liable to unsoundness in the wind and he is likely to become overbent when ridden.

The opposite is always associated with weak muscular development and will again make bridling difficult and the horse unpleasant to ride. Stargazers, who carry their heads excessively high, appearing to have the head pushed onto the neck almost vertically, are likely to make control something of a problem.

A further consideration affecting the horse's ability to bridle correctly is the width between the lower jaws under the neck. You should be able to fit your fist between them. Thick jowled horses also find it difficult to bend the head and accept the bit easily.

The Mouth and Age

Now a look at the mouth (*Fig. 3*). This is something one is expected to do and certainly there is no other way of finding out the approximate age, or whether the seller was telling the truth when he said the horse was a five-year-old. Not very long ago I heard of a case where a child's parents had bought a pony as a six-year-old. They did not have the pony vetted and later, when its condition began to deteriorate and a vet. was at last called in, it was found to be the best part of fifteen years older than that.

It is not easy to arrive at an accurate estimate of the age, particularly

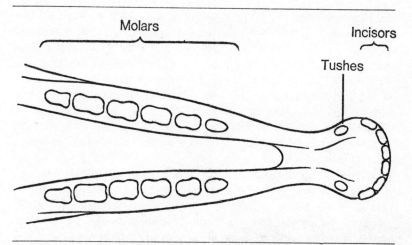

Molars

Incisors

Tushes

Fig 3 The lower jaw

when the horse is over eight or so years, but a little basic knowledge will help to avoid errors or occurrences of the dimensions I have quoted.

The horse has both *incisor* teeth, the biters, at the front, and *molar* teeth, the grinders, at the rear. It is from the former that the age can be estimated. Up to the age of five the horse is in the process of shedding the milk teeth—a process which is completed at five years when he is said to have a 'full' mouth of permanent teeth. Thereafter one must rely upon other indications of ageing.

The diagrams (*Fig. 4*) which accompany this section will help to make the stages easier to understand.

The foal at birth has no teeth, although it is possible to see the central incisors through the gum. These are cut at ten days and are followed by the lateral incisors, somewhere between four and six weeks, and the corner incisors at six to nine months, giving him his full complement of six milk incisors. Milk teeth are easily recognisable by their shape, which is one coming to a definite point at the base. Codrington *(Know Your Horse)* describes the tooth as having a 'distinct neck'. They are also white in colour, rather than yellow as is the case with permanent teeth.

It is not until three years are reached that some of the temporary or milk teeth are clearly replaced by permanent incisors, and the animal will then show two central permanent incisors in each jaw, flanked on either side by two milk teeth. At two years 'marks' or 'cups' are clearly apparent on the tables of the milk teeth, but the permanent central incisors appearing at three years will not show these marks. At four years the temporary lateral incisors are replaced by permanent ones, leaving only two milk teeth, the corner incisors. By this time the central incisors will have developed cups on the tables while the two new laterals will be unmarked. In the male horse the tushes situated behind the incisor teeth are now visible. Mares do not grow tushes except in one or two rare cases.

At five years the remaining corner incisors are replaced by permanent teeth and again all, with the exception of these, display cups on the tables.

Because the newly erupted teeth are immature and have as yet received no wear, these corner incisors will only meet at the front in the five-year-old mouth. The horse now has a mouth of permanent teeth and, as our American cousins would say, from here-on-in the task of assessing the age will be beset with more difficulty, and considerations of wear and changing shapes, among others, must be taken into account.

By six years the corner teeth will have worn level, meeting along the complete surface of the tables and the cups on all teeth will be clearly visible. The tushes, too, are now fully prominent. Now the cups, which have so far been helpful in their regular appearance, begin to change their form. At seven years their distinct outline begins to fade and to lose the formerly hard outline. In addition the upper corner incisor develops a hook overlapping the rear of its opposite number.

The appearance of the cups alters again at eight, becoming very indistinct in the central incisors, but at this time a dark line appears at the forward edge of the table in these teeth. The hook on the corner incisor has worn away at eight years.

The dark line is noticeable on all the incisors at nine years and all the cups have disappeared, although those on the corner incisors can still be seen in outline. At this age another hook begins to appear on the corner incisor as the direct result of wear. The most significant change at this age, and one that presents a sound guide, is the appearance of a dark groove, Galvayne's groove, on the upper corner incisors. This groove extends down the tooth as the horse gets older. In general terms it will have reached halfway at around fifteen years and will have reached the bottom of the tooth at twenty years.

The teeth become longer and project forwards at a greater angle by

The central nippers have just erupted

At birth

Corner temporary incisors are erupting

6 months

Permanent centrals and laterals

Temporary corner teeth

2 years

Central permanent incisors show wear

The temporary incisors are worn

3 years

Permanent central teeth

Temporary lateral & corner incisors

4 years

Fig 4 Ageing as shown by the teeth

central lateral and corner incisors all permanent

corner incisors meeting in front only

5 years

Corner teeth now level

Cup marks on all incisors can be seen

6 years

Hook

The cup marks begin to fade

7 years

Hook of corner teeth worn away

A dark line appears on the centrals

8 years

Galvayne's groove
appears on corner
teeth

Dark line visible
on all teeth

9 years

Slope of teeth
increases

10 years

The shape is
more triangular,
the cup marks
are less distinct

All teeth more triangular
in shape, cup marks
have disappeared

15 years

Slope now very
pronounced

Galvayne's groove
is now at the base
of the corner teeth
& gradually
disappearing

20–25 years

the time the horse is ten, altering their shape and becoming more triangular. As the years advance the slope of the teeth becomes more apparent and any faint outlines of the cups on the tables will disappear altogether.

The incisors become more and more triangular in shape and our estimate of the age must be based increasingly on experience and on the position of Galvayne's groove. At ten the groove may be $\frac{1}{4}$ inch long and from then it will proceed down the teeth at a rate of approximately $\frac{1}{8}$ inch each year.

An important feature to be noted when examining the mouth is that it is neither parrot shaped, the upper jaw and teeth overlapping the lower, nor under shot, when the opposite structure will be seen. In either case the horse is best rejected. These mouth formations make the proper fitting of the bit difficult, and in the case of a double bridle almost impossible.

To examine the mouth part the lips gently, using a hand for each lip, and when you wish to open the mouth insert the thumb and forefinger, held on either side, onto the bars of the lower jaw, i.e. between the incisors and the molars. There is no need to take the jaw in a vice-like grip, the insertion of the fingers is usually enough to secure the horse's co-operation.

The Neck

From our examination of the head we naturally pass on to a consideration of the neck to which it is attached.

Obviously it should be strong, but it should not be of the very short, thick and cresty sort. If it is this shape the horse is more inclined to be stiff in his neck. This type of neck is also frequently associated with animals who tuck their chins in and 'motor-on' quite regardless of the indications or wishes of their riders. If the thickness of the neck continues into the junction with the head the horse may still 'motor-on', but with his nose poked out in front of him. There is very little that can be done to rectify this sort of conformation.

If the neck is too long and too weak it becomes difficult for the horse to carry his head correctly for any period of time. The neck is, in fact, overweighted by the head and for practical purposes is an inefficient piece of machinery which overburdens the forehand and must produce a faulty balance.

Although, again, proportion in relation to the size and set-on of the head is all important, the way in which the neck is joined to the

9 ABOVE: *A Welsh cob under saddle*
10 BELOW: *A New Forest mare*, Priory Pink Petticoats

11 Mrs. H.P. Warren's Highland mare, Seagull

12 A champion Fell pony, Mrs. Newall's Bess

13 A Connemara pony, Conquest of Calla

14 An attractive group of Welsh ponies

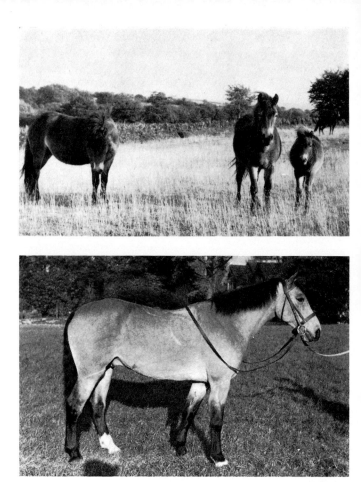

15 Exmoor ponies

*16 An interesting
Arab/Connemara
cross*

*17 A charming
Dartmoor pony*

shoulders, which in turn affects the joining of shoulder and trunk, is an equally vital point. The base of the neck must be of sufficient width and very well formed. Too low a junction with the shoulders, often found when the latter are inclined to be straight, will have the effect of overloading the front end and any sort of practical head carriage will be almost impossible to achieve.

The ideal appearance is when the neck, broad at its base, blends itself without interruption into the shoulders. Such a neck, neither too long nor too short, when accompanied by a well-connected head of proportionate size, will enable the head to be carried fairly high. In this position the balance is properly placed and there is greater control over the forehand.

There are two types of necks to be avoided according to all the authorities. First the *swan-neck*, where there is a pronounced upward curve in the upper third of the neck with the head looking as though it were dropped on vertically. Any horse with a neck and head of this shape just cannot bridle. R. H. Smythe, however, perhaps one of the greatest of equine authorities in the matter of make and shape and the mental processes of the horse, while condemning the type, remarks that the animal 'usually sees well and may be a good ride over jumps . . .'

Secondly the *ewe-neck*, more often found in mares than in geldings. This is where the neck is definitely concave along the upper edge. Smythe admits that it is possible to see some quite adequate performers with necks of this shape, but I feel he would join with every other expert in condemning it.

I would not be so rash as to disregard the advice of these authorities or to advise people to buy ewe-necked horses, but I do believe that much can be done to overcome this defect by intelligent schooling.

Although the conformation is due, basically, to an incorrect structure, many animals are made worse than they need be by bad riding. Quite recently I bought a mare (or rather my wife saw something attractive in a very unattractive creature) in weak condition and with this fault among a host of others.

Having got over the initial shock of seeing so misshapen an animal in my stables I decided, as I could certainly make matters no worse, that it would be interesting to see what a horseman of no more than average ability could do to improve her.

To start with the mare was rather like a ship without a rudder, and our progress down the road resembled that of a drunken man. Gradually, as she began to make up, I started to school her, first on the lunge and then from the saddle. For three months it was impossible to carry out a sitting trot and I concentrated on riding her in our sand school allowing her a long rein and with the minimum of contact. In time she learnt to find her own balance and would circle quite happily stretching her neck downwards and outwards. After six months, which included mounted and unmounted work over cavalletti, the muscles on the top of her neck had begun to develop, a process encouraged by much hand massage, while those on the underside of the neck began to fall away. The defects in her conformation are not eradicated, but their effect has been decreased, and she is now a fairly well-balanced, pleasant and safe ride. Her picture appears in *Plates 21 and 22*, from which it will be seen just how much improvement has been made. She was, incidentally, a cheap horse to buy, and while much time and effort has been expended on her she has increased my own knowledge in corresponding measure.

To sum up this question of necks, a longish neck with a well set-on light head contributes towards speed with a long length of stride. A short neck, though stronger, shortens the stride and, therefore, in theory, the speed; where then speed is not a factor of great necessity a slightly shorter neck is not unacceptable.

The Withers

Before examining the shoulder in detail it is necessary to look at the withers, the formation of which are of the greatest importance in the saddle horse. Unless the wither is well formed it is unlikely that the upper part of the shoulder, or the scapula, will be long and laid back, necessary for maximum efficiency in the free movement of the fore-limbs.

The withers should be fairly prominent and well covered with muscle. Very fine, very high withers are not so good, being deficient in muscle. A horse having them will ride well, but the construction will not have the strength of those more normally formed.

Low or flat withers are *usually*, but not always, found in conjunction with straight shoulders, which result in a short stride and greater concussion, and therefore wear, on the legs.

Flat withers, too, make saddle fitting difficult and in the case of ponies, especially, who are often very deficient in this respect, can give rise to the saddle riding forwards.

The Shoulder

I imagine that everybody knows that the ideal shoulder should be long and well sloped. This is applicable to all horses if the forelimbs are to be efficient and if undue wear and tear is to be avoided. Obviously the conformation also gives a more comfortable and balanced ride, the potential speed will be greater, as will the freedom of the action and ability to extend.

Smythe gives the desirable measurements of a good, well laid-back, shoulder as follows: 'It should have', he writes: 'a degree of inclination, measured from the point of the shoulder to the junction of neck and withers, of approximately 60 degrees. From the point of the shoulder to the centre of the withers, their highest point, should give a reading of 43 degrees. From the point of the shoulder to the junction of withers and back, the reading should be 40 degrees.'

There has always been controversy about the position and length of the humerus, the bone connecting the scapula with the fusion of the radius and ulna of the foreleg. It is largely upon the length and position of the humerus that the position of the fore-leg will depend. The more horizontal and the longer this bone the further back under the body will the leg be placed. In consequence it is argued with some justification that the action will be correspondingly restricted. Whereas if the humerus is more upright and fairly long the leg is placed further forward, which gives greater freedom and extension. But, say the critics of this view, the leg is subjected to more jarring.

The simplest way out is to avoid a horse displaying either of these extremes.

The Foreleg

There is very much less argument over the foreleg *(Fig. 5)*. From the top, the elbow must be free from the body and should not look as though it was tied in. If in doubt turn the horse round when the elbow should turn out naturally. The forearm should be long, with good muscle development and the knee set low to the ground.

A knee high off the ground means a long, and therefore weak, cannon bone. A short, strong and straight cannon is what is required. The knee itself, viewed from the front, must be flat; from behind the pisiform bone should be prominent, so that there is sufficient width for the flexor tendons to pass downwards.

Some horses will appear to be a little 'over at the knee', that is they appear to have a forward inclined bend to the knee. This may be a matter of individual conformation or the result of hard work, but it does not seem to produce any ill effect upon action or soundness.

Fig 5 Conformation defects of the limbs: A. Tied in below the knee.
B. Back-at-the-knee or calf-knee. C. Over-at-the-knee

A horse that is 'back at the knee' is so termed when the leg below the knee curves inwards. It is a definite weakness to be avoided.

Horses that are 'tied in below the knee' are an abomination. This is where the measurement immediately below the knee is less than the measurement taken lower down towards the fetlock joint. It denotes weakness and a certain chance of future unsoundness. Too light a bone under the knee is also hardly advisable. The bone present should be in proportion to the animal and the weight it is to carry, bearing in mind the differences in bone structure between the Thoroughbred and the common horse which have already been mentioned.

In every case the ligaments and tendons, running downwards below the knee, should feel hard and firm, there should be no puffiness apparent anywhere. In a horse that is light of bone, ligaments and tendons will be correspondingly small and weak.

The fetlock joint must be flat on all sides, never fleshy and never round.

The pastern is the shock absorber *par excellence*. If it is short and upright there will be undue concussion to the foot and leg, resulting in unsoundnesses. Overlong pasterns put a greater strain on the suspensory ligament and the tendons which run down the rear of the foreleg. How great a strain is placed on these can be seen from photographs of horses landing over a fence when, on occasions, the rear of the fetlock joint is touching the ground.

A good pastern should have a gentle slope to it, being neither too upright nor too much the other way. The hind pasterns, because of the compensating flexing action of the hock, are a little shorter than those of the forelegs.

The Foot

The foot is a subject in itself and is dealt with in some detail in the chapter on shoeing (*see page 141*). There is no truer saying than 'no foot—no 'oss'. A horse is as good as his feet and if they are bad then no other aspect of conformation can compensate for them.

Look carefully at them and make quite sure that the two pairs, fore and hind, are as near a perfect match in shape and size as is possible.

If one foot is smaller than its companion we may deduce with some certainty that the horse has a record of lameness. If a horse is lame he naturally puts less weight on to the foot which is causing him pain and as a result the foot shrinks because it is not subject to the same spreading pressure as its fellow.

Small, boxy feet which appear to be too small in proportion to the size of the horse are best avoided. They usually *are* too small.

Heels must be open, deep and never contracted. In order for this to be so the bars of the foot must also be deep and well-turned.

The soles of the feet should be thick and strong and not give when pressure is applied with the fingers. The shape of the sole in a healthy foot is slightly concave in the forefeet and more so in the hind ones. Avoid feet with dropped soles. The frog is an anti-concussion and an anti-slip device for the foot and a healthy one will be large, well formed and coming well down to the ground. Shrivelled looking frogs not coming into contact with the ground are bad, as in this condition they cannot perform their proper function.

The wall of the hoof must be strong and show no signs of breakage or longitudinal cracks.

The wall is usually dark grey in colour; white walls, usually found in horses with white legs or coronets, are considered to be of softer horn and are, therefore, more prone to wear. However, opinions differ on this point and providing the feet are otherwise good there is no need to worry.

The coronary band secretes a protective, waterproof oil (the periople) over the hoof wall and healthy feet (those that have not had the wall rasped by the smith or polished with blacking) should show evidence of this secretion.

Feet that turn out or turn in will affect the action. Those that are turned out presenting the more serious fault, as brushing is then almost inevitable. Turned-in toes are not as bad a fault and many authorities will say that such a horse will go better in the deep. This may be so, personally I prefer feet that point straight to the front in any sort of going.

The weight bearing parts of the foot are the frog, the wall, the bars and the outer edges of the sole. If these are properly formed and healthy there will be nothing much wrong with the foot.

At this point I was about to suggest the most desirable angle of slope in a healthy, well-shod foot. I had always understood that the correct angle of the forefeet was about 50 degrees and that of the hindfeet between 55 and 60 degrees. On checking this, however, I found the experts, including three veterinary surgeons, at some variance. The concensus of opinion is around these figures, but it is surprising to find differences involving ten and more degrees. Nevertheless, feet displaying slopes approximating to these figures can, I think, be considered correct.

The Chest

Viewed from the front, should be wide to allow for expansion of the lungs. The shape of the chest depends upon the curvature of the ribs. If the ribs are not well sprung, the horse will be flat sided and the chest cramped and narrow. Under these circumstances the forelegs will be set too close together, 'both legs coming out of the same hole,' and there will also be a predisposition to brushing and a generally inhibited action. Too heavy and wide a chest, often found with heavy shoulders, is not likely to produce a turn of speed in the animal concerned. Horsy people talk about *heart* room when they should talk of *lung* room. The heart does not need an enormous amount of space, the lungs do.

The Girth

To correspond with a good chest, must be deep and the ribs well sprung. The latter should come well back to the loins and one should not have the impression that the horse could do with another rib. Any slackness here is an indication of want of stamina.

The Back

Requires careful examination—after all it is the part you will sit on and deficiencies in this department have a great influence on the ability of the horse to perform under saddle, and upon the comfort of the ride you will receive.

The back is that portion of the horse between the withers and the quarters and is bounded on each side by the ribs.

A back, like any other part, cannot be judged on its own. However good in itself it must be supported by good withers at one end and good loins and quarters at the other.

As it is the only convenient part of the horse upon which we can inflict the presence of our bodies it must, necessarily, be shaped to carry a saddle. Further, as it is easily damaged (and when it is the horse will not be able to give of his best), it must be so constructed as to be protected as well as it may be from its principal enemy, the saddle plus the rider's weight.

Any back which does not carry a saddle well must be a serious fault in any horse whose purpose is to do just this. Abnormalities, such as a pronounced hollow-back, or its opposite, the roach back, make saddle fitting difficult and increase the danger of damage to the structure. Roach backs are also uncomfortable rides and encourage a faulty action.

Excessively short backs may be strong, but restrict the freedom of the hind limbs and are uncomfortable for the rider, who receives the full force of the propulsive thrust. A very long back is equally bad and must be regarded as being potentially weak.

For speed, however, and for comfort, a longer rather than a shorter back is desirable. A little spinal flexion is then possible in the horse, but in an excessively short back any sort of flexion of the spine is impossible. Spinal flexion in the horse is only accomplished in the area behind the saddle between the last of the dorsal joints and the first of the lumbar. Mares, by virtue of their sex, may have somewhat longer backs than geldings.

The Engine of the Horse

Supplying the necessary forward propulsion, is contained in the loins, quarters and hind legs. Obviously, therefore, the 'back end' must give an appearance of power and should never look mean *(Plate 18)*.

The Loins

Which rise from the last rib to the croup, should be somewhat elevated and always muscular. Any tendency to an overlong loin results in slackness and the structure will be a weak one and consequently defective in performance.

The Croup
Is the highest point behind the saddle. In the young horse it will be higher than the withers, while in the mature horse the latter will have developed, ideally, to be on a line with the croup, or even a little higher.

A high croup, giving a sloping effect to the quarters is often termed a 'goose rump'. It may be somewhat unsightly, but authorities argue that it displays a good bone development, which is advantageous for the attachment of muscle, and may indicate a horse having considerable jumping ability.

Animals possessing a large proportion of Arab blood (the pure-bred Arabian frequently has nineteen ribs as opposed to eighteen in other breeds and five lumbar bones instead of six) often have a straight croup, resulting in their characteristic high tail position.

Otherwise the quarters should appear well rounded over the top when viewed from behind, filling out on both sides as the eye travels downwards.

The Gaskin
The gaskin, or second thigh, between the stifle and the hock, supplies much of the power. In general, and for speed, most people would prefer it to be long and muscular, a development usually associated with a low hock, rather than a shorter, and possibly stronger, second thigh which will be found with a longer cannon bone. There are perfectly cogent arguments advanced on behalf of both formations, but for most of us the important thing to remember is that whatever the shape it is most necessary for a horse to show strong development in this area.

Again looked at from the rear, a pronounced lack of muscular development between the thighs, resulting in a horse being 'split up behind', is bad, as is a pair of very heavy thighs, joining very low down and appearing to force the animal to move wide behind.

The Hocks
Possibly the point of greatest importance in judging the efficiency of the back end is the position and shape of the hocks *(Fig. 6)*. Ideally to achieve maximum efficiency and true proportion the point of the hock should be level with the chestnut which lies above the knee in the fore-leg, and, in conjunction with a long second thigh, should be set low.

48

18 Bad and mean quarters without power. The tail is badly set on and there is a notable absence of second thigh

19 A pair of very objectionable 'cow-hocks'

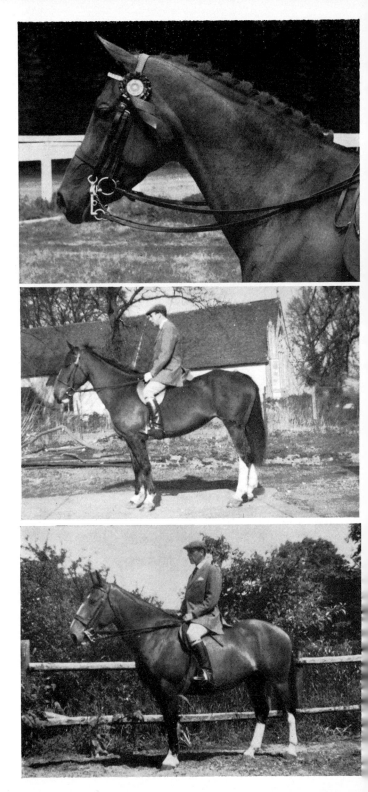

20 *Profile of a winner*

21 *A cheap horse because of her poor condition*

22 *The same mare some months later*

Fig 6 Hocks: A. Straight hocks in front of vertical line. B. Good: hocks in line with seat-bone. C. Sickle hocks projecting behind the vertical line

In perfection a line drawn from the point of the buttock to the ground coincides with the point of the hock and the cannon bone should not deviate from the vertical.

In practice a number of good hunters and jumpers will be found to carry the hock a little to the front of this line and the cannon bone, too, will be slightly in advance of the perpendicular and rather more under the horse. This position may not contribute to speed, but it has strength and supplies the necessary jumping thrust.

Where the hock is carried well to the rear of the line dropped from the point of the buttock there will be a loss in propulsion and a greater risk of damage to the joint. Hocks which are too straight and are in advance of the vertical are likewise a source of weakness.

Sickle hocks, those which are too overbent, or curved on the front surface, subject the joint and ligament to greater strain and are frequently disposed to disease.

Hocks out of true, that is either turned out (bowed) or turned in (cow-hocked) must be less efficient than those that are truly symmetrical *(Plate 19)*. Both result in a loss of speed and possibly contribute to uneven wear in the mechanism of the joint and greater strain on the connecting ligaments. Here again there is a confusing divergence

49

of views among expert opinion. I have, for instance, found one qualified authority stating categorically that cow-hocks are a sign of weakness, whereas bowed ones are an indication of strength, and an equally eminent source saying exactly the opposite.

My own, by no means expert, opinion, is that anything which is very much out of true, any extreme malformation, is bound to prove less effective whatever the shape it takes.

The Perfect Shape

I have included a diagram *(Fig. 7)* which is of assistance in giving us a picture of the proportionate horse. With the help of a tape-measure hours of innocent amusement can be obtained comparing the measurements of one's own animals with this perfect horse.

I have dealt with the subject of conformation in some detail, and in doing so I have tried to give some idea of the reasons why one structure is preferred to another and why it is possible to overlook certain differences according to the type of work the animal is asked to perform.

There is no such thing as the perfectly made horse. There are general rules which apply to all riding horses, but it is not possible to lay down rigid requirements to cover every activity to which the horse is put. The ideal conformation of the racehorse is not necessarily that of the show jumper, and in the former case there will indeed be a difference in conformation between sprinters and stayers.

What is important is that we should try to buy as well-proportioned a horse as our pocket permits, and that where we are compelled to buy one with a fault in make and shape we should appreciate the significance of the particular deficiency in relation to the work we intend to ask of the horse.

A horse of good conformation, if sound, must be of better balance than a badly made one, and, therefore, more easily trained and more pleasant to ride. The more ambitious our aims, the greater, therefore, will be the need for our possessing a horse of good conformation and balance.

As in all things there will always be the exceptions to prove the general rule, horses that appear to exhibit nearly every fault and are yet outstanding performers. The point to remember is that these *are* the exceptions and that the majority of badly made horses are poor performers.

As it is unlikely that one would knowingly buy an unsound horse and it is hoped that no-one will try to sell you one that is clearly

Fig 7 The perfect shape

A=1 Length of head, 2 Point of hock to ground, 3 Point of hock to fold of stifle, 4 Chestnut to base of foot, 5 Depth of body at girth, 6 Fold of stifle to croup, 7 Posterior angle of scapula to point of hip
Length from point of shoulder to seat bone=2½ times length of head
Height from fetlock to elbow=approximately height of elbow – wither
B=1 Seat bone – point of hip, 2 Seat bone – stifle, 3 Stifle to point of hip
  A line dropped from the seat bone meets the point of the hock and continues down the back of the cannon bone

unsound, I do not propose to go too deeply into the subject (which is dealt with more fully in a later section) at this point. If you are wise you will not under any circumstance buy an animal before you have had a satisfactory report from a veterinary surgeon.

Running Him Out

You must, of course, before riding the horse have him run up for you so that you have a chance of assessing the trueness of his action. If he is abundantly lame it is unlikely that even a person of little experience will fail to see that this is the case. If he is just a trifle uneven, or going the tiniest bit short, it is rather more difficult to detect, unless one has great experience or is a competent veterinary surgeon carrying out a thorough examination for soundness.

Providing the horse seems to go sound, concentrate on watching the action. Have him walked away from you and then trotted towards you.

The Action

Deficiencies in action are, in nine cases out of ten, as we have seen, due to faulty conformation.

The action should be true and straight. Watch for any irregularities such as 'dishing', i.e. turning the toe of the foreleg, followed by a throwing out of the foot in an outward circling movement.

It may not be of vital importance, but because it is out of true the affected limb receives undue strain and, of course, the ability to gallop is reduced. Plaiting, or crossing the forelegs one over the other when in movement, is rather more serious. Not only does it seriously restrict the freedom of movement, but there is a likelihood of the horse coming down. Animals that turn the toes out have a tendency to knock their legs about, as will one who goes too close in front or behind. This latter practice, called 'brushing', can be alleviated by special shoeing, but it is a constant nuisance and may mean that the horse always has to wear protective boots.

At the walk, which should be free and long striding, the hind legs should be brought well under the body, coming down in advance of the hoofmark made by the foreleg. A horse with a good walk is rarely bad in any of his other paces and should be able to gallop.

At the trot watch the action of the knee, if it is high much of the energy which should be expended in going forward is being dissipated. The faster paces will, therefore, lack speed and extension and the ride will not be so comfortable. In addition, of course, the limbs are subjected to greater concussion.

The Horse under Saddle

Now have him saddled up. This is an opportunity to judge his behaviour in the stable. Watch him being bridled and note whether he accepts what can be a little uncomfortable with equanimity.

His reactions to the saddle are also a useful pointer to the condition of the back. If he humps his back and looks generally unhappy and uncomfortable it may just be a habit and mean nothing. On the other hand it could be indicative of some derangement or damage to the kidneys or to the spine itself. There are horses who are termed 'cold-backed', and it is suggested that they resent the cold surface of the saddle in much the same way as a person might dislike the feel of a cold shirt first thing in the morning. This is possible, but it is far more likely that these horses are suffering from an arthritic condition between some of the lumbar vertebrae. It is, in fact, quite surprising to learn that very many horses, even if they do not exhibit these signs, suffer more or less constantly from back pain of this nature. All the more reason, of course, why young animals should not be asked to carry weight before they are reasonably mature.

Many so-called 'cold-backed' horses are perfectly all right once they have had a few minutes exercise, although they may be more inclined to buck than others.

Avoid, however, the horse who almost sits down when saddled or when the rider comes to mount. He is undoubtedly suffering from one of the conditions described. After all, the object of our keeping a horse is to ride him and in order to do so we must first be able to get on.

Once you are up, without we hope any objections from the horse, ask him to walk on and get the feel of him. Some horses give one an immediate feeling of security, these are usually the well-made, nicely balanced ones; others, with little 'front' to them, may give just the opposite feeling.

Try the horse at walk, trot and canter *and on both reins*. You will soon see whether he favours one side or the other and by how much.

If you have the opportunity to jump over a low fence, do so—you want to find out as much about the horse in the short time at your disposal as you possibly can.

Now take him away from his home surroundings, turning him away from home. If he is going to be nappy he will try it at this point. If possible ride him down a road where there is some traffic and make sure that he is all he is claimed to be in this respect. If you can possibly find a gentle slope trot the horse down it and see whether his action shortens uncomfortably.

It is unlikely that you will uncover any definite tricks he may possess, but you will have gained a fairly good impression of the sort of horse he is and whether he measures up to your requirements.

Handle him in his box, putting on his rugs, lifting his feet and rubbing his ears. Ask him to move over and note his reactions to these things.

A horse that appears nervy in the box, is fussy about his head or lays his ears back when you adjust his rugs is not necessarily vicious, but to be forewarned is to be forearmed.

If at the end of it all you decide that the horse fulfils the majority of the conditions you have in mind—it is unlikely that he will fulfil them all—then buy him, *but subject to his being passed sound in every way by the veterinary surgeon.*

BUYING A CHILD'S PONY

The purchase of a child's pony is, to my mind, a far more difficult thing to accomplish satisfactorily. If one wishes to risk one's own neck that is, within reason, one's own affair. One should not, however, risk the limbs and maybe the lives of small children.

It is an unfortunate fact that the standard of pony breaking (and it is often *breaking* and not *making*) is appallingly low. I think this is due to the deplorable tendency, which I have already mentioned, of selling and buying ponies at too young an age.

I have seen with my own eyes, as well as having hundreds of instances brought to my notice, young ponies, two- and three-year-old babies, sold to inexperienced homes—often with the most frightful results. I have before me now a letter from a ten-year-old child desperately asking for advice about her pony. She says, 'My pony is three. We bought him at a sale last autumn and he was very quiet. Now when I ride him on the road he whips round and bucks, and if I try to make him go on he rears up. He is also very bad in traffic. My father gets very cross with him and hits him, but it does no good and makes him worse. Now I dread riding him because he frightens me so much. Please can you help me.'

You may well ask, what sort of parent would expose his child to such danger? But there really are people who do just this sort of thing.

This is a bad example, but it is by no means a solitary one. It is typical of a large number of letters that editors of magazines receive every week. All they can do is to reply immediately, urging the parents to get rid of the pony before it maims or kills their child.

We may blame the person who sold the pony, even to the extent of condemning his or her action as criminal, we may blame the parents for their ignorance, what we cannot do is blame the poor, wretched pony.

The fact is that the pony, in spite of the father's treatment, was not properly broken for riding and was certainly not an animal suitable for a beginner to handle on her own.

Anyone with a modicum of knowledge can break a weak, immature animal incapable of resistance. I have no doubt, and God forgive me if I ever should, that had I a two-year-old, unbroken pony I could within three days have accustomed it to wearing a bit and to accepting a child on its back. I would not, however, have a made pony at the end of the operation. At best he is half-broken, and *broken* is the word, and that badly.

Sold in poor condition he may initially appear to be quiet enough, but when he begins to feel better and stronger, because he cannot understand what his rider wants him to do, and she cannot tell him, he becomes confused. Then he becomes nervous, then angry and resentful. Add to these feelings that of fear, fear of noises and sights with which he is totally unfamiliar, and then, because he shows he is frightened, terrify him by beating him until all his instincts urge him to flee, to get away anywhere and anyhow and what have you left? You have no longer an animal willing and happy to put its trust in man, it is now an animal which has reverted to its wild state, only because of its contact with humans it is doubly distrustful, doubly unreliable. Man is now associated with pain and terror.

A beginner's pony, a first pony, should be bought with the object of giving the child confidence. Any old pony just will not do.

A first pony must be quiet, he must not move like quicksilver and if he has little ambition beyond a modest trot he will be none the worse for it. He need not necessarily be very, very old, for it is not so much his age which is important, but his temperament. There are lots of seasoned old reprobates at twenty and many very nicely mannered ponies of nine or ten. The young pony of four or five may turn out to be perfectly satisfactory, but you run more risk of his getting a little above himself than you do with an older and more experienced one.

Here again, Pony Club District Commissioners are usually prepared to be helpful and may know of a suitable outgrown pony in the district.

Failing this go to some reliable person who specialises in providing ponies for children. Don't buy them at sales. Otherwise write to one of the horse magazines, or even to me, and ask advice as to whom you should approach.

Conformation in a first pony is not so great a consideration, providing that it is not the type of pony that is so broad as to make the child both uncomfortable and insecure. Avoid if you can, however, the really badly made pony who just cannot carry a saddle without shooting it up its neck.

Sound it should certainly be, although there are many first ponies that would be as lame as dogs with three legs if worked hard, but who are quite able to do the quiet work demanded of them without becoming unsound.

Do not grudge the extra £10 or £20 if it buys you peace of mind—it is cheap at the price.

For slightly more experienced children a brighter sort of pony can be bought, but his temperament must be good and he must be 100% safe in traffic. In these cases more account should be taken of conformation. Don't buy a great, heavy-necked, cresty sort of pony, he will always be too strong and will ruin even the most sensitive young hands.

In this country we are fortunate to have our indigenous pony breeds and these, or crosses with them, make ideal young people's mounts.

Unless you are set upon showing the pony it is as well not to have one of the miniature Thoroughbred types. They are not nearly so tough and take far more looking after. They may also be too much for the average child rider to cope with comfortably.

There are nine native breeds, all of which vary considerably in appearance, but all of which are hardy and often have lovely temperaments and a high degree of intelligence (although some might call it downright cunning).

My own particular favourite is the Welsh—but then I am a Welshman. There are four principal sections to the Welsh Stud Book, the Welsh Mountain pony, who is the little fellow not exceeding 12 h.h.; his brother the larger Welsh pony up to 13.2 h.h., who is definitely a riding pony; then the Welsh pony of cob type and the larger Welsh Cob. To my mind no pony is more beautiful than the Welsh Mountain —but, as I said, I'm prejudiced. All of them are sure-footed, narrow enough, have substance and are capable of giving a lovely ride and, of course, the bigger ones can carry an adult too. There is also a part-bred section in the Welsh Stud Book in which there are some very nice animals.

The Connemara comes from Ireland and may exceed 14 h.h. He is an excellent riding pony and has a reputation for being a 'lepper'.

A first cross of this breed with the Thoroughbred is an excellent combination and is often bigger.

The Highland varies from the small 12.2 h.h. to 13.2 h.h., which come from Barra and the Outer Islands, to the largest, 14.2 h.h. Mainland pony, with the useful Riding pony, 13.2–14.2 h.h., thrown in between. These are very gentle, biddable creatures of enormous strength, but despite all that is claimed of them I cannot consider them really suitable riding ponies.

If the Highland is the big fellow of the native breeds his countryman the Shetland is just the opposite. Incredibly strong, he only stands 9 to 10 h.h. and so as a riding pony he is only suitable for the very young, and even then he is not entirely ideal. He just is not the right shape to make a comfortable ride and although a delightful 'cuddly' he can have an independent spirit.

The New Forest can stand as high as 14.2 h.h. and is an excellent and clever pony.

From the North come the Fell (13.2 h.h.) and the larger Dales pony. Shaggy, up to almost any weight, and if not elegant in appearance, capable of giving a fair ride, although they will lack the scope of some of the other breeds as far as the keen pony clubber is concerned.

Last, but by no means least, of our native ponies are the Dartmoor and Exmoor. These are small ponies, about 12.2 h.h., and the Dartmoor is a really lovely riding pony. So, too, of course, is the Exmoor, who is usually stockier and is claimed to be the oldest of the mountain and moorland breeds.

There are, of course, part-breds of all these breeds who may exceed the heights I have given and yet still retain the essential type. With this enormous variety to choose from I often wonder why so many unsuitable and nondescript ponies are about, and why people bother to buy such animals.

I am the last person to discourage a child owning a pony, or parents buying one, and I am only too well aware how insistent the young can be when they contract 'ponyitis'.

Even so, the expense connected with a pony does not end when the purchase cheque is made out. It goes on, month in and month out, for as long as the pony is owned. Too many ponies are bought by ignorant and indulgent, or perhaps exasperated and exhausted, parents under the mistaken impression that so long as there is a bit of rough grass a pony costs no more than his purchase price.

'Lives out' does not mean lives on air. He must be fed in the winter and properly cared for, he needs a shelter and his feet must be regularly attended to, and if grazing is hired it must be paid for.

All of which means additional and continued expenditure which must be considered before, and not after, the pony is bought.

The totally unhorsy parent is also well advised to view his offspring's assumed expertise in matters equine with some scepticism.

Little girls, and boys if they are interested, are not qualified to look after and manage a large animal on the strength of their having traipsed round the lanes on a quiet pony once a week for a year. At least not without some adult help or supervision. If parents are not able or willing to give this then the child is better off continuing with his or her weekly rides at the local riding school.

These are important considerations to be taken into account before acquiring a pony.

If, on the other hand, the parents are keen, prepared to learn and to accept advice, and are determined that their pony shall not suffer through ignorance, or lack of means or proper facilities, then go ahead and buy one.

It is more than well worth the expense and the effort.

HORSE AND PONY BREED SOCIETIES

Arab Horse Society (Secretary: Brig. F. H. V. Purcell, M.B.E., Loughmoe, Shelley Close, Itchen Abbas, Winchester, Hants.)

Cleveland Bay Horse Society. (Secretary: O. Wellford, Midge Hall, Roxby, Staithes, Saltburn, Yorks.)

Connemara Pony Breeders' Society. (Secretary: John Killeen, 4 Nunn's Island, Galway, Ireland)

English Connemara Pony Society. (Secretary: Mrs. L. Barthorp, The Quinta, Bentley, Farnham, Surrey.)

Dartmoor Pony Society. (Secretary: Dr. E. L. Roberts, Lower Hisley, Lustleigh, Newton Abbot, Devon.)

Exmoor Pony Society. (Secretary: Lt.-Col. V. C. A. Munckton, Capland Orchard, Hatch Beauchamp, Taunton, Somerset.)

Fell Pony Society. (Secretary: Miss P. Crossland, Packway, Windermere, Westmorland.)

Highland Pony Society. (Secretary: G. D. Cheyne, 51 High Street, Dunblane, Perthshire.)

Hunters' Improvement and National Light Horse Breeding Society. (Secretary: C. G. Wright, 17 Devonshire Street, London, W.C.1.)

National Pony Society. (Secretary: Cmdr. B. H. Brown, Stoke Lodge, 85 Cliddesden Road, Basingstoke, Hants.)

New Forest Pony Breeding and Cattle Society. (Secretary: Miss D. McNair, Beacon Corner, Burley, Ringwood, Hants.)

Northern Dales Pony Society. (Secretary: C. Nixon, Hutton Gate, Guisborough, Yorkshire.)

Ponies of Britain Club. (Secretary: Mrs. G. Spooner, Brookside Farm, Ascot, Berks.)

Shetland Pony Stud Book Society. (Secretary: T. H. F. Myles, 61 George Street, Perth, Scotland.)

Welsh Pony and Cob Society. (Secretary: T. E. Roberts, 32 North Parade, Aberystwyth, Cardiganshire.)

PRINCIPAL HORSE SOCIETIES

The British Horse Society. (The National Equestrian Centre, Stoneleigh, Kenilworth, Warwickshire.)

British Show-Jumping Association (address as above).

The Pony Club (address as above).

The British Horse Society is the recognised national equestrian body in this country. Its committees cover The Pony Club, Combined Training, Dressage, Riding Clubs, Instruction and Examination, Riding Establishments, Horse and Pony Breeds, Shows, International Equestrian Fund and a Joint Measurement Scheme. The Society offers free advice to members and operates preferential insurance schemes as well as many special privileges.

The present and future interests of every horseman and woman are furthered by the efforts of the B.H.S. and all riders should be members. Full membership costs £2 per annum, associate membership £1 per annum.

Horse-keeping - which method?

Well before a horse is purchased plans must have been made for his accommodation and a method of keeping him decided upon.

The final arrangement will depend largely upon the time one has available; for horse-keeping, whatever method is adopted, makes heavy demands on time. It will also, of course, depend upon the work the horse is to do and the facilities that are available.

Keeping at Livery

The easiest way to keep a horse, and the most expensive, is to get someone else to keep it for you at livery. There will be horse-owners who have no alternative but to employ this method but, expense apart, it seems to me to take much of the fun and interest out of horse-owning. It may be very nice to drive up to the stables and have your horse, saddled and bridled, waiting for you, but it is somewhat impersonal and the arrangement denies to the owner the opportunity, and the undoubted satisfaction, of establishing a really close relationship with the horse.

Full livery is necessarily expensive, but there are stables which will charge much reduced rates if they can use the animal as a school horse. There are two disadvantages to what might otherwise be a convenient arrangement. First, the school would like to make use of the horse at weekends, when they have a greater number of clients, and this is probably the time the owner also wants the animal; secondly, it is very difficult to keep a horse reasonably schooled if half-a-dozen different people, all possibly novices and all endeavouring to communicate in different ways, are allowed to ride him. The horse either gives up the unequal contest and becomes just another unambitious plug, or he may develop a number of annoying resistances and habits which become more deeply ingrained as time goes on. If, of course, his use can be restricted to a qualified member of the stable staff the matter assumes a very different complexion.

Nevertheless, there are parts of the country where livery is the only possible answer and people living in these areas must make the best arrangements they can if they are determined upon horse-ownership.

Certainly in these cases it is better to have the horse properly cared for at a livery stable, which may also have facilities in the way of schooling areas, jumps, etc., and where he has the company of his own kind, than to try and keep him on a quarter acre of rough scrub land at an inconvenient distance from one's home.

The B.H.S. *Supplement of Riding Schools*, already referred to, is a great help in choosing the sort of livery accommodation required.

A STABLE FOR THE HOME-KEPT HORSE

If, however, one has the necessary space at or near one's own property the most enjoyable way is to look after the animal oneself.

The horse that is going to be in fairly hard work, either hunting or taking part in competitive events, both of which pursuits require him to be maintained in hard condition and in the winter to have his coat removed by clipping, will need a stable of some kind, whether he is to live in entirely, or be kept on the New Zealand rug system. If there are no existing stables or buildings which can be converted to the purpose there is only one solution—the erection of a new stable.

Pre-Fabricated Structures

Fortunately there are a number of obliging firms, specialising in ready-to-erect wooden stabling, which are very willing to submit plans and quotations for either a single box or a range of stable buildings. Most of them are also able to lay the necessary concrete foundation and erect the building for you if you feel this is beyond your ability. Otherwise, of course, a local builder can be called in to do the job for you. All this, however, increases the cost and I am assured, although not convinced, bearing in mind my own ineptitude with a hammer, that any average handyman can put the affair up without too much difficulty. I say I am not convinced because I once witnessed the efforts of six strong men, all useful handymen, two boys, two further directing geniuses and one woman (who may have been the trouble) trying to erect a range of two boxes supplied by a well-known firm. The language, which the presence of the lady did little to ameliorate, was horrific, the whole operation appeared to be highly dangerous, and while they did eventually get the thing up, the cost in time alone was far in excess of what a small builder would have charged.

In fairness, many people do manage the job most satisfactorily, but it is as well to make an honest assessment of one's ability before deciding to 'do-it-yourself'.

Extremely affluent horse-owners may prefer to build in brick, which is a job for a professional builder, but there is at least one firm manufacturing stabling in pre-cast concrete.

Planning Permission

In almost every part of the country it will be necessary to obtain planning permission for permanent buildings and local authorities vary considerably in their requirements regarding drainage, distance from human habitation, etc. It is, therefore, essential to find out from your local council offices what regulations have to be observed.

Regulations regarding horse-keeping, whatever the type of building employed, are much stricter in built-up areas, where the question of other people's amenities are to be considered, and it is as well to find out well in advance of acquiring a horse what the authorities will ask of you.

Conversion of Existing Buildings

The conversion of existing buildings allows for more personal ingenuity and is generally far cheaper. My own stables, although far from exemplary, are very satisfactory, and the cost of conversion amounted to only a few pounds. We had a three-sided Suffolk cart-shed of some age, but it was, within reason, structurally sound. It had a storage loft and a pantiled roof which was made completely water tight, and insulated at the same time, by fastening roof felt on the inside across the roof beams. It was made into two large boxes, about 14 ft. square, by means of railway sleepers. The sleepers were set upright in a trench to divide the area into two and to make a front wall, and made secure by means of timber stretchers set along their length.

Any gap between the sleeper wall and the ceiling level was filled in with some rough, but perfectly adequate timber, and gaps between individual sleepers were sealed with a plastic filler. The half-doors were filched from other odd buildings on the place, at least the bottom halves, and were fitted easily enough. The top halves were rather more difficult, so much so, in fact, that in the end they never did get put up. If I had really thought them necessary I would have persevered, but as I never shut the top door, even in the worst weather, it would have been a waste of time anyway. These stables have been in constant use for over eighteen months and we have never had a horse with even a suspicion of a runny nose.

By putting the sleeper wall back from the overhang of the roof we also managed to have a verandah in front of the boxes and, apart from our own convenience, this allows the horses to have their heads out on the wettest day without discomfort.

It is, in fact, quite surprising what can be achieved by the intelligent alteration of the most unpromising buildings. Of course, it is very necessary when converting an existing building to make sure that all projections, old nails, etc., are removed, otherwise one is asking for trouble.

First-class stabling is very nice to have, but it is no substitute for good horsemastership.

Fundamental Requirements—Types and Sizes

Nevertheless, however humble the building there are certain fundamental and common-sense requirements which it should meet and there are certain forms which are better than others.

Loose boxes are vastly preferable to the more old-fashioned stalls. I can think of nothing more soul destroying and likely to produce a neurotic animal than to make him stand in a confined space, facing an expanse of wall, for the greater part of the twenty-four hours in a day.

Stalls are all very well for ponies who normally live out and who make use of them for short periods devoted to grooming and such like, but they are hardly ideal for the horse who spends most of his time in the stable, and certainly not so for the animal stabled like this on his own. Where a pony occupies a stall for anything beyond a short period he should be secured by means of a rope passing from his headcollar, through a ring or hole in the manger and then through a manger log which may just rest on the straw. A manger log is not a 'log' at all, but a sphere of *lignum vitae* with a hole through the centre. Once the rope is passed through the log it can be tied with a simple quick-release knot, in case the pony ever gets a leg over the rope.

This method allows the pony a certain amount of liberty within the stall, without his being able to turn right round, and also lets him lie down if he wishes to do so.

My own ideal size for a loose box would be no less than 14 ft. x 12 ft. for a horse and 12 ft. x 10 ft. for a pony. Many pre-fabricated boxes are, however, somewhat smaller and I would always think it advisable to spend a little extra and have a good size box. There is certainly more freedom for the horse and less chance that he will get himself cast in a bigger box. The fact that you have to use more straw to make a satisfactory bed should not be a consideration.

More important is to have a good airy box and this you will not have if the roof level is too low. I would like a 12 ft. minimum eaves height, but I admit this may not always be possible to achieve.

Doors should certainly be high enough to prevent the animal jumping out of the box, but not so high that he has to crane his neck to see over the top. A height of 4 ft. 6 ins. is about right and 4 ft. is a good width. Narrow doorways are an abomination against which horses can knock their hips. Horses can suffer considerable damage, even to the extent of bone fractures, by knocking themselves in this way.

Two bolts are necessary on this bottom half of the door, one of the normal pattern at the top, and one of the kick-over type at the bottom. This will prevent the crafty fellow who has learnt to undo top bolts from disappearing in the middle of the night and also discourages the gentleman who kicks the bottom of his door for the sake of hearing the glorious rattle it makes.

Siting

The siting of boxes is of great importance to the well-being and the mental serenity of the horse. Boxes should face to the south, out of the head winds and where they receive as much of the sun as we are likely to get in this particular section of our vale of tears. In addition, they should be sited so that their inmates can see as much of what is going on as possible. Horses, like humans, become bored, but can do less about it than their masters. The horse will be much more alert, interested and happy if he can see people, dogs, children and all the comings and goings of the normal household from his box.

THE ESSENTIAL TRINITY

There are then a further three factors to be considered, whatever the type of stabling. They are *ventilation, insulation and drainage.*

Ventilation

As far as the first of these is concerned we need *ample* ventilation without draughts. Draughts are anathema to horses just as much as they are to human beings. Apart from causing aches and pains they contribute materially to colds and chills and therefore cannot be tolerated. If

23, 24 and 25 *A selection of heads of various types*

*26 A horse protected by a well-made
New Zealand rug*

the box is high enough and the top door left open there should be plenty of ventilation. An additional aid would be a set of louvres high up on the rear wall to take away the upward rising bad air which may accumulate in the box. If there is a window in the box (always placed next to the doorway) it should be of the type which opens inwards from the bottom hinge so that the air enters in an upward direction and not directly on to the horse. The more fresh air we can have in our stables the healthier will be our horses.

In very cold weather it is far better to increase the ration of heating foods, to compensate for the extra used by the horse to keep himself warm, and to put on an extra blanket, rather than to shut the top door. The unclothed parts of the animal, his neck and his buttocks, may look a little rough, but he will remain healthy and free from colds.

Old fashioned grooms and some horse dealers shut the top door, put on plenty of clothing and create a fug worthy of a bar parlour. As a result the owner, or client, can be shown a horse who exhibits a glorious satin-like sheen, but that horse is much more likely to catch cold than his toughened, if not so elegant, brother who enjoys plenty of fresh air whatever the weather.

Insulation

Insulation implies the use of materials which will keep the building relatively warm in cold weather and relatively cool under the opposite condition. In order to achieve this object it is necessary in wooden structures to have the inside lined. Apart from creating an insulating cavity between the outer and inner walls it also contributes to the strength of the structure against the depredations of horses with a propensity to kick at the wall for the sheer hell of it. Older stable buildings are usually well and solidly built, but there is always a temptation when converting less well-constructed buildings to use corrugated iron sheeting for the roof. This material attracts heat, when there is any, and doesn't keep the cold out. It is a bad insulator and not to be recommended. Asbestos sheeting is not over expensive and is far more efficient in these respects, but, of course, is unsuitable for any part of the building other than the roof.

Drainage and Floors

The problem of drainage is relatively easy if one is building from scratch. The simpler the system the better it is likely to be. Old fashioned stables had floors of very beautiful (and now very expensive) blue Staffordshire brick which were often ruined by having drains set in the middle. The drains were frequently blocked and the box consequently permeated with unpleasant smells.

The best idea is to have a very slightly sloping concrete floor ($1\frac{1}{2}$ to 2 inches slope is enough) and an open drain, which can be swilled and brushed out, *outside* the stable door. If the drain is inside the door it makes it uncomfortable for the horse to stand looking out. Many modern stables, in fact, have no drainage system at all and manage very well without. The wet straw is brushed straight out of the door on to the concrete fronting the boxes and that in turn is brushed clean and the refuse transferred to the muck heap. I doubt, however, whether the council of a suburban area would approve of this method; most of them require elaborate, and sometimes impossible, drainage systems to be installed.

In many countries overseas, and I have also seen them in this country, floors of hard-packed earth or clay are employed, quite often having a base of rubble. Obviously they cannot be so effective from the viewpoint of drainage, but they are far less likely to cause injuries than brick or concrete and have greater insulating properties. Providing the floor has a thick covering of straw, much of the water will be absorbed before it makes contact with the earth surface, and while the pundits tend to condemn the system I am by no means persuaded that it is impossible to keep healthy horses this way in Britain.

Far more important from the horse's point of view is that whatever the system employed the box is properly and regularly cleaned and kept sweet.

Fittings and Tools
In all types of stabling certain fittings will be required and a number of simple cleaning tools are also a necessity.

These fittings or tools can be elaborate or simple depending upon what the owner can afford. Elaborate ones may not always contribute to healthier horses, but they often make the stable work a lot easier.

First one requires a manger, or at any rate a receptacle, in which to put the horse's food. In the old type of stabling mangers are often massive, porcelain affairs built into the corner of the box. Obviously they are very durable and are nearly always sufficiently deep to prevent a horse sweeping his food out to either side—a wasteful procedure indulged in by some horses. Their disadvantage is that they are difficult to clean easily and quickly. Horses are fastidious eaters and like us do not appreciate eating, as it were, from a dirty plate.

For newly built boxes galvanised mangers which fit into a corner are very satisfactory. They are usually fitted with two 'anti-waste' bars, one on each side, and can be easily dropped into a wooden framework set across the corner. They have the great advantage of being easily removable and, therefore, very easily cleaned.

A manger is, for the sake of safety, set at breast height. There is a school of thought which holds that as the horse in nature feeds from the ground it is illogical to feed him from manger height when stabled. The answer, of course, is that the *stabled* horse is, as far as he is concerned, in a *natural* state, or at least an accustomed one, and seems to have adapted himself to eating from this position very well. Other advantages which are argued in favour of manger feeding are that the horse cannot, having had his meal, kick the manger about, damaging both it and himself and that he is less likely to deposit his droppings into a manger, possibly spoiling the food, than into a similar feeding receptacle placed on the floor.

The first point I concede, but it does seem to me that it is just as possible for an animal to put his droppings into a manger as into a feed tin on the floor. Providing the horse is correctly positioned at the moment of lifting his tail the difference in height would not appear to be of any significance.

For the very simple reason that I do not possess mangers I feed my horses from heavy, round feed tins of adequate depth which can be obtained from most ironmongers, particularly those in farming areas. They are cheap, easily removable and, therefore, easily cleaned after every feed. They are placed firmly on the straw in the corner and are removed when the horse has finished feeding. No extra work is involved in this as we make it a rule always to see whether a horse has eaten up within an hour of his being given the feed. Once or twice they have been kicked, but no droppings find their way into them. If they were left in the box all night they probably would get used as footballs and they might contain droppings in the morning, but they don't get left in the box and so the matter doesn't arise. Neither does the close proximity of the bedding induce the horse to eat it—another theory advanced by the anti-ground faction.

A cardinal rule of feeding, which appears in the majority of horse manuals, is that horses should be watered before being fed. And in principle this is sound because if the horse had his feed and then immediately drank a bucket of water it would have the effect of washing undigested food out of the stomach. But this in fact would only arise where water was not always available in the box, the horse being watered at fixed times.

Modern opinion says 'Keep water in the box all the time', and it is right. At one time much controversy raged as to whether horses should drink hard or soft water. I always considered it to be a somewhat pointless argument and my horses have always drunk water from the tap. Very few horses, however, like very cold water and I always leave water in the buckets for about half-an-hour before putting it in the boxes.

Having digressed a little we must consider how water shall be made freely available, and the simplest way is to keep a filled bucket in the stable.

Oak stable buckets are heavy and so not easily knocked over if put on the ground. They need regular cleaning, however, if they are not to become slimy, and even with an inner rim of iron fitted round the top horses have been known to chew at them. Galvanised buckets are a boon to bored horses, they rattle delightfully when kicked and crumple most satisfactorily when sat upon. Rubber or heavy plastic buckets are much better and stand up to more ill usage, but they need scalding with a soda solution before use, otherwise they make the water taste.

I can personally attest to the truth of this having had to use water carried in rubber buckets to the house during the severe winter of 1962–63. Everything from tea to steamed puddings tasted of rubber. I have never forgotten it and would hate to inflict such a hardship on anyone, much less my horse.

Rubber buckets are also light in weight, which is an important consideration. Oak buckets get even heavier with age and use and when filled are beyond the carrying capacity of a girl or a lightly built woman. They do, of course, look very smart outside the stables, painted in one's colours and filled with geraniums.

To avoid the possibility of buckets being knocked over they can be hung from a hook on the wall, but this must be a hook of proper design with the point turned back, elongated, and presenting no sharp projection on which the horse could injure himself.

If you can afford self-filling water bowls in the stable, which will involve the installation of a permanent water system, this is ideal for the horse and will save hours of time for the owner or groom.

If your stables are old ones they may be fitted with hayracks fairly high up on the wall. Pull them down and sell them for scrap. Horses fed hay from these affairs, apart from having to imitate a giraffe to get it, receive all the dust and seeds in their eyes with consequent ill effect. Feed hay from a haynet. You can then calculate how much hay you are feeding and can be assured of the minimum of waste. Suspend the net from a galvanised ring, either screwed into the wall or bolted through it, and have another ring to which the horse may be tied for grooming or when saddled before going out.

Where the box has a window, of the type already mentioned, it must be protected with an iron bar grille. Electric light switches should be of the type designed for outside use and should be placed *outside* where no horse can play with them. Electrical fittings inside the box must be out of the horse's reach and as an extra precaution covered with a wire mesh.

The door, bolted as I have already described, can have the top edge covered with zinc to discourage chewing, and mesh grilles can be purchased to close across the top half.

The reasons given for using these grilles, which, of course, prevent a horse standing with his head out of the box, are to prevent a horse biting you as you pass by, to prevent a horse contracting the habit of weaving, and also to prevent him biting his next door neighbour.

My own comments on these points are: my horses are not wild animals: I do not expect them to bite me. Should they forget their manners and nip me hard I bite them back and they don't do it again. (This is not as silly as it sounds and is psychologically a sound practice. Very quickly one takes the muzzle in both hands and inflicts a sharp nip on the tenderest part. The effect is salutary and long lasting, and it is amusing to watch the horse puzzling out the 'action-reaction' factor.) Weaving is caused by boredom. Short of keeping the top door permanently closed I can think of no way better calculated to encourage the vice. It doesn't often happen or assume serious proportions. When it does it is more sensible to erect a grille which projects outwards between the boxes and so separates the antagonists.

Possession of proper stable tools (apart from grooming kit, which is dealt with elsewhere) contributes to the ease with which the stable can be cleaned out. Absolute essentials are a barrow, a stable shovel, a pitchfork (two prongs with blunted ends), a four tine fork, and a broom. A muck skip (there is a very good rubber one on the market, and if you can run to two of them one can be used for carrying the feed to the manger), or even, a muck-sheet, a piece of strong sacking or canvas, which can be used for the same purpose, is also helpful and, indeed, necessary. You will also need a sack, split open down one side and the bottom to carry straw from the store to the box. Without this inexpensive piece of equipment you will not only find the operation difficult, but will also leave a trail behind you which will have to be cleared up.

For the more affluent there is a stable-barrow to end all stable-barrows which was designed by my friend, Lt.-Col. C. R. D. Gray, owner of the Stetchworth Stud and manager of the Hadrian Stud at Newmarket. This barrow, which is obtainable from a number of Newmarket firms, is big enough to take all the dirty bedding from a box, and a lot more besides, at one time, but is so light and so accurately balanced that it can be wheeled and tipped up when full with hardly a perceptible effort.

The rest of this equipment is easily enough obtained and requires little comment, although it is as well when buying broom heads to go for the best, they last so much longer. Best of all are the, admittedly expensive, nylon brooms used for road sweeping by many local authorities. They take a very long time even to show signs of wear.

Bedding and Mucking Out

For most of us the removal and replacement of bedding is the job most deserving of the description, 'stable chore'. Unfortunately, apart from possessing the necessary tools and planning an intelligent yard lay-out there is not a lot we can do to diminish this necessary labour. Nor, in fact, should we seek to suit our own convenience in this respect, or any other, at the expense of the horse.

Good beds are necessary for the well-being of the horse and our only consideration should be to obtain the best material to provide them. Poor bedding, or an insufficient quantity of bedding, does not induce horses to lie down and can cause injuries from contact with the floor when they do.

Nice, happy, contented horses express appreciation of their lot by lying down frequently and for long periods. Not only is it good for their legs, but also for their mental state.

Whatever form of bedding is used one should aim at providing a dry, warm and resilient bed which is absorbent and deodorising. Again, the best quality material will amount to nothing if good stable management is not practised.

70

Straw Beds

Straw is the most common form of bedding and of the varieties obtainable wheat straw is the most satisfactory. In pre-combine days it was cut long and this property enabled one to make a really good bed with little effort. In some parts of the country it is still possible to obtain wheat straw of a good length, but in many more the shorter variety has to be accepted. Even so it is the most resilient and the least palatable.

Oat straw, which can be used for mixing in chaff, is very much more attractive to equines as a food and most horses will become addicted to bed-eating where it is provided as bedding.

The consumption of straw is bad for the wind, upsets one's calculations of the bulk quantity of food required by the horse and is generally regarded as one of the equine sins. The bed can be made less attractive by spraying with disinfectant. These considerations apart, oat straw can be used, but it flattens easily and one needs a great deal of it to provide a good covering. It is best avoided if possible.

Barley straw in the old days was not considered suitable because the awns on the ears are so prickly as to cause skin irritations and if eaten they give rise to colic. Combined barley straw, however, is almost free of awns and makes a good enough bed.

Rye straw is tough and hard-wearing, but is not generally obtainable.

Straw, used for bedding, has an advantage over other materials in that the resultant box cleanings are saleable. In many areas manure merchants will arrange to clear the muck heap periodically and to supply fresh straw in return. Admittedly this is usually of the short, combine variety, but the system has its merits and there are many areas where long straw is impossible to obtain.

The Use of Bracken, Sawdust, Peat Moss, etc.

In some parts bracken (cut when green) is used for bedding, but it is scratchy stuff, non-absorbent and often full of insects. It makes a very poor bed. Sawdust is often used where it is easily available, but requires a deal of labour and management if it is to be satisfactory. If sawdust is considered it should not come from other than seasoned woods. Green woods produce a sawdust which ferments easily and becomes very hot as it gets wet and hard packed. Wet patches and droppings must be removed quickly and the bed needs forking and turning daily.

Wood shavings are better as they are less likely to ferment, but they are not absorbent.

71

These two materials can be used in conjunction with each other and in this case the sawdust forms the under layer.

Peat moss is in popular use and like sawdust is highly absorbent and is the most efficient deodoriser of all. Whilst it does not get hot, like sawdust, it does, however, need the same attention. Lack of proper management, resulting in soaked patches being left in the box, will cause rotting of the feet and skin disorders on parts of the body coming into contact with the bed.

All absorbent beddings such as those described above are remarkably efficient drain blockers and precautions must be taken accordingly. A further disadvantage is that a muck heap formed of these materials is unsaleable and may even cause disposal difficulties.

The advantage is that horses do not eat these types of bedding—which is, I suppose, something to be thankful for.

Some years ago there was a waterproof plastic covered mattress on the market, originally intended for cows, and there was talk of similar mattresses, suitably strengthened to withstand shod hooves, being produced for stables. The makers claimed that it was warm, resilient and easily washed down although, of course, an area of the box would have to be covered with straw upon which horses could stale, as they have an understandable aversion to staling either on surfaces which they feel might be slippery or where they might get their legs splashed.

It never came to anything, but in the future it is not beyond possibility that something other than natural materials may be found which will do the job as well, or perhaps better, and save us all a lot of work.

In my view straw beds should be cleaned out every day. The soiled straw and droppings go to the muck-heap and the slightly wet stuff, which can be used again, put out to dry. The bed is then remade with fresh straw after the floor has been washed down and sprinkled with disinfectant.

At the risk of repeating myself I would stress that beds should be generous. A thin bed may seem to be economical, but it is an economy made at the expense of the horse's well-being and comfort and is, therefore, a false one. Straw should be laid with the stalks criss-crossed to give greater resilience and should be well banked up round the edges of the box. This practice not only makes a cosy draught-free bed, but prevents, in certain measure, the horse becoming cast, i.e. getting himself turned over against the corner in such a way that he cannot get himself up again.

The Deep Litter Method

There are people, however, who employ the deep-litter method, removing the droppings etc. and putting down fresh straw on the top. One is, in fact, making a compost heap within the stable, the whole thing being cleaned out in one go when it becomes inconveniently high or, as I suspect, at the end of the season when the horses go out to grass. Adherents of the method claim a great saving of labour with no ill-effect upon the horse, who, they point out, always has a deep, resilient and warm floor covering.

There are obvious arguments against the practice and while I am all for the saving of labour and am well aware that there are many healthy horses kept in this fashion, it does not commend itself as a system which I would personally employ in its entirety. However, I know of a number of horse-owners who practise the method on a weekly basis, leaving the bulk of the mucking out as a weekend job.

Exercise for the Stabled Horse

In one respect, however, there are no short cuts when a horse is kept stabled. I refer, of course, to exercise. The horse must go out once a day, every day, if he is to remain healthy in mind and body.

If he is in hard work, one day off a week may do him good and help him unwind, although I often think it is more for the convenience of his master that he has a day off than for any other reason. If he has not had a hard week a day in the box is just a period of frustrating boredom as far as he is concerned.

Unlike his master he has no need for the consolations of religion on Sundays.

THE COMBINED SYSTEM

Fortunately, for the many people who cannot always exercise every day and have little time to spare for stable work there is an excellent way of keeping horses which reduces labour in these respects. It is the so-called 'combined' system. The horse is given a hunter clip, i.e. the legs and saddle-patch are left unclipped, he is kept in at night and then turned out in a New Zealand rug during the day. As a result stable-work is made less onerous and the horse is able to exercise himself (*Plate 26*).

The system has almost everything to recommend it, for it allows the

73

use of a fit horse during the winter months without the owner having to spend a disproportionate amount of time looking after it.

More important the horse is, I believe, just that little bit nearer to his natural state. Certainly the method is beneficial to his mental state and he is unlikely to develop tricks due to boredom.

The system, of course, does not preclude labour entirely and the horse must have his regular feeds just as a stabled animal does. The fact that he is out at grass for part of his day, grass which in the winter months has no nutritional value, does not mean that any economy in feeding can be contemplated. In fact, in cold weather, he will need more heating foods to maintain his body heat.

He will, of course, get dirty and there will be a certain amount more work involved in getting him cleaned up for a hunting day. His coat, too, may not carry quite the same bloom as does that of a stabled horse, but these things must be accepted, and providing he remains fit and healthy, and is as well turned out as possible, the question of appearance is of secondary importance when compared with the obvious merit of the system as a whole.

Obviously the system can be operated with variations. My own mare for instance is 'quartered' (i.e. given a quick brush, mane and tail made tidy and feet picked out) after her morning feed and is then exercised. On her return she is put out in her paddock, where she has her mid-day feed, and is then brought in during the early afternoon to be properly groomed and strapped.

If for any reason she does not have her hour or two of freedom she is noticeably fidgety and usually indulges in a fit of sulks.

Alternatively, if the box opens on to the paddock, the horse can be let out during the day, and if the door is left open can come in and out as he wishes.

At the other extreme it is possible to keep the horse out day and night in a New Zealand rug. I think you would then need two rugs per horse as they can get very wet and muddy, but it has been accomplished quite satisfactorily, although I have never tried it myself. In this case an adequate shelter, well strawed, is necessary and the horse will need generous feeding. I would also, I think, carry out only a high trace clip, leaving the coat on the top of the back and the upper side of the neck as well as on the legs.

Horses kept in this fashion will hardly appear as the epitome of elegance, but so long as they are never brought in hot and have equable temperaments, they will remain free from colds and chills.

74

Choice of a New Zealand Rug

The rug itself is the integral part of the system, and, therefore, its purchase and subsequent care demands the closest attention. Surprisingly, for very many are used, the majority of the so-called New Zealand rugs available are very poor in design and sometimes in quality too.

Their greatest failure is in the shaping, and the seeming inability of the manufacturers to relate purpose to design. It is essential that the rug should fit really well, that it will not shift unduly in use, that its fastenings do not chafe or exert constant pressure on any one part of the horse and that the wretched thing is waterproof.

Very few fulfil these requirements. A good rug, which cannot be made cheaply, should give more than ample freedom at the neck and particularly over the shoulder. If it is tight in these places the movement of the horse will cause it to first rub away the hair and ultimately cause a sore place. The only way I know of avoiding shoulder rubbing is by shaping the rug at the shoulder and giving it an extra fullness by means of a dart. The rug must be deep enough at the sides and of sufficient length to cover the dock by some three inches. It should then be darted to fit round the quarters and prevented from blowing up either by a cord, which can be tightened and is inset into the rear end, or a tail or fillet strap passing round the upper thigh below the tail.

There are only two patterns which I would use and neither of them employ a surcingle to keep the rug in place. Surcingles are a snare and a delusion on a New Zealand rug. In fact when they are fitted the rug is no longer a 'New Zealand' pattern, but just a waterproof rug. Either the surcingle is fastened so loosely as to be useless, or so tightly as to cause a sore back because of the constant pressure exerted on the spine.

I would use a rug employing a Pape's pattern fastening (the Australian design) or one of the Emston type (a true New Zealand rug). They are the most satisfactory in design and in use.

For the materials, I like the drab coloured canvas, not that frightful green tarpaulin which becomes board-like after one or two wettings. The lining, which should reach only half way down the flanks to avoid it getting muddied, should be of good, heavy, wool cloth. The check type of collar lining is as good as any. The leg straps, which must be of ample length, need to be of stout, good quality leather. I always think the grey chrome leather, or the very supple red buffalo hide, are the best, and the easiest to keep soft under adverse conditions.

The maintenance of the rug is all important. Straps must be kept soft by the continual and liberal application of Kocholine, or some similar preparation, and all hooks and metal fittings always kept covered with a thin layer of grease. Once a year have the cloth re-proofed, and when the rug is in use go and see that it is in place and properly adjusted as frequently as you can.

To prevent chafing and provoking a possible rodeo display loop the leg straps one over the other to keep them away from the tender parts between the hind legs.

Cleanliness—Next to Godliness

Whether you adopt this system or keep your animal permanently stabled during the winter months, or perhaps during the summer in the case of show jumpers, the maintenance of the stable itself is vital.

The golden rule with the stabled horse is cleanliness in all things.

Most of us are meticulous enough in our own homes and with our own children. Horses are much like children in many ways and require almost as much attention. Babies, in good homes anyway, are not left for long periods in wet and soiled nappies; our families (sometimes under protest) wash regularly and wear clean clothes. We eat clean, untainted food from clean crockery and our living quarters are dusted and kept free from dirt.

The horse asks no more than we give to ourselves, but it is our responsibility to provide for his needs. After all, it is we who put him in a stable for our own convenience and enjoyment. In return that stable must be kept clean. He needs a dry bed, fresh food and water, given in clean receptacles and his body must be kept clean by regular grooming.

There is a school of thought which recommends leaving cobwebs in stables as fly-catchers. Cobwebs are not tolerated in our houses and there is no reason why they should be allowed in a stable. This is one of the more stupid horsy maxims which are adhered to only for the convenience of the lazy horse-master. If one is so worried with flies an insecticide spray is much more efficient.

Sandbaths and Storage

If the layout of the yard permits a small space to be set aside for a sandbath so much the better. All horses seem to appreciate a roll in sand and the cost of this facility is not large.

For the rest of the yard; water supply, feed house and tack room should be within easy reach if time is to be saved. Where it is not possible to store bulky forage, i.e. hay and straw, under cover it should be kept off the ground so that the air can circulate underneath. This is easily accomplished by stacking the bales on planks raised from the ground on bricks. A plastic stack cover will prevent the forage becoming wet, but it should be removed and the air allowed to get at the bales as often as possible. If this is not done the condensation, which forms easily on the inner surface of plastics, will encourage mildew.

Siting of Manure

The siting of muck-heaps is even more important. Obviously they do not want to be too far away, but neither must they be placed so close to buildings as to be unhealthy or likely to cause damage to the structure. Wooden buildings, particularly, can be considerably spoilt if they are in too close contact with the ammonia fumes given off by the heap.

Very elaborate manure pits can be constructed with concrete floors, brick or concrete walls, drains and a permanent covering to keep off the rain, but simple and effective ones can be made on a patch of concrete using railway sleepers to encompass the heap.

In either case the manure should be well packed down and the edges tidied up. In a well-packed heap decomposition will be more rapid and the increase in heat produced will discourage fly breeding. Needless to say the heap should be removed regularly.

OUT AT GRASS

We now come to the last method of horse-keeping and the one open to the most abuse—the horse kept at grass all the year round.

It is, of course, the natural way for a horse to live. The difference is that in his wild state the horse roamed over extensive areas, feeding and exercising himself as he went. He was not confined to an acre of rough orchard and expected to work during the week and gallop about at rallies and the like at weekends.

Far too many horses and ponies are bought by people who do not realise this fact or its significance, and to whom the phrase 'lives out' means 'lives on air'.

The proper management of the grass-kept animal requires as much knowledge and almost as much supervision as that of the stabled horse.

The first essential, of course, is to have an adequate amount of *good* grazing. A requirement that is but rarely fulfilled. Two to three acres per animal, properly managed, and that means rested at intervals, when alternative grazing will be required, is by no means too much.

In the horse's feral state the problems of horse-sick pastures and red-worm infestation do not arise because of the enormous areas concerned, but in domesticity, where the animal is confined, it becomes a very real problem. The management of grassland is dealt with elsewhere, as it is a subject in its own right and of the greatest important to the horse-owner; all I would stress at this stage is that adequate grazing is essential and that back gardens and the odd half-acres of waste ground do not constitute *adequate* grazing.

Given that one has sufficient space, or the use of it, there are four prime conditions to be observed, apart from the quality and extent of the herbage. They are (a) proper water supply; (b) shelter from prevailing winds, such as trees, hedges or in their absence a shelter; (c) pasture properly enclosed and free from all bodies which might be a cause of injury, and (d) constant and regular supervision.

If these conditions are fulfilled a pony, particularly one of the native breeds, although not those having a high percentage of Thoroughbred or Arab blood, can be kept out in the worst weather without taking harm, so long as supplementary feeding is practised during the winter months.

To revert to the four conditions mentioned. Water is best supplied by a field pipe to a trough which has no sharp edges and which can be emptied for cleaning. A heavy galvanised tank filled by means of a hose-pipe may be pressed into service if a proper trough is not available, but is more difficult to clean. Water is an essential to health and should be clean, so it must not be allowed to collect a covering of scum during the summer, or be positioned where it can become a catchment for falling leaves in the autumn. Stagnant ponds, usually of dirty water, are not suitable as a watering arrangement.

Horses and ponies at grass, even in the bitterest weather, will, if they are receiving supplementary feed, spurn an artificial shelter, preferring to use that afforded by trees or thick hedges. During the winter nature creates a film of waterproofing grease beneath the heavy coat which gives adequate protection against rain. Animals kept entirely at grass, and therefore not intended for hard work, do not need a rug, nor should they be clipped and groomed. Cold winds are, however, a different matter and if the paddock does not have natural shelter against the prevailing ones then a field shed must be provided. This need be nothing more than a three-sided shelter, but it must be sited to give every possible protection.

In the summer months shelter is equally important to provide shade and a cool place away from the worst attacks of flies.

78

Safe fencing is a more obvious necessity, although it is often one that is neglected. If the field lacks a good, thick surrounding hedge then it will be necessary to fence it artificially.

Post and rail fencing is obviously good, but is hardly cheap. Plain, heavy guage wire strung tightly from stout wooden posts is acceptable, cheaper and the next best thing. The lowest strand of wire should not be less than one foot from the ground otherwise there will be a danger of animals getting their feet caught. Barbed wire and chicken mesh fencing are not suitable under any circumstances.

Whatever type of fencing is used it is always advisable to round off the corners of the field. Right angle corners can be a source of danger to galloping horses letting off steam.

All posts will require a thorough soaking in creosote as a preservative measure, and the application should be renewed each year. Creosote will also discourage horses from chewing, a habit many of them contract when bored or when there is insufficient feed in the paddock. Trees can also be treated in this manner for horses and ponies often seem to find the bark quite irresistible. If animals are allowed to chew at the trees they will, of course, soon kill them. Many authorities hold that wood-chewing is an indication of mineral deficiency and can be rectified by supplying large lumps of rock salt for the horses to lick. I am not sure how well-founded a supposition this is—I suspect it may be less accurate than most of us accept—but, as it can do no harm, I like to have rock salt available both in the box and the paddocks.

Foreign bodies in the way of large stones, tins, stakes, etc., must be removed—if they are not it is almost certain that the horse will injure himself on them. Horses at grass are not, in fact, very sensible and if there is any sort of trouble they can get into they invariably do. Therefore, be particularly vigilant in these respects and make a careful examination of the grazing area before putting animals out. Hedges must, of course, come in for the closest scrutiny to see that they contain no poisonous shrubs or trees, such as the yew. Ivy, too, should be removed. It is not so poisonous to horses as yew, but its effects are bad enough to be worth avoiding. Ragwort and deadly nightshade should also be removed, as these plants can be fatal if eaten.

I have already indicated that horses at grass are the most accident-prone of all animals and this faculty for damaging themselves is just one reason why regular supervision is so essential. Horses are at best rather helpless creatures in a domestic state and although the thought of putting stabled horses out at the end of the winter may be welcomed with a feeling of relief, it does not mean that the owner can forget them.

At least once a day, preferably twice, and ideally three or more times, they should be visited to ensure that everything is in order.

Water has to be checked for quantity and cleanliness, the animals inspected for injury, fences looked at, and if necessary repaired, and in addition feeds and hay must be given when this is necessary.

Regular visits to the field in any case pay dividends in the saving of time and temper. An animal who is frequently handled, and possibly fed, when at grass is far less likely to become one of those exasperating creatures who refuse to be caught. Once the animal associates the visit with feeding time, which is not necessarily or always followed by work, he is far more likely to be amenable and co-operative in this respect. In addition regular inspections of this kind help to maintain and reinforce the contact between master and horse.

Although the method of keeping horses at grass permanently has advantages in the saving of labour involved one must appreciate that it restricts the owner's usage of the horse.

Living out is the natural existence for the horse, and in a wild or semi-wild state is perfectly satisfactory, but when we confine a horse to a relatively small area this is not much more in accordance with his natural state than is shutting him up in a stable.

Wild horses who had, or have, the freedom of vast areas found sufficient nourishment in the variety of grasses and herbs contained in these areas, a variety that in the domesticated state we endeavour to reproduce and to improve in nutrient value by agricultural skills, in a very much smaller space. It is a fact, however, that with the exception of professionally operated stud farms, a great number of horse pastures are of poor quality.

The Feral Versus the Domestic State

It is also a fact, and one conveniently ignored by many owners practising this method of horse-keeping, that in his wild state nature maintains the horse in the condition best suited to the exertions he is likely to make. The wild horse keeps himself in trim by wandering *slowly* many miles in search of grazing, a procedure denied to the animal kept in a small paddock. In addition he does not carry a weight upon his back, he very rarely gallops and except when panicked does not jump.

By domesticating the horse and asking him to do these things for our pleasure we have, over a period of time, imposed upon him a life quite at variance with his natural existence. In consequence we must prepare and condition his body to perform the work we require of it. We achieve this object by feeding him artificially with foods designed to increase his energy and to replace the loss of body tissue which occurs during work. We groom him and in the cold weather we remove his coat and his natural protective grease covering, replacing it with rugs while he is in his stable.

Exercised, groomed and shorn of the coat which would prevent him from working hard without losing condition through excessive sweating, and properly fed with a balanced, if artificial, diet, the horse is physically capable of considerable effort.

Despite the fact that man, over many centuries, has produced breeds of horses aimed at perfecting the qualities and characteristics suited to his purpose, the domestic horse cannot be expected to work unless he is conditioned to do so.

In many cases, particularly that of the English Thoroughbred, the breed has become so far removed from the wild horse that they can no longer withstand the rigours of what to them is no longer a natural existence. Our native ponies, on the other hand, are still to some extent bred on the moors, mountains and in the forests and are therefore nearer to their natural environment and less dependent upon man for their well-being. Even so, while they retain the qualities of hardiness, lost by the Thoroughbred, they are not fitted to perform hard work unless physically prepared for it.

Grass alone does not possess the necessary energy and tissue replacing properties needed by the horse in work. In summer, grass is a soft, bulk and laxative food producing a soft condition. Where grazing is lush animals quickly enough run to fat, a condition in which undue strain will be placed on organs and limbs. If, therefore, an animal is to be kept at grass during this period of the year and also subjected to work, then grazing on lush pasture must be restricted and the animal fed artificially in relation to the work he is to do. If this work does not exceed a few hours gentle hacking in a week his additional food requirement will be small and he will come to no harm. If, however, the animal is to be in regular use, carrying an exuberant child or teenager to gymkhanas, mock hunts, club rallies and the like, it will be necessary to curtail his grass consumption to a few hours a day and feed him a greater quantity of body-building and energy-producing foods.

In winter, or more correctly from October to April, the grass will contain little nourishment and will do nothing but provide bulk. Much of the horse's food intake will be expended in producing sufficient

81

body heat to maintain health and, indeed, life itself, and the animal will require considerable and regular feeding for this purpose alone if he is not to lose condition. The winter coat will prevent him from indulging in fast work without his becoming distressed. It should not be groomed, other than for the purpose of removing the worst of the mud, lest the protective grease is removed also. It is, however, possible for him to be worked quietly, provided that his intake of heating foods is increased accordingly.

In conditions of snow, or conversely in a very dry summer spell, his inability to obtain sufficient bulk from his pasture will necessitate the feeding of hay.

As I have said elsewhere, the tragedy is that while literature on the subject is by no means sparse and horse-magazines, as well as Pony Club branches and Riding Clubs, continually stress the importance of understanding the fundamental requirements of the animal kept at grass, there are still people who ignore all the proffered advice because it doesn't suit their convenience to act upon it.

Quite recently I wrote an article on conditioning horses for long distance rides. In this I stated that the hard, muscle fit condition, necessary for such exertions, could not be obtained by keeping a horse solely at grass with a minimum of exercise and possibly a few handfuls of horse cubes. Not unexpectedly I received a number of letters telling me, in hardly more polite terms, that I was talking through my hat or that what I had said could not possibly apply to the writer's pony or horse because they regularly rode 30 miles off a handful of grass.

I do not say that it is impossible to work horses off grass. It is quite possible, and some horses put up with it better than others. What I do say is that it is wrong to do so, because, to suit your own selfish convenience, you are imposing undue and possibly unseen strains on a body not properly prepared to sustain them. Apart from the damage that can be done to ligaments, sinews, bone structures and internal organs which are unprepared for work, muscles are much more likely to be strained.

The results of muscle strain may not be immediately apparent, but there is every chance of a rheumatoid or arthritic condition being set up which will not only cause pain in the future but will incapacitate the horse and prevent him from functioning to his full ability.

In the keeping of horses, love (usually the wrong kind) is no substitute for knowledge, and ignorance is just as much 'the devil's trade mark' as it ever was.

Feeding Horses & Ponies

I have tried to make it clear in the preceding sections that by domesticating the horse we have imposed upon him a mode of life which is in contradiction to his basic nature. In his natural state he existed very well on a diet of grass, herbs and the like and can still do so, in some cases, so long as he has a sufficiently large area over which to graze and is not called upon to do more than travel slowly from one grazing ground to another with very occasional short bursts of speed.

In domestication, however, he is made to carry weight, often at speed, and sometimes over obstacles. To do so satisfactorily the efficiency of his organs and the strength of his body and muscle structures must be increased, and he has to expend a great deal more energy than it is ever necessary for him to do in nature. It is in fact a basically unnatural procedure for him for which his natural food is unsuited.

If he is to perform his work properly, and without risk of damage to himself, he must, therefore, be fed food other than that which sustained him in his natural state. Unnatural food, in fact, to correspond with the unnatural demands made upon him.

The Four Life Requirements and the Utilisation of Food

The food consumed by the horse in freedom, grass and herbs, is used to fulfil the four fundamental requirements of life and under normal climatic conditions is adequate for the existence led by the wild horse, or, if the acreage is sufficient, for the domestic horse not called upon to do more than very light work. These four requirements are:

1   To maintain the body temperature;
2   To replace natural wastage of the tissue.
    (If the food intake is insufficient for the maintenance of these two factors death results);
3   To build up body condition;

4   To supply the energy required for movement and for the internal processes of digestion, circulation, etc.

Of these four factors the first two are paramount and in times of scarcity they will be maintained at the expense of the others. To a certain extent the body can lose *condition* (i.e. become thin) and also lose the strength, or *energy*, to move with any speed, without death immediately ensuing.

A condition of this sort will occur in very severe weather when a greater proportion of the food intake will be needed to maintain the *body heat*, and the proportion which would normally be devoted to *building up the body* will be correspondingly reduced, resulting in a loss of weight.

Conversely in the spring and early summer, when feed is more plentiful and the weather warmer, less of the feed intake will be needed to promote *body heat* and the horse will gain in *condition*. In this natural state only a small proportion of food is used on the expenditure of *energy*.

In the same way it follows that if the horse were to be divorced from a life in which he needed to expend little energy and put into hard work (requiring a high degree of energy output) without compensations being made in his diet, then similar circumstances would obtain.

The *energy* expended by the body would demand a greater share of the total output supplied by the food intake, the requirements of *body temperature* and *tissue replacement,* being prime essentials to life, would continue to take their share, and there would be little left for *body condition.* In other words the food intake would be insufficient to sustain condition as well as supply the energy made necessary by the imposition of work.

If the process were continued, the horse after becoming very thin, would show increasing signs of weakness, lack of energy and debility. Finally, the process of tissue replacement would cease, the horse's temperature would drop below normal and the animal would die. It would take time for events to run their full cycle, but death would be inevitable.

When, therefore, the horse is put into work which involves an expenditure of energy, that loss must be made good by the introduction of an additional energy producing food if he is to maintain his body condition.

If on the other hand the work is stopped or reduced and the horse is still fed on energy promoting food there will be a surplus in the food intake. This surplus will be used to build *body condition* (the needs of *temperature* and *tissue replacement* will have been met), and the horse will become fat.

If the process were allowed to continue the digestive system, perfectly designed to cope with a natural diet and existence, would become overloaded, the blood heated and so on, with correspondingly unpleasant results.

First Principles

The principle which emerges is that *intake of energy food must equal energy output* and vice versa. In other words feeding of energy foods must correspond to exercise.

The diet of the horse in his feral state was balanced to contain the constituents which were needed to maintain him in the physical condition necessary for his limited requirements. We have already seen that when removed from this environment and required to perform physical work greatly in excess of that which is necessary in nature, it is essential for him to receive additional energy-giving food if he is not to suffer in condition.

It is also, of course, equally essential that his artificial diet should be as balanced as his natural one and contain the same constituents. In addition this artificial diet must be fed to him in a way that as nearly as possible resembles the manner in which he would naturally consume his food. The horse cannot change the digestive system which served him so well in nature, and if we are to maintain him properly we must conform to its requirements and limitations.

Diet Constituents

The constituents comprising a balanced diet are six. They are PRO-TEIN—FATS, STARCHES and SUGAR—WATER—FIBROUS ROUGHAGE—SALTS—VITAMINS.

Proteins perform three main functions: (a) replacement of muscular wastage; (b) formation of body tissues; (c) production of energy and heat.

Fats, starches, etc., in simple terms, can be regarded as producers of energy and heat and it is, therefore, easy to see that while foods containing these elements in concentration are necessary to the working horse, those foods supplying protein are essential. No food, in fact, consists entirely of protein or entirely of fats, starches and sugar, but too large a proportion of starch and sugar makes the protein element more difficult to digest and all three elements are valueless as producers of energy unless protein is also present.

Water is as essential to life as solid food, in fact more so, as can be appreciated when we realise the horse's body consists of 80% water. The horse, we are told, can do without food for thirty days, but without water he cannot live much more than a quarter of that time. The maintenance of a proper and sufficient water supply is, therefore, all-important. Without it the natural processes of the body and of digestion (all foods to be fully utilised pass into the system in solution) must break down.

The average intake of water varies according to temperature and circumstance but, on an average, a horse will drink between eight and ten gallons per day. In hot weather, however, the amount required may be double this figure.

Fibrous Matter has no particular food value, being woody in substance, nor is it easily digested. Its function and, therefore, its presence in the diet is, however, necessary because it is through this agency that the concentrate foods are broken up and absorbed into the system.

The precise function of *Salts* (minerals) and *Vitamins* is not easily determined, but that they are necessary to the organism is accepted. Any marked deficiency in these respects has an effect upon the health which may result in general debility or in such ailments as rickets in young stock.

The foods which, by experience, have been found to supply these constituents and when fed in the proper proportion form a balanced diet for the horse in work, and we will presume stabled, can be divided into three groups: BULK FOODS—ENERGY FOODS—AUXILIARIES.

Bulk Foods consist of hay, chaff (a mixture of chopped hay and oat straw), the various proprietary brands of horse nuts and cubes (these are, in fact, claimed to incorporate the essential constituents in balanced form as well as supplying bulk) and to a degree we may also regard bran and green food as performing some of the functions required of bulk feed. Grass is a bulk food and, when of good quality and properly managed, provides a balanced feed for the horse not in work during the summer when its growth and nutrient value is at its highest.

While all these foods contain proportions, in varying degrees, of the essential constituents of a balanced diet, they are the principal source of fibrous roughage, hay containing between 25–35% woody fibre. They may also contain relatively high percentages of proteins, but do not on their own supply sufficient energy for hard work, although in some cases nuts, particularly those designed for racehorses, may replace oats and other heating foods satisfactorily.

Energy Foods, those containing a high percentage of starches and fat (starch is, of course, converted to sugar by the action of saliva and the gastric juice) are, for practical purposes oats, barley, maize, beans and peas. They do, however, vary considerably in protein value and the proportions of *digestible* protein to starch (the protein/starch equivalent) they contain.

Oats, for instance, which are the best energy providing food, contain 11% protein and 57% starch equivalent. Although, therefore, the heating and energising element is high the *proportion* of digestible protein is low in comparison, say, to best quality hay which may contain 19% protein and 37% starch equivalent. These figures reinforce the necessity of feeding in balance and the impossibility of feeding energy foods alone without providing sufficient protein in conjunction with them.

Auxiliary Foods are those such as bran, containing a high percentage of salts; linseed, which is a fattening food, and the various forms of green food from grass to carrots and other suitable roots. In addition there are a great many artificial feed-additives and vitamin supplements on the market. They are directed at repairing various mineral and vitamin deficiencies and are undoubtedly useful if used carefully. There are also supplements which, besides tempting the shy feeder, are good feed variants and may serve as additional sources of energy or condition forming concentrates.

Cod-liver oil, an excellent condition builder, can be fed in the form of Codolettes. These are cakes which are particularly attractive to the equine and from which the unpleasant taste of cod-liver oil has been removed. Molasses or molassine meal is also good for the coat and is a means of providing easily assimilated energy food. Shy feeders can often be tempted with molasses and horses are very fond of them. Glucose can be used for horses being prepared for hard work, and seaweed, in powder form, is claimed to supply minerals and trace elements and to improve condition. Seaweed concentrates have only recently been marketed extensively, but there is much evidence to show that they are an effective food.

Before considering how and in what quantities these various foods should be fed it is as well to have a little more detailed knowledge of their properties.

Hay falls into two groups—meadow hay and seed hay. Meadow hay is made from fields laid permanently to grass and seed hay from arable land, of which it is one of a rotation of crops. The former will contain a greater variety of grasses, but the latter will have a higher percentage of clovers.

Of the two seed hay is preferred. It is the more nutritious if properly saved and, therefore, the most expensive to buy. For horses in really hard work I think it is essential, but meadow hay is quite good enough for ponies and animals whose work is not demanding. Hay is not very digestible and seed hay is even less so than meadow. A really good mixture must, in fact, be fed judiciously as it can cause digestive troubles.

In either sort the quality and, therefore, the feeding value depends largely on how the hay was made. Unfortunately our weather conditions in this country are not always conducive to good hay-making. Much of the nourishment in hay is contained in the flower and the seed. Ideally, hay should be cut when the grasses are in flower, usually around early June. If the hay is cut too late the flower will have gone to seed and the seeds will have been scattered.

Wet hay also causes complications. Nourishment is reduced and the drying process causes much loss of seed and flower and consequently goodness. 'Mow burnt' hay, that which has been stacked too soon, heats in the stack and if it does not catch fire it will be badly browned and is useless as horse feed.

Musty hay, caused by stacking or baling before it is dry, will be refused by most horses.

Good hay, of either kind, should be greenish in colour, it should smell sweet and be neither too dusty nor showing any sign of mould. The grasses should be in flower and when a bale is opened the hay should have some definite spring to it. Hay made from poor land will be noticeably woody and coarse. Hay, apart from providing bulk, is the basis of the stabled horse's diet and good mixtures will contain high percentages of the essential feed constituents.

Lucerne hay, known as *alfalfa* in America where it is widely used, is not easily come by in this country, although it is the most valuable nutritionally. It can, too, be fed as green food, when it is equally good. It has the highest protein content and the highest ratio of protein to starch of all hays (i.e. 19% protein, 37% starch equivalent). *Sainfoin* has almost the same content.

A good mixture of *red clover* and *rye grasses* contains approximately 12% protein, whilst *pure clovers* contain some 2% more than this. The very best *meadow* hay may have 13% protein content and 48% starch equivalent (i.e. almost 1 to 4), while the poorest will have perhaps something nearer to a 7% protein content and a 20–22% starch equivalent. All hay has a relatively high percentage of salts varying from between 6–7%.

The importance of buying good hay, which will form possibly between one-half and two-thirds of the diet of the stabled horse, cannot be over-emphasised.

There is then the business of buying 'old' hay as opposed to 'new', on which the old horse-master set such store. Generally speaking old hay is anything between six and eighteen months old, at which age it is reckoned to be in the best condition. Before it is six months old it is reckoned to be too soft and too grass-like in character. If, therefore, you want horses in hard condition, new hay is too soft and too much like grass, which produces a soft condition, to do the job. After eighteen months hay deteriorates and is of little nutritional value.

In the forage trade, however, hay becomes 'old' after September 29th (Michaelmas Day) and so it is as well to ask when it was made, otherwise you may be talking at cross-purposes and not get what you want.

Not very long ago I was speaking to a riding club when this question of old hay came up. They were all, or the great majority, horse-owners, but while knowing the difference according to the book practically none thought it to be of great importance. I got the impression that they considered themselves lucky if they could just get hay, meadow or seed, old or new, at something like a reasonable price.

I am sure that a great many horse-owners regard hay in much the same light, whereas the buying of it should be of the utmost and primary importance.

Chaff is a mixture of chopped hay and oat straw and unless made at home, which entails the possession of a chaff-cutter, is usually of little value. Chaff sold in bags is very often of the poorest quality consisting mostly of straw and sweepings. I am sure it is possible to obtain good quality chaff and there are doubtless many forage merchants who sell such feed; I just haven't come across one.

The advantage of feeding hay in this form is that it encourages the horse to chew his food instead of bolting it down. It is also claimed to be an economy and less wasteful. Bran to some degree prevents bolting of the food and horse nuts certainly do, so unless you have a chaff-cutter, or can buy a secondhand one cheaply, the provision of chaff is not an essential on this score.

From the economy point of view hay mixed with oat straw obviously goes further than hay on its own, but there should be no great wastage if hay is always fed from a net. The value of chaff, in comparison with good hay, is, of course, not so great.

Horse Nuts are the result of the first serious attempt at providing a scientifically balanced diet in one form. I don't think the makers would claim that a horse's diet should consist solely of these nuts or cubes and I imagine that most horse-owners use them, as I do, in conjunction with hay and concentrates. That they are convenient, however, and an excellent foodstuff cannot be denied.

Horses that become uncontrollable at the smell of an oat can eat nuts with equanimity, and they are ideal for ponies. In theory, horse nuts can eliminate the need for feeding oats, and it is certainly true that horses in light work manage very well in this fashion, but I do not think they contain sufficient energy food for animals doing more than this. As a general conditioner and a diet variant they are, nevertheless, valuable. Most of the firms manufacturing these foods make, in addition to the standard product, cubes of a higher energy content for race-horses, and another variety suitable for breeding stock. Although always well-packaged, nuts, like any other food, must be fresh—stale or dusty nuts are not welcomed by horses.

Oats are usually accepted to be the best grain for horses and to contain the maximum nutrient elements in the most easily assimilated form. Oats bought whole, that is unbruised, should be 100% dry, exhibit no signs of must or mildew and be plump in appearance. The best quality oats are supposed to be those termed Scotch Oats.

Oats can be fed whole, but in this state are more difficult to digest. Whole oats should never be fed without the accompaniment of chaff or bran, otherwise a greedy feeder will bolt them without mastication. It is usually better to feed oats 'bruised', which is half way between whole and 'crushed'. Oats that are crushed, really crushed, lose most of their flour content in dust and, therefore, most of their nutritional value.

Barley is often dismissed as a food and yet in many countries is the horse's staple grain, as it is in India. It is not so 'intoxicating' a grain as oats and if introduced into the diet gradually, not more than ½ lb. a day to start with, and fed bruised it is very good indeed. Barley should not be fed whole as in this form it is very indigestible. Boiled barley is excellent for putting flesh on thin horses.

Maize is another grain not in general use in this country, but is again used almost exclusively in the Americas. It is a heating food and 7¾ lb. of a mixture of two parts maize and one of beans is the equivalent to 10 lb. of oats. The addition of beans compensates for the protein deficiency in maize.

In this country maize is often fed as 'flaked maize', looking rather like thick domestic corn-flakes. In this form it is a good conditioner, a producer of heat, and will help to make the diet more interesting. It is, however, somewhat indigestible and must not be given unaccompanied by other foods.

Beans and Peas contain a higher protein/starch equivalent than any other food (beans 25·5/48·5 and peas 22·5/53·5), but they are excessively heating. They are fed split or crushed in very small quantities to racehorses, but are not usually necessary for horses doing less energetic work. For horses (perhaps show jumpers) at grass during winter 2 lb. of beans per day would be a useful addition to the diet. I have heard it suggested that beans might be given to ponies under similar circumstances, and so they might, providing there was no likelihood of a child riding the animals concerned. New beans are too indigestible to be fed —they should be at least one year old.

Bran is an excellent food, particularly if it is good broad bran. It is the ground husk of the wheat grain and contains a fairly high percentage of salt (5·8%), besides being easily digestible. It has the peculiar property of being a laxative when fed damp and having the opposite effect when given dry. It is usually mixed with other foods.

Because of its digestive and regulating properties bran is particularly valuable and is the bulk constituent of the bran and linseed mash. It is not a food which keeps well as it absorbs moisture very easily and in this state becomes sour. It is, therefore, unwise to buy bran in anything but small quantities.

Bran mashes, which are laxative in effect and easily digestible, are usually given at least once a week to horses in work and also after periods of great exertion when the digestive apparatus does not function so effectively. A mash is made by adding boiling water to the bran (3 lb. per horse), adding a handful of household salt (1 oz.), stirring well, then covering the bucket, to keep the steam in, for about 30 minutes.

Linseed contains a very high percentage of fat-forming material. Its oil or fat content is, in fact, as high as 37% and it is also high in protein content. These properties make it an ideal conditioning food which increases body weight and also gives a bloom to the coat. Because of the high oil content it is useful in the feeding of ailing, badly debilitated animals or ones in an exhausted condition, as it makes little demand upon the digestive apparatus. Linseed cannot be fed raw and is, therefore, given to the horse boiled and mixed with either bran or oats, or a mixture of the two.

To make a bran and linseed mash, soak the linseed overnight (1–1½ lb. per horse). Boil the next day for some three hours stirring very frequently over a low heat. Linseed not only burns easily, but makes a terrible mess if it is allowed to boil over; add to this mixture 2 lb. bran per horse, stir well, cover and allow to stand for about half-an-hour. A linseed jelly is made by adding the soaked seed to boiling water, 1 lb seed to 2 gallons of water is about the right proportion. A little cold water is then added and the whole thing brought to the boil again and allowed to continue boiling for 20–30 minutes.

The jelly is mixed with either oats or bran or a mixture of both. For conditioning animals in very poor condition or for preparing show animals, linseed jelly may be fed every day, but the ration should not exceed more than ½–1 lb.

Linseed can also be fed in the form of cakes.

Green Food is always good for the horse—it is cooling to the blood, a good cleanser of the system and an aid to digestion. Horses always enjoy it, particularly when stabled, and this in itself is sufficient reason for feeding it. In winter, carrots—sliced lengthways to prevent the animal blocking his small gullet, as he might do were he to be fed them cut in circles—turnips, mangolds and swedes, fed whole and left with the horse for him to chew, are all excellent. There is no great feeding value in roots, as will be understood when we realise the large percentage of water they contain (carrots 87%, swedes 88% and sugar beet 93%), but they are succulent and take the place of fruit in the human diet.

Sugar beet (soaked and pulped) is often used as a bulk feed stuff and is claimed to be a great conditioner. In view of its high water content this claim cannot be justified and its actual feed value is virtually nil.

In addition, seize every opportunity to let the animal have a nibble at fresh, clean grass. Ten minutes a day employed in this fashion is worth all the bottled tonics in the chemist's shop. Do not, however, feed grass clippings during the spring and summer. Some people hold that if fed fresh no harm is done. Possibly this is so, but I would not risk it. Grass cut by a lawnmower impacts and ferments in the stomach and can cause severe colic.

The Digestive Apparatus and Methods of Feeding

The methods and principles of feeding are dependent upon the peculiar digestive apparatus of the horse and the positioning of his relatively small stomach.

In the simplest terms, the stomach, small in relation to his size, is placed behind the diaphragm, a section of muscle separating it from the chest cavity proper. The diaphragm is in contact with the lungs in front and at the back almost touches the stomach and liver.

Immediately following a feed the stomach and the bowels, which will still be digesting the previous feed, will become distended and the stomach will press against the diaphragm.

This will induce no discomfort while the horse is at rest, but should he be saddled and taken out immediately, the effort of moving will cause him to breathe more deeply and to expand his lungs. Now it follows if the lungs expand they will exert pressure on the elastic structure of the diaphragm, which in turn will press against the now distended stomach. As a result not only is his breathing impaired, but there will be interference with the digestive processes going on in the stomach and the bowels. The result will be indigestion which may become so acute as to develop into a severe case of colic. At its worst, that is if fast work were to be carried out on a full stomach, the lungs would become choked with blood and a rupture of the stomach could occur. The general rule, therefore, is *do not work after feeding*. It would be possible to take the horse out if the pace were restricted to a walk, but otherwise do not exercise within one hour of feeding.

Although the horse has a small stomach its bowel structure (there are two bowels, the small and large) is capacious. The whole apparatus is designed for the absorption of food consumed slowly and almost continuously over long periods.

At grass the horse passes food via the mouth, where it undergoes the first process of digestion by being broken up by the molars and saturated in saliva, with almost unbroken regularity to the stomach. Once the stomach is filled to about two-thirds of its capacity the food is passed into the bowel at the same speed at which fresh food enters the stomach.

The gastric juice manufactured in the stomach dissolves the food and the stomach muscles move to assist the process. The food, now having the consistency of thick cream, passes into the small bowel where it becomes further liquefied and the unabsorbed pieces of food pass finally into the large bowel where, after a further processing, they are passed out of the body as droppings devoid of all absorbable nourishment.

Ideally the stabled horse should be fed in a similar manner, a handful of food being thrown in his manger every ten minutes, but this is obviously neither convenient nor possible and he must be fed at periodic intervals. As a result he tends to eat rich, not easily digested foods rapidly, and, if given the opportunity, unwisely. If he were given, to cite an extreme instance, one large feed per day his stomach would be too small be contain it. As a result it would become distended to an extent where the muscles assisting the digestive process became incapable of effort. The process would break down, the food would ferment giving off gases and the animal would suffer such acute digestional pains as might result in a rupture of the stomach.

The capacity of the stomach and that of the digestive system to cope with the food intake is not more than 4 lb. in total at one time, of which no more than 3 lb. should be grain, and feeds should not exceed this weight. *Feed little and often* is then the second rule and rather than give two big feeds, give the same quantity split between three or four feeds.

Hay, which acts as a digestive aid, may be given in larger quantities because it is eaten more slowly. The bulk of the hay ration is usually given at night when the horse will have a longer period to eat and digest it.

The need to water before feeding is not relevant as the horse should have water constantly available, for reasons already explained.

Inspection of the Teeth

A further lesson does, however, emerge which is connected with the mouth, or rather the teeth. If the horse's teeth are not properly cared for, that is if they are allowed through uneven wear to become sharp, then they will lacerate the mouth and possibly the tongue, mastication will be discouraged and the digestion of food affected.

In extreme cases *quidding* will occur, when, through diseased teeth, the food is partially chewed and then dropped from the mouth—in which case the digestive system doesn't even get under way.

Care of teeth is, therefore, an elementary duty incumbent upon the horse-keeper.

Proportions of the Food Intake

Full assimilation of the food given will depend very largely on the horse receiving a proper quantity, particularly in regard to bulk, which is correctly combined with other foods to give a balanced diet, in which there is neither a notable deficiency nor excess. Good, clean food is more easily digested than that of inferior quality. To feed tainted food causes particular trouble due to the horse's inability to vomit. Digestion cannot take place without water being present. Overworked horses, and those in poor bodily health, will have digestions in a similar condition and will be unable to assimilate food properly.

There is now the very important question to consider as to how much food the horse needs, in what proportions and at what intervals.

In these respects there can be no hard-and-fast rules since horses are individuals and vary enormously in their requirements. There will be some animals who thrive on practically nothing and others who need an awful lot of feeding to keep in anything approaching condition. Formulating the correct diet for the individual is the art of the good feeder and the job of every horse-owner.

It is possible, however, to give a general guide to the quantities of food which various horses will require. In theory the amount of foodstuffs required by an animal is dependent, not upon height or weight, but upon the skin surface area. A large skin surface suffers a correspondingly large loss of heat, and as the maintenance of body heat is a prime need of life, it must be replaced by food.

It can easily be seen that a heavily built, 15 h.h. cob, presenting a large surface area, will need a greater food intake than a lightly-built hack of the same height. In the same way a pony weighing perhaps half the weight of a hunter will need more food in comparison because the surface area is greater per lb. body weight.

The only real indication of an animal's needs is his bodily condition. Nevertheless, the following figures, necessarily approximate and average, will be a guide to the novice horse-keeper for the horse in normal work.

HEIGHT H.H.	Under 12	12–13	13–14	14–15	15–16	Over 16
APPROX. DAILY BULK FOOD INTAKE LB.	14–16	16–18	20–22	22–24	24–26	26–28

The proportions of bulk, energy and auxiliary foods of which the bulk intake consists will again vary according to the individual and the amount and type of work being done.

For a horse in regular exercise and hunting one day per week, the proportion of bulk food to the remaining two would be on an equal basis with a possible increase in the energy and auxiliary intake at the expense of the bulk on the day preceding the meet. In lighter work the bulk diet might be as much as two-thirds bulk to one third of the others.

For the horse doing much fast work, or work demanding the expenditure of great energy, the energy feeds would be increased and the bulk foods considerably reduced, but not below about one third of the total intake. As we have seen, bulk is essential in feeding and the digestion cannot support a large intake of energy foods without its being present to a considerable degree.

How Much Corn?

The quantity of oats a horse receives depends on the work he is doing and his individual make-up. The number of feeds into which the energy ration is divided depends on that quantity and is governed by the horse's inability to digest more than 3 lb. of grain in any one feed.

There is no hard and fast rule by which we can assess the amount of corn an animal should receive. The best way, in my experience, is to start on a low ration and gradually increase it until the horse is rather above himself. Then one cuts it back until the horse is again sensible.

There is a school of thought which calculates the corn ration as 1 lb. per 1 mile of exercise. This is not a bad formula to follow, providing one remains flexible and does not persist in feeding a fresh horse more corn than he can carry, or needs.

In general I believe that the majority of horse-owners have a tendency to overdo the ration, which is quite as bad as going the other way. An over-fresh horse is not a co-operative one, and if the rider is fighting to control his horse for the greater part of the exercise period it is hardly conducive to the attainment of the *entente cordiale* which should exist between the two. A couple of light-hearted bucks and a squeal or two on a cold morning can be regarded as a spot of fun between the two partners and is forgivable in any fit horse.

If however, the horse has not settled in ten minutes or so then I would suspect he is getting too big an energy ration in relation to his energy output.

Examples of Feeding

As an example of feeding let us consider the case of a 15.2 h.h. hunter who is exercised every day and hunted once a week.

If we decide that his bulk daily intake shall be 26 lb. it will be safe to apportion half this quantity to bulk, in the way of hay, and half to energy and auxiliary foods. I would expect an animal of this sort doing, perhaps, one and a half hours exercise per day, to need 8 lb. of corn and, therefore, a further 5 lb. of auxiliary food, as his daily ration.

As this is something of a border line case it might be thought that the feed could be safely enough divided into three. I think it could, but four would be better.

The auxiliaries in this case might consist of bran, nuts and carrots, which could be given in the proportions of 2 lb., 2 lb., and 1 lb. respectively. Dividing this into four feeds my suggested diet/work sheet for a week day would appear as something like this:

TIME	OATS	BRAN	NUTS	CARROTS	HAY	TOTAL ENERGY ETC.	TOTAL BULK
7 am	2 lb.	½ lb.	½ lb.			3 lb.	
8.30 to 10 am	Exercise after quartering						
10 am	Mucking out				3 lb.		3 lb.
Up to 12 pm	Grooming						
12.30 pm	2 lb.	½ lb.	½ lb.	1 lb.		4 lb.	
4 pm	2 lb.	½ lb.	½ lb.			3 lb.	
7.30 pm	2 lb.	½ lb.	½ lb.			3 lb.	
10 pm					10 lb.		10 lb.
				TOTALS:		13 lb.	13 lb.
				BULK INTAKE:		26 lb.	

The bulk of the hay has been given at night so that the horse may have plenty of time to digest it and to keep himself occupied through the hours of darkness.

The addition of molasses, molassine meal, the occasional ounce of household salt, or any other pet supplement of the horse owner, can be divided up between the last three feeds without affecting the bulk intake materially.

If the horse was inclined to bolt his food 2 lb. of the night hay ration could be chopped and divided between the first, third and fourth feeds.

Many people may have to ride before breakfast, or would prefer to do so, in which case one exercises first and feeds afterwards. For my own part I concentrate better after breakfast and I see no reason why the horse should not feel the same.

The important thing is that whatever timings are decided upon they should be adhered to most strictly. Horses have a built-in alarm clock in their stomachs and expect their routine to follow a regular pattern.

The horse in question, however, hunts on one day a week and this will involve some alteration in the diet. As the horse is going to expend an extra amount of energy on his hunting day it is only reasonable that he should be given the opportunity to store up some extra by being given an increased ration on the *preceding* day. On the actual day he will not have the opportunity to eat his accustomed quantity. Partly for this reason and partly to replace any excess output over intake he may have suffered it is also wise to slightly increase the ration on the day *following* his exertions.

If Saturday was the hunting day the diet sheet for Friday should be altered to show an increase of 1 lb. oats in each feed. This addition to the bulk intake would, however, have to be compensated by a corresponding reduction in the bulk foods.

In my own case I would cut out the ½ lb. nuts and ½ lb. of the carrots in the midday feed and reduce the morning hay ration by 1 lb. and the last hay net by 2 lb.—a total bulk reduction of 4 lb.—to correspond with the increase in corn.

On Saturday the horse would receive his normal first feed, possibly with the addition of a handful of chopped hay. We have already noted that the digestive functions of the tired horse are considerably reduced in efficiency and for this reason the animal on its return from hunting will be given an easily digested feed. I would suggest a linseed mash, and later he may be given his last hay net as usual.

An extra 2 lb. of oats over and above the normal ration may be split between the four feeds on the Sunday and the hay ration reduced accordingly. If the horse has had anything like a day's hunting he will not need exercise on Sunday, but he should be walked out for half-an-hour or so and allowed to nibble at some clean grass.

The once-weekly linseed mash should be enough to keep his bowels in order, but if experience shows that he still tends to constipation then a bran mash may need to be introduced once a fortnight, or even more frequently.

In the event of bad weather stopping hunting and making exercising difficult the corn ration must be cut at once and replaced with non-heating auxiliaries, green food and hay.

But what of the horse owned by the working girl who may have neither the means nor the opportunity to hunt during the winter and confines her equestrian activities to Saturday and Sunday, being unable to ride during the week?

The principles, of course, remain unaltered, but the method of application must necessarily change. Let us say that our young lady has trace-clipped her horse and intends turning him out in a New Zealand rug by day and bringing him in at night. As the horse may be doing no more than say a total of six hours work under saddle per week he will not require the same amount of energy food as in the previous case, although he will be using a considerable quantity of his food intake to keep himself warm.

Given that his necessary bulk intake is the same as his stabled brother (i.e. 26 lb.) and that the young lady has a member of her family willing to do the feeding while she is at work, the weekly diet sheet could be as follows:

DAY	NUTS	OATS	BRAN	CARROTS	HAY	TOTAL
Tuesday	3 lb.	3 lb.	2 lb.	1 lb.	17 lb.	26 lb.
Wednesday	3 lb.	3 lb.	2 lb.	1 lb.	17 lb.	26 lb.
Thursday	3 lb.	3 lb.	2 lb.	1 lb.	17 lb.	26 lb.
Friday	3 lb.	5 lb.	2 lb.	1 lb.	15 lb.	26 lb.
Saturday	3 lb.	5 lb.	2 lb.	1 lb.	15 lb.	26 lb.
Sunday	3 lb.	5 lb.	MASH* 2 lb.	1 lb.	15 lb.	26 lb.
Monday	3 lb.	4 lb.	2 lb.	1 lb.	16 lb.	26 lb.

* *Either Bran or Linseed*

The ration could be divided into *three* feeds a day with the greater portion of the hay ration being given, as usual, at night. The fact that the horse may consume some additional bulk in the form of grass, which will be sparse and devoid of nourishment during the winter months, would not under normal circumstances be material. Additional additives can be given without altering the diet, as in the previous instance.

As a point of interest the intake of energy foods, i.e. oats and a percentage of the nuts, corresponds fairly closely to the 1 lb. energy food per 1 mile theory. In the course of the six hours work he receives per week the horse may be considered to cover 36 miles approximately at a rate of 6 m.p.h. For this energy output he is receiving a weekly energy intake of 28 lb. oats and 21 lb. nuts, of which possibly one-third of the latter might be regarded as producing energy.

Feeding and Care at Grass
At this juncture let us consider the needs of the horse at grass, either doing no work or doing a limited amount.

During the optimum growth and nutritional period, between May and August, a horse doing no work manages very well on *good and ample* grazing without additional feed. In very dry spells, particularly on poor quality grazing, additional feeding will be necessary to maintain the horse in condition.

Ponies are, however, something of a law unto themselves, in this as in other things. The average pony of native ancestry is tough and hardy and is able to get a living from poor land and still keep in surprisingly good condition. This is not to say that I condone the practice of putting two or three ponies on an acre of scrubland. I do not by any means, but there is a most certain danger in going to the opposite extreme and putting them out on really lush grazing.

Susceptibility to Laminitis and Grass Restriction
Horses at grass, using little energy, put on condition and become fat and soft, but ponies, always greedy feeders, the most efficient converters of food and by nature unused to such high living, rapidly attain a rotundity which is past belief. Now this is bad for the pony, particularly if he is being ridden. He is firstly over weight and, therefore his legs are overburdened as well as his soft and out of tone internal organs. What is even more important is that he might develop *laminitis* under these conditions. Laminitis is a very serious and painful disease

of the feet (usually the fore-feet). The sensitive laminae encased by the non-elastic horn of the foot are subject to intense inflammation and as the foot cannot expand the pain is very great. There are a number of factors which cause laminitis, but in ponies too great an intake of rich grass is the most prevalent.

Fat ponies are also a cause of much frustration in the matter of saddle fitting. Saddles were made to fit backs having at least some outline of the conventional and expected shape, not for billiard tables.

Ponies should not, therefore, be allowed lush grazing. It is far better to restrict their intake by bringing them in for specified periods and giving no food at all than to allow them to get overfat.

The Working Pony
Ponies are often worked far harder than most people appreciate during the summer. One has only to go to a small gymkhana to see how much work they get through in a day. I did this very thing to satisfy myself on the point, choosing a group of children who had a five-mile hack to get to the gymkhana ground. Their ponies were brushed and cleaned from their field by 9 o'clock and they arrived at the ground at 10 a.m. They spent the morning cantering and galloping about with occasional rest periods, taken while the riders ate ice lollies and lunch, usually still sitting on the pony.

During the afternoon they took part in at least six gymkhana events, leaving the ground at 5 p.m. and arriving home at 6 p.m. Now that is a very fair day's work for any horse, and, in my book, too much work for a pony. I would not advocate the feeding of oats to ponies, but if they are to work they must be fed accordingly.

I would suggest that a pony kept at grass during the summer and worked every day in the holidays should be kept in the following way.

If the grazing is sparse and poorish he may stay out for the whole 24 hours, but should be given *at least* one feed a day consisting of 3 lb. nuts and 1 lb. bran as well as the occasional carrot. On this diet he will not become too much for the child, as he most certainly would if he were fed on oats. Oats and ponies are not a good combination. If he is doing no work he will not need supplementary feeding on this sort of grazing.

On lush grazing the pony must be brought in during a part of the day to prevent him getting too fat. This must be carried out whether he is in work or not. Alternatively he can spend periods on very poor pasture if this is available. If he is being ridden it is probably wise to bring him in for the whole day, giving him the feed mentioned above split into two, and turning him out at night.

In every case common sense must be exercised and the pony allowed grass and feed in relation to the work he is to do.

In winter ponies will lose condition if kept on small acreages (or even large ones) without additional feed. A hay ration of 10 lbs or, if he will eat more, in excess of that figure, is not too much and at least one feed of 3 lbs nuts and 1 lb. bran is necessary per day.

If the pony is worked during the winter at weekends, the energy ration should be increased on Friday, Saturday, Sunday and Monday, and it may be necessary to feed the pony twice a day. As an example I give a suggested diet for a 13 h.h. pony out at grass during the winter and worked for a total of four hours on Saturday and Sunday.

DAY	NUTS	BRAN	CARROTS	BRUISED BARLEY		HAY	TOTAL
Tuesday	3 lb.	1 lb.				14 lb.	18 lb.
Wednesday	3 lb.	1 lb.	One or			14 lb.	18 lb.
Thursday	3 lb.	1 lb.	two			14 lb.	18 lb.
Friday	4 lb.	1½ lb.	sliced	½ lb.	In two	12 lb.	18 lb.
Saturday	4 lb.	1½ lb.	in each	½ lb.	feeds	12 lb.	18 lb.
Sunday	4 lb.	1½ lb.	feed	½ lb.	per day	12 lb.	18 lb.
Monday	4 lb.	1 lb.				13 lb.	18 lb.

As before the largest part of the hay should be fed as the last feed.

It should be remembered that summer grass is a soft food producing soft condition. Horses kept at grass during the summer are fit for nothing more than very slow work. If the horse is to do hard work he is better kept in on a hard diet and restricted to an hour or two at grass each day. To work soft horses is to impose severe strain on the heart and other organs and upon the legs.

The Importance of Worm-control

However well his horses are fed and cared for the efforts of the horse-master will be of little avail unless he also appreciates the susceptibility of his charges to parasitic infestation.

Worm infestation, to the point where debility or even death can ensue, is a direct result of domestication and its control is of just as much importance to the well-being of the horse as is the correct relationship of food to work. One would think that so much effort and ink had already been expended on this subject that no horse-owner could possibly fail to understand its importance.

Surprisingly, however, this is not the case, for there is still a large number of horse-keepers who have little, or no, knowledge of worms or of the need to control them. There are even more (those with the ability to swallow lumps of undigested fact) who know a great deal in *theory*, but never get beyond that stage—an all too prevalent state of affairs.

All domestic horses harbour parasites which, in general, use pasture as a main vehicle in their life cycle. Much can be done by proper grass management to combat the danger but, as yet, there is no sure way of eliminating parasites entirely without possessing an unlimited acreage and incurring enormous expense. At present, therefore, the main area of attack must be confined to the horse itself.

There are three common types of worms met with in horses: *White worms*, *Whip* or *Seat worms* and the *Red worm*. In addition there is the *Stomach Bot*, which is not a true worm, but can be conveniently dealt with in company with the others.

The White Worm *(Ascaris)* is the most common in horses. Because of its size and colour (it is white and can be up to a foot long and as thick as a pencil) it is easily discernible in the droppings.

In small numbers it will cause no harm in the adult horse, but if it

103

is allowed to increase the horse will lose condition, the coat will stare and there is a possibility of intermittent colic. In severe cases a stoppage or even a rupture of the gut may occur. By the time the worms can be seen in the droppings the infestation is becoming established and should be dealt with at once. If proper worm prevention is carried out this stage should never be reached.

The eggs of this worm are laid in the gut and passed out in the droppings. They hatch on pasture, or in badly managed bedding, and in the former case re-enter the animal with the grass he eats, or in the latter make their way into the manger or the hay.

The small worms having entered the gut penetrate the intestinal wall and move through the internal organs until they return to their starting point, and the whole cycle commences once more.

Whip or Seat Worms *(Oxyuris),* which are very thin and can measure nearly two inches long, occur in the rectum and are not harmful in their effect as far as general condition is concerned. They do, however, cause intense irritation which is manifested by rubbing the tail and a discharge around the anus.

It is not necessary to call in a veterinary surgeon to effect a cure as the treatment is quite simple. An enema consisting of a handful of salt in a gallon of warm water, given after the dock has been thoroughly sponged, is usually effective.

The treatment should be carried out three times with an interval of five days between treatments. Cloths or sponges which are used should be thoroughly disinfected afterwards to prevent re-infestation.

The Red Worm *(Strongyle)* is common and is by far the most dangerous. There are two types, the Large (up to one inch) and the Small strongyle (about a quarter of an inch). In cases of severe infestation death will ensue. The adult horse in good health develops a certain resistance to the red worm, but young animals are particularly susceptible to the attacks of this parasite and have rarely developed sufficient resistance to their attacks.

Strongyles live and breed in the intestines. In similar fashion to the white worm the eggs are passed out in the droppings and, developing on pasture or soiled bedding, gain re-entry into the system. The large strongyle larvae pass through the organs and blood vessels, and in sufficient numbers will cause stoppages of the blood stream. Eventually they regain the intestine and recommence the cycle.

The small strongyle develops in the gut wall where a percentage remain, together with the adult, large stongyle, and feed on blood. The result of a heavy infestation is anaemia, pronounced loss of condition and diarrhoea, having a very strong and unpleasant smell. The stomach will be distended, the skin tight, the coat stary and the membrane of the eye pale in colour.

In neglected cases the worm may penetrate and close a main artery, cutting the blood supply to the bowel, when death will be almost inevitable.

Clearly the need to keep small or large pastures clear of droppings and not to graze them with horses indefinitely and entirely is of paramount importance, but even if this is done red worm can still be regarded as an almost permanent parasite, whose potential danger will be increased if the host, i.e. the horse himself, is in poor condition.

In the case of red worm and of the less dangerous white worm, effective control can only be exercised by regular treatment.

In the past it was considered sufficient to dose the horse against worms twice a year. This is not, however, nearly frequent enough, particularly where the horse is exposed to recurrent infection, as he will be when allowed access to pasture. It has now been proved that the horse can acquire a new red worm egg burden within two months and it follows that to keep the animal free from infestation suitable medication will have to be administered at intervals of between six and eight weeks.

There are a number of old fashioned worming treatments for both white and red worm, and probably even more proprietary remedies which are marketed in easily administered form.

The discovery of Thiabendazole, which eradicates the all important adult red worms in the gut, has simplified control enormously, but in my view it is *always wise to consult a veterinary surgeon before embarking on any particular course of treatment.* It may be necessary to use more than one type of worm pellet or powder, as it is possible for the worms to develop a resistance to a drug given regularly. For this reason, although it is not the only one, veterinary supervision is necessary. No treatment should be given before the vet has had an opportunity to assess the degree of infestation present by taking a faecal worm count.

While worm control is essential for the horse at grass, or for one having even restricted access to pasture, it is equally necessary for the stabled horse. As we have seen it is still possible for the worm cycle to be maintained under stable conditions, although extreme cases of infestation are unlikely if stable management is of a high order. It should be remembered that hay made from worm infected land is capable of red worm transmission and that the practice of piling bedding beneath the manger facilitates the movement of the worm from the soiled straw to the manger.

The absence of discernible red worm in the droppings does not imply that the horse is worm free.

The importance of control cannot be over-emphasised and preventive measures, or at any rate egg counts, under veterinary supervision, should be as regular a part of horse management as are the visits of the blacksmith.

Stomach Bots are caused by the bot-fly laying its eggs on the legs of the horse at grass. The eggs are carried to the stomach, where they hatch, by the horse licking at the affected part.

The brownish-yellow eggs can be seen adhering to the hair of the legs and are easily enough removed by clipping the hair away. Bots are not dangerous unless they occur in very large quantities when a horse, despite feeding well, will display loss of condition together with a dry and staring coat. A simple remedy for clearing a severe internal infestation is to give a drench, after food has been withheld for a day, of a pint of linseed oil to which two tablespoons of turpentine have been added, but the services of a veterinary surgeon will probably be safer and more efficacious.

Conditioning & Managing the Stabled Horse

Horses are either stabled or kept on the New Zealand rug principle in order that they may be more easily and effectively conditioned for a particular purpose, such as hunting.

Animals kept entirely at grass cannot be properly conditioned for anything more than very moderate work. In winter the grass-kept animal is not clipped, for obvious reasons, and his heavy coat makes it impossible for him to work at anything but very slow paces. In summer, unless he was kept on very sparse grazing and adequately fed and exercised, he would probably be too fat and too soft. To work him in this state would be to run the risk of overstraining his legs and internal organs.

To get a horse physically fit is not, however, achieved just by putting him in a stable, clipping off his winter coat and stuffing him with food a week or two before the opening meet. It is a long, slow process, the length of which depends on the initial physical state of the horse.

In the past, and the practice is still carried out today, it was customary for hunters to be put out to grass after the season, usually in April or early May, depending upon the weather, and not worked until they were brought up again towards the middle of August or the beginning of September. Today there are many people who use their horses all the year round and this more flexible approach has advantages. A horse kept in moderate work during the summer, with probably three or four weeks holiday at grass, will never get into the gross, soft condition of the animal who is out for the entire summer season. As a result his muscles never entirely lose their tone and he will be more easily brought into hard condition.

If, of course, a horse has had a very hard hunting season, as a hunt servant's horse might have, then there is a case for putting him out for a good, long rest which will allow him to unwind both mentally and physically. Otherwise, if a horse finishes the season in good condition, having not done an excessive amount of work, there is no reason why, after a short rest period, he should not spend the summer hacking or competing in the various events which are available.

Nevertheless, whatever his state and circumstances, a horse must obviously be sound before he can be made fit, and he must be carrying plenty of flesh. It is no use trying to work on a thin horse, he will just go on getting thinner. Therefore, if one's horse is not carrying enough weight he must first be given an opportunity to put the matter right before one thinks of setting him a conditioning programme.

In getting a horse fit, as in most things connected with the equine race, or the human one for that matter, it is advisable to define the objective and then to plan (to the extent of committing the programme to paper) the methods by which the objective is to be achieved.

The objective in this case, as we have taken hunting as an example, is to produce on 1 November, or thereabouts, a hard, muscle-fit horse, big, but without carrying more than a covering of surplus fat.

Within a week or two of the opening meet he will then be hunting fit. There is a deal of difference between this and a horse who is racing fit. The latter will be lean and trained to a very high peak of fitness—the ultimate fitness, in fact. To achieve this sort of condition requires great skill, and to maintain a horse at this peak for even short periods demands both skill and experience. For the purpose of racing it is a necessary physical state, but not for hunting or anything outside the racecourse. Racing demands maximum effort, of limited duration, over short distances. Hunting, eventing or long-distance riding calls for sustained effort, with occasional bursts of speed, over long distances for an extended period.

A horse that is racing fit at the beginning of the season will be like a toast-rack half way through, that is if he and his rider survive the first day. Conversely, a hunting fit horse would be unlikely to make much of a showing in a fast run two mile 'chase. The condition, therefore, must fit the purpose.

We shall condition the horse by the intelligent combination of three factors:

Feeding, Exercising and Grooming
Feeding will build up his body and supply the material required for the making of muscle as well as producing the necessary energy.

Exercise will develop, strengthen, and tone the muscles and will remove the burden of surplus fat. Fat, incidentally, is not converted

108

into muscle. Muscle is muscle and fat is fat; there is no question of the latter being changed into the former. By exercise, too, the legs, the sinews and tendons, etc., are hardened, the wind is made clear and the horse is accustomed to carrying weight.

Grooming and strapping not only develops and tones muscles, but cleans the body so that it can work to maximum effect. A dirty, pore-blocked skin is no aid to efficient body function. Feeding has already been dealt with at some length and the importance of it being regulated according to the amount of exercise has been stressed.

Nevertheless, at the risk of being repetitous and for the sake of the horse, I will emphasise the need for a gradual increase in the feeding of hard food. A horse that has been having additional feeds during the summer and has been doing exercise can have his ration increased *slowly*—in proportion to the extra work expected of him. The horse that has been at grass for some months must be taken even more slowly, otherwise his digestive capacity will become overloaded. Ideally, he should have at least two weeks of very light work, possibly lungeing, and one or two small feeds per day to get his digestive system in something like working order. He can also be stabled for a few hours a day before being brought up entirely.

I am not much in favour of the old practice of 'physicking' a horse (the administration of a pretty drastic laxative) up from grass in order to clear him out before starting hard feeds. In many cases the shock to the system does a lot more harm than good, and as I wouldn't like it myself I don't see why the horse should either.

The average horse occasionally gets too much EXERCISE, but more often too little.

It is impossible to lay down the exact amount of exercise a horse should take at any one time during the process of conditioning, because it depends entirely upon the mental and physical characteristics of the individual. The following factors, however, will always apply: Exercise will be progressive in speed and duration and must always be related to physical condition and the intake of energy foods.

Many people will appreciate the necessity of observing these fundamentals and will conscientiously enough endeavour to carry them out. Unfortunately there are far too many owners who consider only the physical well-being of the horse and neglect, or even overlook entirely, the importance of his mental state. Horses, like children, are easily bored and idle minds are just as much a source of mischief as are bodies in a similar state of lethargy.

109

The aim in training the horse, and the skill, is in the twofold development of MIND and BODY, and in recognising that the full value of exercise lies not only in quantity, but also in quality.

Exercise should be an enjoyable and an instructive business for the horse and these two requirements will not be met by trotting round the same convenient route each day. Variety in the programme is essential, and for this reason, as well as others, it is advisable to have one's conditioning programme planned out well in advance of its commencement. Obviously the programme must be flexible to some degree to allow for the 'best laid plans of mice and men' being upset, but the very fact that one has a programme makes it easier to achieve the objectives.

Lungeing, loose schooling and work in the manège or jumping ring can all be combined with road work and hacking over broken country, negotiating small obstacles as they present themselves.

The greatest ally in preparing horses for work is time. Condition is achieved by slow processes which cannot be hurried and the more time that can be devoted to the programme the more satisfactory will be the result. Slow work is always beneficial, fast work is rarely so.

Riding exercise requires just as much attention to detail as does feeding. The first essential, to my mind, is that when it is planned to give the horse a specified period of exercise, i.e. one hour, he should receive one hour and not forty minutes. If it takes ten minutes to saddle up, and another ten minutes to unsaddle and put the horse to rights on returning to the stable, then one needs to devote one hour twenty minutes to the exercising period.

It is as well, if one is to do the job properly, to find out the speed of the horse's paces in relation to the distance covered. On average a horse walks one mile in sixteen minutes, trots one mile in eight minutes and canters one mile in five minutes. These times, of course, vary slightly with individuals and can be verified by timing over a measured distance if it is considered necessary. Armed with this knowledge routes can be planned to coincide, roughly, with the time available.

Walking and trotting are the two paces from which the greatest benefit is derived. At neither should the horse be allowed to slop along, but on the other hand he does not want to be over restricted.

The walk can be on a long rein, and occasionally on a loose one, while the trot should be slow, but very active. Roadwork, at an intelligent combination of the two paces, will harden the legs and slow trotting uphill is excellent for the wind. Trotting over broken ground and negotiating drainage grids along road verges is an excellent balancing exercise for both horse and rider. When going downhill proceed at the walk.

At the trot the rider should change the diagonal frequently in order that the horse should develop his muscles equally. Changing the diagonal is a very simple process and a common-sense practice.

The trot is a two-time pace, that is the horse moves the two diagonal pairs of legs alternately with a short interval of suspension as he springs from one to the other. The right diagonal is the off-fore and near-hind, and the left diagonal the opposite pair. A rider, when rising to the trot, is said to be on the right diagonal when his seat touches the saddle as the off-fore and near-hind strike the ground. The rider changes the diagonal by remaining in the saddle for an extra beat before rising again. In other words he bumps once. Conversely, of course, the rider will still change the diagonal if he keeps his seat out of the saddle for two successive beats.

The first method is usually preferred because it is held that the rider does not lose contact with the horse. Having decided long ago that the horse was not specifically designed to carry weight on his back, and having the greatest sympathy and respect for that part of the equine anatomy, I do not, personally, carry out this method of changing the diagonal, preferring to have my seat momentarily raised for the extra beat. I do not think I lose contact, as my legs are still available, and even if I do it is hardly a matter of great import. From the horse's viewpoint I am sure it must be more comfortable not to have an extra twelve stone bump (which is what in many cases the average rider's change amounts to) and I am equally convinced he is more relieved than worried by the minimal loss of contact involved.

For those who are not very clear as to which diagonal they are riding on a brief glance at the position of the horse's shoulder is informative.

When the left shoulder is to the rear as the seat touches the saddle you are on the right diagonal and vice versa.

While exercising it is good for the horse's concentration as well as for his manners to indulge in a little schooling. On a quiet road ask him to move diagonally from side to side, it is an excellent introduction to moving on two tracks and gets him used to answering to the leg.

If the head is moved slightly in the required direction and, to start with, the action of the outside hand (i.e. the left hand if one is moving from left to right) reinforces the leading inside hand by moving slightly forwards and then pressing intermittently below the withers,

111

the horse will be encouraged to move his shoulders as well. The outside leg acts, again intermittently and gently, behind the girth.

Make a habit of opening gates, starting with ones that are properly hung and do not have to be lifted out of the mud by brute force.

It is equally valuable to ask for variations in pace and even for very short periods of collection or posture shortening, in so far as the horse is capable. Do not, however, overdo these little requests and always having asked for and received a shortening of the stride and posture, reward the horse by allowing him to work on a long rein.

Above all avoid riding over the same ground day after day and never get into the habit of always cantering over a certain piece of ground If you do, the horse, in the first case, will become bored and may begin to make resistances from pure devilment, and in the second case will, in time, always canter or gallop when he comes to the spot, whatever his rider's wishes may be.

The introduction of a steady canter and an occasional short burst at speed, apart from getting the itch out of a horse's heels, has the effect of clearing and toning the lungs and bronchial tubes. Hence the expression a 'pipe-opener'.

Never, of course, should a horse be brought into the stable sweating after exercise, as he is likely to catch a chill. For this reason it is best to walk the last mile home to give him a chance to cool off. If he is still hot on returning to the stable then one must pay for the sin of omission by walking him round until he has dried off.

The act of grooming removes the natural grease from the coat and, therefore, its waterproofing property. The horse kept at grass and ungroomed suffers not at all from rain, but this is not the case with the stabled horse whose protective grease has been removed and who is, therefore, far more likely to catch cold if he gets wet.

On rainy days, however, the bringing home of a wet horse is unavoidable and under these circumstances it is better to trot briskly home, bringing the horse back warm, to rub him down with a handful of straw, put a mesh rug on, or alternatively cover his back with straw, and finally throw a top rug, inside out to prevent it getting wet, over the lot. The animal should then dry out quite happily.

Do not, if the horse should be hot, remove the saddle immediately or the cold air on the heated back will either give him a chill or cause other troubles. It is far better to leave the saddle on with the girths loosened and remove it when the animal has had time to dry off completely.

27, 28 and 29 Massage technique; ABOVE LEFT: *the locked finger position used for leg rubbing;* ABOVE RIGHT: *leg stretching;* BELOW: *manipulating the withers*

30 Use of the clippers

31 The correct way to pick up a foreleg

Grooming, the third factor in conditioning, is not only necessary for the sake of appearance, but also for the health of the stabled horse, who is kept under artificial conditions and, by reason of the work he is asked to do, consumes large quantities of artificial foods. As a result of the latter his body has an increased quantity of waste matter for disposal. Much of this waste is got rid of through the increased rate of breathing by the lungs and through excrement, but just as great a proportion is possibly dispersed through the skin. In order, therefore, to fulfil this function the skin must be kept clean.

Although the cleanliness and stimulation of the skin is a large part of what is loosely termed 'grooming' it is not the whole. Massage, hand rubbing and wisping also play their part in bringing a horse into hard condition. It is these practices which bring the skin to a high peak of functional efficiency and also stimulate circulation and promote the growth and toning of muscle structures.

The items comprising a full grooming kit are as follows:

DANDY BRUSH—a stiff wisk, nylon, or whalebone brush used for removing mud from the legs. It is too stiff and scratchy to use on the body of clipped animals of any but the most common parentage. The brush is not used on the mane or tail as it pulls out the hairs.

BODY BRUSH—a soft bristle brush used on the body and for brushing out the mane and tail.

WATER BRUSH—a soft, boat-shaped brush used damp on the mane and tail and often to put a final shine on the horse.

CURRY COMB—a metal comb of toothed blades set on a metal back and sometimes having a wooden handle or a handstrap. Its purpose is to clean the body brush, not the horse.

TWO SPONGES—one for cleaning the eyes and nose and the other for cleaning the dock.

STABLE RUBBER—a linen cloth used as a final polisher.

MANE COMB—a small metal comb, used usually for trimming.

HOOF-PICK—a good big one is preferable to the rather ineffectual folding ones.

One might also add the newer form of rubber or plastic curry comb which is used on the horse and is excellent for stimulating and cleaning the skin. A good chamois leather is also useful to give a final polish and an old dandy or water brush can be helpful when washing out the feet.

The normal procedure for grooming a horse is to start high up on the neck, behind the ears, and work with the body brush from front to rear.

The whole secret lies in placing oneself far enough away from the horse to be able to get one's whole weight behind the brush. If you stand too close this is impossible. Use the body brush in the right hand holding the curry comb in the left. After each three or four strokes clean the bristles on the comb.

Many horses, particularly the well-bred ones, are very ticklish under the tummy and between the hind legs and will object to the brush by either trying to nip their persecutor or by aiming a crafty cow kick with the hind leg. Fortunately this latter is unusual, but if the animal is really ticklish dispense with the brush altogether and use the hand only. If you keep the unoccupied hand against his neck, or even grasp the headcollar, you will prevent him biting you.

Use the body brush for cleaning the head and ears and for heaven's sake use it gently, being very careful not to bang the boney projections with the wooden back. It is well worth spending time encouraging the horse to drop his head and accept the cleaning quietly. Very many horses become head shy because of rough treatment by some impatient idiot wielding a brush inexpertly. In the stable a horse should come to you of his own accord and allow his head to be touched and the bridle to be put on without fuss.

If you can persuade the horse to accept brushing calmly it is unlikely that you will experience trouble either bridling him or clipping him. However exasperated you become never catch hold of his ear, and certainly don't pull it. If he is nervous about his head it is probable that he was made so by somebody twitching his ear and his fear will only be confirmed by receiving the same treatment again. Never bang the body brush on the horse and be particularly careful not to do so anywhere near his loins, where there is risk of damaging the kidneys.

The legs, if muddy, can be cleaned with the dandy brush, but again be careful not to knock the horse with the edge of the brush lest he retaliate by kicking. Now brush out the mane and tail and then 'lay' them with a damp water brush. Clean the dock, eyes and nostrils using both your sponges.

A final polish is attained by wiping the horse over with a damp rubber or chamois leather.

Brushes will require cleaning from time to time and the best way is to place the bristles in a shallow dish, containing a strong solution of soda, overnight. When the grease has been removed wash the bristles only in water and then place the brushes (just the bristle part) in a dish containing salt and water, which will harden them again.

A good brush should have the wooden part made in two pieces which allows the bristles to be wired into the base of the brush. Solid back brushes have the bristles plugged into the base and are cheaper to buy, but lose bristles at an uneconomical rate. No brush lasts for ever, but a good one has three or four times the life of a cheap one.

The feet are usually picked out before one actually commences cleaning the body and the dirt removed can be caught in a skip. To pick up the foreleg, stand alongside the horse facing the tail, and pass your hand down the back of the leg. Nine horses out of ten will oblige by picking up the foot. Hold it firmly in the hand and clean it out using the hoofpick from heel to toe with the point (a blunt one) pointing away from you. The tenth horse may not be so obliging and may even put all his weight on the foot you wish to pick up. If he does not respond to a shove against his shoulder, aimed at getting him to shift his weight to the other side, a pinch on the back of the leg, above the joint, may persuade him to remember his manners, and if this fails a sharp tap behind the knee or a push with the elbow will secure his co-operation.

To pick up the hind leg, face the rear again and run the hand down the quarters to the hock and from thence down the inside front of the cannon bone. As the foot is raised move the joint a little to the rear and let the hand slide round the hoof. Don't ever pull the leg either too far to the rear, to the front or sideways; it is uncomfortable for the horse and makes it difficult for him to keep his balance. Where the feet are particularly dirty they can be washed out with either an old brush or the corner of the water brush.

Washing the hooves should not be overdone as it tends to remove the natural oil secreted from the coronary band. There is, however, no harm in helping nature and appearance by regularly oiling the feet with hoof oil (obtainable from saddlers). Don't, however, use boot polish on the feet, as this only seals the foot and prevents the absorption of oil. After washing a foot out make very certain that the heels are well dried, if they are left wet there is a risk of chapped heels which will cause the horse to go lame.

Geldings will require to have their sheaths washed out periodically and this is best done wearing a domestic rubber glove and using a thin sponge dipped in warm water. Failure to carry out this cleansing of the sheath may result in discomfort for the animal and an accumulation of the scaly substance which forms on the penis may prevent him drawing properly when passing water. When this occurs the urine will be passed directly on to the belly, where it can cause a painful skin condition.

Grooming is best carried out *after* morning exercise when the horse is warm and the skin pores are open, but wisping and massage is better left to the later afternoon or even early evening.

The reason for this is that wisping encourages circulation which will naturally slow down during the night hours.

The purpose of wisping is to (a) develop and harden muscles, and (b) stimulate the skin and the circulation. It will also produce a shine or bloom on the coat which is caused by releasing the oil from the glands which surround each hair.

A wisp is made from a tightly woven rope of hay, about eight feet long. To make one, open a hay bale and shake it out somewhat, then start twisting a rope, putting your foot on the bulk of the hay. Now make two loops at one end and twist the rope between them. Secure the end of the rope by passing it through each loop and then tuck it in firmly. With a little practice the result should look something like the illustration *(Fig. 8)*.

If you find this beyond your accomplishment a chamois leather

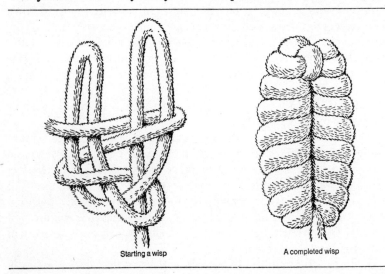

Starting a wisp   A completed wisp

Fig 8 A hay wisp

116

stitched firmly to make a small bag, and then stuffed with hay until it is firm, is just as satisfactory. Saddlers will also supply a rather more sophisticated article in the form of a hay stuffed leather pad.

To use the wisp, first damp it and then bring it down energetically on to the horse following the lay of the coat. Use it on the quarters, shoulders and neck, but not on the loins, head, belly and legs. Most horses enjoy wisping and when a rhythm has been achieved the muscles will visibly contract and decontract in time to the strokes of the wisp.

Massage Technique

Although I use the wisp a great deal I also carry out a further massage technique with the forearms. This is hard work and one must literally roll up the sleeves, but the result is worthwhile. I am also a believer in a twice weekly muscle rubbing and stretching session *(Plates 27, 28 and 29)*.

I begin by rubbing the body all over with a closed hand, using a small circular motion and quite a lot of pressure. The pressure is increased in that area of the circle nearest to the heart and decreased on the area furthest away from it.

As one becomes more experienced it becomes easier to discover a tightening of the muscles in various places and these areas can then be given more attention until they become relaxed.

The second stage concerns the legs below the knees and hocks, and I begin by alternately squeezing and releasing the bulbs of the heels. From here I work upwards to the coronary band and the pastern, employing stiffened fingers and quite a lot of pressure. The hands are then locked round the leg and worked again *upwards* with the heels of the hands making a small circular motion. This is carried out on all four legs up to the knee in front and the hock behind, and from front and rear. Usually it is combined with an application of the Radiol spirit lotion.

To complete this stage each leg is stretched forwards and backwards. Initially the horse may resent this and the limit of the movement will be small. Under no circumstances should the leg be forced to move further than is comfortable, otherwise there is a danger of pulling the muscles. In time, however, the horse will relax and will find it quite easy to stretch his legs in this way.

If he finds continued difficulty in the exercise, however, it is possible that the trouble lies not in the leg itself but in the spine, and one should desist accordingly until the source has been treated.

It is not generally realised, I am sure, that the spine and the muscles of the back can be so easily damaged and are the reason for so many resistances in the ridden horse. It has now been established that the majority of horses do suffer at some time in their lives, if not throughout them, from pain, often amounting to an arthritic condition, in this most vulnerable part of the body.

Much of the trouble is caused by the horse carrying weight before the bone structure is properly formed, i.e. at too early an age, by injudicious riding before the back is properly conditioned to carry weight, by badly fitting saddlery and by plain bad horsemanship.

Because I am almost as obsessed with this subject as other people are with finding a suitable bit to inflict upon their horses' mouths, the last stage in my massage and manipulative routine is directed at the neck, the back muscles and the spine.

I start at the top of the neck, moving down to the withers, kneading the crest with my fingers and rolling it from side to side. I then use the thumbs and the heels of the hand to flex the spine from the withers to the croup. Quite quickly the horse begins to move under the pressure and to respond to the movements to a noticeable extent. Obviously the operator must exercise tact and work very carefully when he finds tension and tenderness in any area and must exercise special care in the region of the loins.

A Programme of Conditioning

Where the horse-owner has carried out the conditioning programme himself he should be as physically fit as his horse and this is an important point. It is no good having a fit horse and an unfit rider, and there is no more distressing a sight than to see a fat, perspiring man trying to cope with a well-conditioned horse. Riding is a partnership between the two and if it is to be successful, or enjoyable to both parties, they must be in equal physical condition.

The form a programme of conditioning takes is dependent upon so many factors, the initial condition of the horse, the purpose, the time available and most importantly, the needs of the individual, that it would be impossible to give a specimen programme which treated the subject anything but generally.

The following programme is, therefore, given only as the roughest guide and to show how the exercise and feed intake should be gradually increased until the horse is in peak condition.

For the purpose of this example we will presume that a 16 h.h. horse is brought up ten weeks before the commencement of hunting and has been in very light work through the summer.

WEEK	FEED INTAKE	EXERCISE	GROOMING
1 & 2	4 lb. 2 lb. nuts ⎫ 3 feeds 2 lb. bran ⎬ per day 1 lb. carrots ⎭ 18 lb. hay 1 Bran Mash per week	1 hour (20 mins lunge, 40 mins slow hacking —walk/trot)	Cleaning 45 mins Wisping or massage 45 mins. Harden back with surgical spirit
3 & 4	5 lb. oats ⎫ 2 lb. nuts ⎬ 3 feeds 2 lb. bran ⎧ per day 1 lb. carrots ⎭ 17 lb. hay 1 Bran Mash per week	1½ hours (15 mins lunge, 45 mins slow hacking, 30 mins school work on the flat	ditto
5	6 lb. oats ⎫ 3 lb. nuts ⎬ 3 feeds 2 lb. bran ⎧ per day 1 lb. carrots ⎭ 15 lb. hay 1 Bran Mash per week	ditto	ditto
6	7 lb. oats ⎫ 3 lb. nuts ⎬ 4 feeds 2 lb. bran ⎧ per day 1 lb. carrots ⎭ 14 lb. hay 1 Bran Mash per week	1½ hours (30 mins school work including cavalletti, 1 hour hacking at approx. 6–7 m.p.h. Include about three—½ mile canters per week)	ditto
7 & 8	8 lb. oats ⎫ 3 lb. nuts ⎬ 4 feeds 2 lb. bran ⎧ per day 1 lb. carrots ⎭ 13 lb. hay 1 Bran Mash per week	2 hours (20 mins schooling including a little jumping 1 hr 40 mins hacking at approx. 7–8 m.p.h. including a steady canter. One—6 furlong gallop per week)	ditto
9 & 10	10 lb. oats ⎫ 3 lb. nuts ⎬ 4 feeds 2 lb. bran ⎧ per day 1 lb. carrots ⎭ 11 lb. hay 1 Bran Mash per week	As above; if possible increase to 2½ hours	ditto

Part of the hay ration may be given as chaff. Additives such as molasses or molassine meal, or other proprietary foods can be given as required and variety introduced as necessary. Oats are given bruised and all feeds are dampened.

During weeks 1–2 allow the horse an hour a day to pick at grass. Reduce the time to ½ hour during weeks 3–4 and thereafter allow the horse no less than ten minutes a day in which he can be led out to a piece of clean grazing.

Clipping and Trimming

In winter nature provides the horse with a thick winter coat and this, combined with the grease which accumulates on the skin, protects him from cold, wind and rain very effectively. The thick coat is no hindrance to the horse in a natural state, for he does not expend energy to an extent that would make him sweat.

By stabling him, feeding him on energy foods and working him at very much faster paces than nature ever intended we are imposing an unnatural or artificial environment, and, in consequence, we must resort to unnatural methods if the horse is to function efficiently.

For the stabled horse the winter coat is a positive drawback and if it is not removed the horse will lose condition through heavy sweating during work.

The coat is, therefore, removed by clipping and the operation not only permits the horse to work faster without distress, but makes it easier for the horse-keeper to keep him clean. In addition, of course, a clipped horse is dried very much more quickly than one with a coat like a bear. Another reason given for clipping is prevention of disease, which should not be applicable in the case of properly kept horses.

The winter coat begins to grow in September and needs to be 'set', or established, before clipping. Most horses, but by no means all, can be clipped in early October and will then need a second clipping either just before or after Christmas. This, at any rate, is usually the case with fine-coated Thoroughbreds, but a very common horse may need clipping more frequently.

The type of clip employed depends very much on the type of horse, the work he does and under what conditions. At least it should do, but more often than not it depends upon the ideas the owner has upon the subject. There are two principal clips and two subsidiary ones, with variations between them, all arising from the artistic eye or the inept hand of the machine operator.

120

The *full* clip involves removing the entire coat. The *hunter* clip leaves a saddle patch on the back, which may vary from a full patch to a three-inch wide strip on either side of the backbone in the saddle area. In addition all four legs are left unclipped. The height to which the unclipped hair is left is roughly governed by measuring, on the hind leg, one stretched hand's breadth from the hock upwards to determine the line at the rear, and one similarly stretched hand from the stifle downwards to obtain a leading edge, which will be some four to five inches higher than the line at the back. On the forelegs the line is obtained by taking one outstretched hand from the elbow down and two from the knee upwards.

The lover of the compromise may, if he wishes, clip his horse completely the first time and give only a hunter clip the second time.

The reasons for carrying out a *hunter* clip are usually given as follows: (a) the saddle patch is left on to prevent galls or scalding; (b) the legs are left unclipped as a protection against thorns, cuts, cracked heels and chills. Whether these reasons hold water is again a matter of opinion and depends very much on the sort of coat one is dealing with.

A fine-skinned horse will, I believe, benefit by having his saddle patch left on, but it is a dubious advantage with a horse carrying a very thick coat. Not only will it encourage excessive sweating under the saddle, often the cause of saddle sores, but it is very difficult indeed to get dry.

As far as the legs go it is more difficult to find thorns and cuts in a mass of hair than without it, and if you miss them they may turn septic. Hairy legs are also not easily dried and wet heels quickly become cracked heels.

Again it depends on the horse. The fine-coated Thoroughbred will probably do better with his legs unclipped and the hairy commoner may benefit from having them clipped out.

Having said this much I will descend from the fence and say that on Thoroughbred horses I use the hunter clip and on anything else I still employ it, only I clip the legs out with the coarser leg blades which do not cut nearly so close as those used on the body.

There is then the *blanket* clip *(Fig. 9)* where a patch approximating to the area covered by a galloping sheet is left as well as the legs. It is suitable for Thoroughbreds. Lastly there is the *trace* clip *(Fig. 9)* in which the hair is clipped from the belly and flanks and usually up the under side of the neck as well. This is a useful clip for hunting ponies kept at grass and for harness horses.

121

Fig 9 The blanket clip and the trace clip

I believe that horses can be clipped by hand-operated clippers and, indeed, long ago when the practice first commenced they were clipped with scissors and even shaved with a razor. Today, however, most of us will use an electrically-operated machine, of which there are two types. There is a heavy duty machine with a powerful engine, and a smaller hand machine in which the engine lies within the compass of one's hand (*Plate 30*). The former is suspended from the ceiling and the clipping head is driven by means of a flexible shaft. For stables with more than three or four horses it is undoubtedly the best tool for the job, but otherwise the hand machine is perfectly satisfactory and efficient. Satisfactory and efficient that is, when properly used and maintained.

The success of the clipping operation depends to a very large degree on the efficiency of the machine and it is well worthwhile reading the manufacturer's instructions and carrying them out.

In 90% of the cases where the machine breaks down, or will not cut, the fault lies with the operator and not the machine. The usual cause is for the tension nut to be screwed down too tightly, which overstrains and overheats the very small engine. During use the machine will get warm and you will have to stop to clean the air vents and give it time to cool. While it is running frequent application to the blades of a thin machine oil assists efficient working.

We will presume, however, that you have your machine in good order with sharp blades (if it is yours I advise you never to lend it, even

122

to your best friend; if you have managed to borrow one you must persuade the lender that I am being unduly fussy).

You will then have two prime requirements. First, a well-lit box (daylight is always preferable), and secondly a clean horse who is cool and absolutely dry. It will be no good clipping after exercise.

A dirty coat will be more difficult to cut and causes the machine to work a great deal harder. There is, in fact, no reason why the horse should not be shampooed with an animal shampoo some few days before you intend to clip. If the weather is not too cold, the horse is rinsed well and dried thoroughly he will come to no harm, whatever the diehards say, and it will make the job of clipping very much easier.

Let the horse become accustomed to the noise of the machine before starting to clip. The object is to do the job as quickly as possible, but without upsetting the horse. A horse that is frightened may begin to sweat and then no clipper will cut. When he evinces no apprehension at the noise, turn the machine off, and spend ten minutes running it over his body. Begin the clipping on the shoulder, a place that is not unduly sensitive, keeping the blades flat and working against the lay of the coat. Do not *push* the machine or you will be putting additional strain on the engine. The operator's job is to guide the machine, not to do its work.

If you are leaving the saddle patch and the legs unclipped, put the saddle on and trace the outline with a piece of chalk and mark the leg lines in a similar way. The edges can either be trimmed with the clipper or with the scissors.

Do not clip either the tail or mane. If you do they will have the appearance of a shaving brush for months. When you reach the quarters make a V-shape above the dock and not an abrupt, straight line across it.

Clipping the belly and between the hind-legs can be a ticklish business for both operator and horse. It is possible to clip a quiet horse single-handed, but it is usually helpful to have an assistant. When these difficult areas are reached he or she can then pick up a forefoot, holding it by the toe with the tips of the fingers, so that the horse cannot lean his weight upon the raised leg or use it as a prop *(Plate 31)*. In theory the horse should then be unable to move any of the other three feet from the ground. In practice this happy state is not always so easily achieved, but, generally, the method will allow the operator to clip the sensitive parts with comparative ease and safety.

As an additional precaution, when cleaning out between the hind legs, it is as well for the operator to hold the tail about two-thirds of the way down. It is then possible for him to pull the horse on to the leg nearest to him which will frustrate any attempt to kick.

I have already mentioned the inadvisability of cutting into the mane and tail and if there is any danger of this, as there might be with a fidgety horse, these areas are best done with a small hand clipper. Some people clip the mane at the withers and cut a piece out, just behind the ears, for the bridle. This is an unnecessary practice with a properly pulled mane and once done has to be clipped at least once a week to keep the mane looking tidy.

Where there are wrinkles in the skin, under the elbows, for example, the skin must be stretched flat and pulled with the hand. It is never very sensible to pick up the skin and cut towards the fingers.

The parts between the forelegs are best dealt with by having the assistant pick up a foreleg and stretch it forwards. The wrinkles that remain are then smoothed as described.

If the legs are left unclipped one is usually advised to trim the heels and the heavy hair on the fetlocks and the back of the tendons with scissors and a comb. This requires some skill and both scissors and comb must work upwards against the hair.

On common horses with a preponderance of coarse hair on the legs many people do, however, trim with the clippers; again, of course, moving upwards. This practice is frequently condemned although the only valid argument against it is that one must be constantly at it throughout the season and the legs do look a little bristly. The best solution to the problem of the hairy-heeled brigade is, in my opinion, to use the clippers with the coarse leg blades, the appearance then is much the same as that obtained with scissors and comb.

Somewhat understandably the clipping of the head is the thing to which many horses object. It should, therefore, be left until last.

The most common form of restraint used to persuade the horse to keep his head still whilst the operation is carried out is the twitch. In its simplest form this is a piece of wood about a foot long with a hole bored through one end. Through this hole is threaded a loop of cord, or binder twine, and the loop is then slipped round the upper lip and the wooden shaft twisted until the string is tight. The shaft is then either held by the operator or slipped back under the halter. Alternatively the twitch is applied to the ear. In both cases the idea is to distract the horse's attention from the work in hand by the use of a stronger counter-irritant.

124

There may be occasions when this barbaric practice is necessary, but to apply a twitch is always a confession of failure. I am wholeheartedly against its use. Few of us would think of employing a similar restraint on a child who was frightened of the barber's chair and we should not think of doing so with a horse.

It is possible that by using the twitch our purpose will be achieved, but the horse will not forget and each successive clipping will be rendered more difficult and require increasingly severe measures to accomplish satisfactorily. More importantly the basis of trust and respect which should exist between horse and trainer, and which to a large degree is built up in the stable, is broken and will not easily be reformed. Horses that have been twitched are frequently head-shy thereafter. This is particularly the case if the twitch has been applied to the ear.

Patience, quiet handling and the establishment of trust between man and horse are the only satisfactory way in the long run.

The ears themselves should not be cleaned out inside, as this will remove the natural protection against wind and rain. It is sufficient to run the clippers along the edges, holding them together so that the hair is removed in one sweep.

Once the clipping has got as far as the back a rug should be thrown on to keep the horse warm. If he is cold he is unlikely to keep still.

However clean the horse seemed to be before clipping commenced, the skin surface, after the first clipping, will be covered with grease and dirt. The easiest way to remove this is to make the horse sweat, which can be done by piling on all the available clothing and giving him a little sharp exercise.

There is no need to gallop him into a muck sweat, give him twenty minutes or so and then bring him home; he will begin to sweat when the clothing is removed. Now take a damp wisp and strap him thoroughly. The wisp, if kept constantly damp, will remove all the surplus grease.

Trimming Manes and Tails

For the sake of appearance manes and tails are thinned by pulling out the hair, which if carefully done does not hurt the horse *(Plate 32)*.

The Arabian horse, who has a mane and tail of very fine hairs, is never trimmed in this way and very often a Thoroughbred horse is left with a full, unpulled tail.

The secret of pulling tails lies in never doing too much at once, a fortnight is not too long to allow, and always pulling the hairs from underneath and not from the top.

The tail should be kept well brushed out and it is as well to wash it thoroughly before you start tidying it up. In this respect avoid the 'whiter than white' detergents and use a medicated horse shampoo. The latter will remove scurf and dirt most effectively, whilst the former can set up irritations of the tender skin on the dock.

Remove the hairs one by one, never pulling too many at a time or you will make the tail sore and the animal may well object unpleasantly. Each day damp the tail with the water brush and put on a tail bandage to encourage it to lie flat *(Plate 33)*.

Tail bandages are made from either stockinette, which is the least satisfactory as they slip, or in a three-inch cotton flex cloth which stays in place very well. Don't leave bandages on for more than an hour or so and certainly not over-night, otherwise the continued pressure kills the hair. It is also neither necessary nor advisable to wet the bandage. If you do it contracts as it dries and becomes too tight.

The tail can either be left as a switch or it can be 'banged'. A 'banged' tail is one that is cut off straight at the bottom and a switch one that is pulled down its entire length and allowed to end in a natural point. Most switch tails resemble the caudal appendage of a rat.

The 'banged' tail, which you will gather is my preference, is pulled at the top only and is full at the bottom. To 'bang' the tail first get someone to lift it up so that it assumes the position it will occupy in movement. Now calculate a hand's breadth below the point of the hock and with a large pair of scissors, the paperhanging variety are the best, cut the hair off in a straight line, but holding the scissors inclined slightly upwards from rear to front. The tail when held out will then finish in a straight line. If you neglect to hold the tail up you will end up by cutting it too short.

Manes are thinned by again pulling out the surplus hair from the under-side *(Plate 34)*. The way to do this is by laying the mane over to the opposite side (i.e. if the mane normally lies on the off-side brush it over to the near-side) and then pulling the hairs with the aid of the small mane comb. Take about half-a-dozen in the comb, push the comb up to the roots, twist and pull. If too many are pulled at a time, or the hair is broken, instead of coming out at the roots, it will grow in upright spikes and will take months before it lies down properly.

When thinned the length of the mane should be about five inches and anything over this length is best removed with a sharp penknife rather than a pair of scissors.

Manes can, of course, be removed altogether and are then termed 'hogged'. On a thick-necked, cresty sort of horse this does improve the appearance and it saves the labour involved in plaiting the mane for special occasions. To keep it tidy, however, it wants doing once a week unless the animal is to bear a distinct resemblance to his erect-maned pre-historic ancestors.

The mane is hogged by first cutting off the hair with scissors as closely as possible. The clippers are then run up each side, from the withers to the poll and then a third cut is made up the centre. The whiskers round a horse's muzzle are, or should be, left untrimmed, they perform a function rather like a radar beam by assisting the horse to gauge the distance of objects from his mouth.

Plaiting

For some reason horsemen feel it incumbent upon them to plait their horses' manes on special occasions. It is a time-consuming operation, but if properly done looks smart and neat.

Most books and manuals lay down the specific number of plaits which is acceptable. With respect, this is nonsense. The number of plaits will depend upon the length of the horse's neck and to some degree what pleases the owner's eye. A long neck looks better with fewer plaits than a short one, a weak neck is improved by plaiting loosely to give a false line, a strong neck can have the plaits made tightly. On a well-proportioned neck I use six plaits and one more on the forelock, on a short one perhaps eight plaits plus one for the forelock.

There are two ways of plaiting manes, first by sewing up the plaits with a needle and thread (a method beloved by the diehards, who often leave someone else to do the plaiting) and secondly with rubber bands. Of the two I must admit that the former looks neater, but confess to often using the latter method.

To plait the mane, sewing the plaits, a large-eyed needle is necessary and a reel of linen thread the same colour as the mane. First damp the mane, then divide it into the number of plaits required. Make the first plait and just after half-way down it plait in a ten inch length of thread doubled over. When you have completed the plait you will be left with two loose ends of thread, loop the ends round the plait and pull tight.

127

Thread both ends through the needle, double the plait under, and bring the needle through it as close to the crest as possible, pull the thread ends through, remove the needle and tie the plait firmly, cutting off the spare thread ends.

Rubber bands are easier. The band is looped round the bottom, the plait turned under and the same band looped round the whole thing.

Tails, if left untrimmed, can also be plaited at the top, and many are the individual idiosyncrasies manifested in design and execution.

The only way to learn how to do this is watch an experienced artist at work. As I have never mastered the art myself my instructions are hardly likely to prove of any value.

One thing, however, I do know, is that a tail plaited badly looks frightful and that one plaited too tight is uncomfortable. In the latter instance a horse will display his discomfort by either clamping his tail between his buttocks or by carrying it bent to one side or the other.

Stable Clothing

Before the stabled horse is clipped he should be provided with a light sheet, a linen one is the most suitable, which will keep dust out of the coat and encourage it to lie properly.

After the coat is removed it will be necessary to provide heavier rugs for warmth. The basic requirement will be a canvas or jute top rug, fully lined with blanketing, an under-rug of wool or a large horse blanket, which is usually striped and weighs 8 lb., and, ideally, one of the open-mesh Aerborn rugs made of cotton. The complement of clothing will be completed by the addition of a set of wool bandages, five inches wide, and a cotton tail bandage.

The mesh sheet is probably the greatest advance ever made in horse-clothing. It acts on the principle of trapping pockets of insulating air between the body and an outer rug, thus acting as an insulator which keeps the body warm in cold weather and cool under the opposite conditions. By the same principle it discourages 'breaking-out', that is the profuse sweating indulged in by some horses after exercise or hard work, or sweating induced by nervousness when travelling.

In reasonably clement weather a horse who is properly and sufficiently fed will be kept warm enough with an Aerborn rug and a canvas top rug. In very cold weather a blanket can be added and laid between the two.

The great difficulty with stable clothing is to ensure that it is kept in place during the night. The most common method is by using a body

32 A pulled tail

33 A correctly applied tail bandage

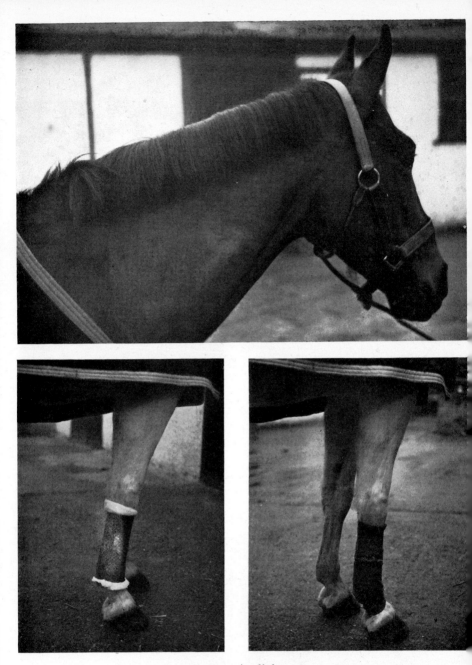

34 ABOVE: *A pulled mane*
35 *An exercise bandage and* 36 *A stable bandage, used to keep the legs warm*

roller, made of either webbing or leather, fastened round the barrel of the horse.

Rollers can, however, cause sore backs if not properly maintained, and the reason is usually to be found in the absence of stuffing in the pads on either side of the spine. Rollers should be fitted as carefully as saddles and there should be no area of the pads' surface bearing directly on the backbone.

If they are fastened too tightly, and they usually are, it causes the horse discomfort when he lies down and ends up with the securing straps being burst. The necessity, and the temptation, of girthing too tightly can be overcome by using a breast strap attached to the forward edges of the roller which will then prevent the movement of the latter to the rear.

The best type of roller is that where the two pads are joined by an iron hoop and where each is hinged so that they will conform to any shape of back.

Rollers like these, and also ones with fixed pads separated by an iron hoop, are known as *anti-cast* rollers and are supposed to stop a horse rolling right over and getting into a position where he cannot rise of his own accord.

They will prevent a horse rolling over, although the hoop is likely to get somewhat bent in the process, but their most important advantage lies in their allowing freedom to the backbone.

The method I use is to have the top rug fitted with two web surcingles which are sewn to the canvas. The forward one is padded on either side of the spine for some eighteen inches and a loop of web left over the top of the backbone.

No pressure is, therefore, sustained by the spine and this surcingle, combined with the second one, which is set some fifteen inches to the rear and fastened quite loosely, keeps the rugs in place admirably. Providing the rear surcingle does not hang down in festoons there is no danger of the horse catching his foot in it.

Most saddlers make well-shaped horse rugs allowing for the protuberance of the withers and the dip in the line of the back, as well as being generous in the cut of the neck hole. Unfortunately no trade is more bedevilled with cheap-jacks selling inferior articles at what appear to be attractive prices, and many of the products of these people are so skimped and badly cut as to be useless.

To fit properly a rug must be long enough, almost up to the dock, deep enough, well down the flanks, and must not be tight round the neck and shoulders when fastened at the breast.

As a rough guide the following sizes are appropriate:

Over 16 h.h.	6 ft–6 ft 3 in (Heavyweights possibly 6 ft 6 in)
15.2 h.h.–16 h.h.	5 ft 9 in–6 ft
15 h.h.–15.2 h.h.	5 ft 6 in—5 ft 9 in
14.2 h.h.—15 h.h.	5 ft 3 in–5 ft 6 in
13.2 h.h.–14.2 h.h.	5 ft–5 ft 3 in and proportionately thereafter.

For high days and holidays, including taking your friends round the stables on Sunday mornings, one may indulge oneself and one's horse in a day rug. This is a wool rug, of almost any colour you like, which can be further embellished by the addition of the owner's initials and replaces the canvas top rug on these occasions.

The use of wool leg bandages, used primarily to keep the extremities warm after exertion, is dealt with elsewhere in this section.

Care of the Stabled Horse After Exercise

A horse tired after strenuous work, such as a day's hunting, an endurance ride or the speed and endurance phase of a three-day-event, requires special, immediate and swift attention. It is in this state that the horse can most easily suffer from slaphappy management. The rule is always to see to your horse's needs first and your own afterwards.

If the horse is brought in dry and cool, remove his bridle and saddle and offer him a warmed drink, if he likes a bottle of stout in it, so much the better. If at this stage he wants to roll allow him to do so. Sponge the sweat marks from the saddle patch and round the girth and dry thoroughly. Put his rug on and make him comfortable by spongeing his head and throat and again drying them. Strip his ears, that is hand rub them, to get the circulation going. Sponge between the hindlegs, under the tail and round the sheath and do the same round the elbows, taking good care to dry the horse thoroughly.

Now inspect the legs for injuries and attend to them at once, including even the smallest scratch. If the mud is dry brush it off smartly, have a look at the feet and then give a quick all-round, upward (toward the heart) hand rubbing with Radiol spirit lotion. Check the heels are dry and bandage the legs (*Plates 35 and 36*). If the circulation is stimulated and the extremities then kept warm the temperature will not drop.

Lastly, groom the horse briskly with the body brush and, if necessary, hand rub the mud off the belly, and put his clothing on. He can then be given his feed, a soft bran or linseed mash, which will not strain his tired digestive system, and left alone for an hour or so.

When you have done this go back to the horse and check that he has (a) eaten up and (b) has not started to sweat again—if he has you must set about drying him. Feel his ears to see if they are warm and if they are not hand rub them until they are. He can now have a haynet strung up and you can have your dinner, after which you must inspect him again.

If the horse is brought in hot, as he may be after a competitive event, he can be sponged down to remove the sweat and must then be dried off by hand and by walking about. He should have a light sheet put over him to prevent his catching a chill. Very often, particularly after racing, a mesh rug is thrown over the horse which in itself has little value. The mesh sheet is only effective when it has an outer covering, and only under these conditions can its insulating properties be brought into play.

Whether horses, or parts of them, should be washed is a point upon which the experts differ, often violently. I have no objection, *provided the horse is properly dried*.

If mud is washed off the legs after hunting (usually it can be brushed off if it is dry) it is, of course, very important to dry the legs, and particularly the heels, most thoroughly. To this end a little bran packed into the heel, after it has been dried, and covered by the leg bandages is an effective drying agent and will prevent cracked heels.

It must be realised that when the body is in a weakened physical condition the bodily functions are weakened correspondingly. It is of paramount importance, therefore, that the rate of circulation and the body temperature are maintained and that the digestive apparatus is not overburdened by unwise feeding.

Handling the Horse in the Stable

I am increasingly convinced that the foundation of a satisfactory partnership between horse and rider can more easily be laid by having a proper relationship in the stable than in any other way. I am not saying that it is impossible to build up a partnership in the field without the rider also acting as a groom to his horse, but I do say that a real understanding between the two is attained more quickly if a basis of trust has already been established by a contact, apart from that experienced during work.

The horse is by nature gregarious and in the herd all, with the exception of the herd stallion, are prepared to follow and to be led without the exercise of personal initiative. When the horse is removed from his herd he does not leave his herd instinct behind, and if we are wise we recognise this and use these instincts to our advantage. In the herd the horse looked to the dominant stallion for leadership and submitted to his authority. Taken from this environment the horse seeks, if we allow him, to transfer this allegiance to his human master, who cares for him, corrects him when necessary and supplies him with food—always a preoccupation uppermost in the horse's mind.

Man is, therefore, always the dominant personality in the relationship, always the leader.

Leadership of any kind is, however, dependent upon mutual respect and trust. Discipline comes into it, certainly, but discipline is not a matter of unquestioned obedience to authority. There is a sort of discipline based on fear, but it is never a truly satisfactory or successful one. When the real question is asked, or to use a modern parlance, when the 'crunch comes', it disintegrates.

Discipline is a two-way bond and a man cannot exercise it over men or animals until he has first disciplined himself.

In the case of the horse there is another characteristic to be considered. He is by nature quick to panic, and he is highly nervous of unexpected sounds or swift movement; if man, therefore, is to be his leader, man must recognise not only this characteristic, but must also realise that at no time must he undermine the horse's confidence in him by being the source of fear.

All living things require a basis of security. A child needs the security of a home and parents, a fox finds security in his earth, a timid hare finds hers, without appreciating its insecurity, in her form and the domesticated horse finds his in his own familiar paddock and, even more strongly, in his stable. This is why a horse in new and strange surroundings, or even a horse in familiar ones, may display reluctance to leave his box, the centre of his security, and will always evince the greatest eagerness to get back to it when turned towards home.

In addition he is made even more secure, or he can be, by his proximity to his human leader, if, that is, he has learnt to trust him.

Where this trust exists it is possible for a horse to overcome fear, or at least to have it allayed, by relying upon his two-legged leader. Properly handled horses will respond to human leadership in almost the same way as a child. Instinctively, if frightened or hurt, a child calls for, or goes to, its mother, and much the same relationship can exist between horse and man.

132

As an example, my horses' paddock is adjacent to an open space fronting the church, and it is the custom of the local Salvation Army band to play in this space on certain Sunday afternoons. The horses had only recently been running out in this paddock when the band appeared one Sunday. The drum banged, the trumpets blared enthusiastically and both animals were prepared to jump the church to escape what for them could hardly be the consolation of religion. I happened to be in the paddock, inspecting the trees, which they are both partial to chewing, and called to them. Almost at once they galloped over and stood by me. I patted them and spoke to them until they lost the wild eye that betokens extreme alarm, and finally they walked back to the fence with me. They were then separated from the band by a matter of only a few yards and spent the rest of the afternoon happily listening to the proceedings. They are now the band's most regular and attentive admirers. By coming to me when they were frightened they were showing the trust they had formed for their 'leader'.

If we recognise this need for leadership and for security in the horse it will influence our handling of him in the stable. Nothing we do will disturb his sense of security, so blows, raised voices, sudden movements have no place within the four walls of his box. This is not sentimentality, but just sound common sense. Break the security of his box and we remove an elemental prop in his existence and at the same time we lose his trust. To a point we may continue to dominate him, but for the wrong reasons.

We should be prepared, with a nervous horse, to spend hours doing nothing more than sitting in his box with him, talking to him or just reading a book until he comes to accept us as a necessary adjunct to his surroundings. We should handle him frequently, and when we feel we have reached a certain point, we can begin to ask him to move over in response to the voice, to lift his legs in the same way and with the aid of a carrot or two one can teach him to take two or three steps backwards. This is easily done by standing in front of him holding the carrot behind his nose. As he drops his head for the titbit a slight backward push on his nose coupled with the word 'back' will induce the required reaction.

Later he will learn that a touch behind the girth is a request to move his quarters away and it is not too difficult to teach him to make one or two side steps. All these little exercises, carried out in a relaxed atmosphere, are teaching him to co-operate willingly, preparing him for future work, and accustoming him to the acceptance of discipline.

When he co-operates willingly in small things he will co-operate as a matter of habit when more is asked of him.

When approaching the box always speak first to warn the horse of your arrival, when in the box move quietly, but purposefully, and always make sure the horse knows where you are before walking round his quarters. Few horses will kick viciously in stables and when they do it is always the fault of some groom who has mistreated them. A horse that has his legs banged with a brush may kick when he sees his groom with one in his hand preparing to brush the particular leg. An animal that has had its tail pulled out in handfuls may react in the same way when you handle that part of him. If you scuttle round the back of him he may be frightened into making a defensive kick, although in nine cases out of ten it is more likely that he will run forward, *away* from the suspected danger rather than attacking it.

The horse's defence, unlike a dog's, never lies in attack, but always in flight. Always, whether ridden or in the stable, he will try to get away from pain, or the fear of it; very, very rarely, if ever, does he turn and retaliate.

Nevertheless, when moving round the quarters precede the movement by placing the hand on him and walk round as close to the horse as possible. If by chance he should kick you will be too close to receive much more than a bump and you will avoid the full strength of the movement. Some horses will lay back their ears when food is brought round. Disregard it and walk quietly to the manger, speaking firmly to him. The reason for his apparent bad temper is a temporary reversion to the wild state. When feeding, horses do not share their particular patch with others, but rather drive intruders off. Temporarily, you, carrying the food, become in his mind a source which may deny him his rightful share, and so he makes faces. A firm word and a resolute step may not remove the scowl from his face, but it will prevent it becoming anything more unpleasant.

The horse is probably more responsive to the human voice than to anything else. He has an acute sense of hearing and although he doesn't understand what you say he will recognise the tone in which you speak to him. This is a great weapon in the horseman's armoury and should be developed and used accordingly. Normally, the quiet, soft voice can be used; if we want a reaction, however, the tone must be firmer, not louder, and can have an executive snap to it.

The contact of the hands on the horse's body is also important, a horse relaxes under the firm, confident hand, whilst he becomes nervous and jumpy with one that is not so confident, or is rough.

Biting is not to be encouraged and should be checked. I, as I have already mentioned, administer an immediate retaliatory nip on the muzzle which works wonders. The feeding of too many titbits is a frequent cause of biting and bad temper. Horses, particularly ponies, tend to bully if the expected titbit is not forthcoming and then to bite in temper. Reserve the titbits, therefore, as rewards for work well done and as a bed-time treat.

Horses may also nip when being groomed, particularly if they are ticklish. This can be avoided, not by shouting at the animal, but by being a little more gentle in your work and keeping a hand on the neck.

As our object is to win the animal's confidence it is hardly an expression of trust or good will to tie him up when you are grooming him. Leave the horse's head free and you will find he submits to your handling it with far better grace than when under restraint.

Never hit a horse in his box, your voice is sufficient punishment for most misdemeanours. The man who takes a horse into the box and punishes him for a resistance committed outside (such people talk about 'squaring him up') is not only a fool (the horse cannot understand why he is being beaten), but is also a coward.

When turning a horse in the box remember that you must give him as much room as you can, and when you lead him in and out, take him through the door straight, so that he cannot bang his hips.

I have said that most horses are by nature followers and are willing and even glad to co-operate, occasionally, however, one comes up against a 'leader-horse' who may not submit so easily.

Such a horse needs a skilled, extra sensitive, horseman to manage him. If he gets less than this he may be turned into a rogue and become virtually unmanageable, on the other hand with the right master he can be the horse of a lifetime.

Managing Grassland

While for reasons of economy and feed value it is most desirable to practise good management of pastureland, a little study of the subject will bring one to an inevitable conclusion. The more grass one has the easier it is to manage it properly, whilst the person possessed of a very small area will find management correspondingly difficult, even though the need for proper control is of more importance.

Drainage
Nevertheless, any effort at improving the quality of the feed is well worthwhile, since good pasture will feed twice as many animals, twice as well, than the same acreage of neglected land. The first consideration is drainage, which is no problem on most chalky, sandy or gravel based soils, but a very large one on clay soils. Clay sub-soils absorb only a little moisture and the topsoil quickly becomes waterlogged in wet weather; there is also practically no aeration possible in the sub-soil. Under such conditions it is impossible for plant life to thrive and no satisfactory crop will be obtained until the land is drained.

At the least this entails the existence of good, clean ditches, but in many cases pipe drainage is the only real solution, and an expensive one at that, although it pays in the long run through the results achieved.

Soil Analysis
The majority of pastures, particularly old ones, suffer from deficiencies of the essential components for abundant plant life, namely, lime, phosphates and potash. It is, however, no good embarking upon a scheme of improvement until the extent and type of deficiencies have been determined by a scientific soil analysis.

This can be obtained by requesting the assistance of the County Agricultural Officer, who will not only arrange for the analysis to be made, but will also advise on the best methods of fertilising and future management. Apart from the important factor of soil analysis as a basis for improvement, a visual examination of the pasture will provide a guide as to the line which should be followed.

Quality of Pasture

A good pasture will carry leafy grasses in great variety, as well as clovers, and there will be a noticeable absence of weeds. Moderate and poor pasture will display these attributes in correspondingly less abundant a fashion. Matted grasses, thick feg, mare's tail and sorrel indicate an acid soil in need of lime. This is, also, the case where there is a preponderance of buttercups and surface moss. A phosphate deficiency is shown by the absence of clovers.

Re-seeding

Nothing much can be done with really poor pasture and it is better and cheaper by far to plough it up and re-seed it. If this method is decided upon preparation of the seed bed is a vital factor. After deep ploughing, to bury the old turf, heavy rolling should be alternated with harrowing, until a fine top tilth is acquired. After seeding the seed should be covered by a light harrow and the surface then rolled again. Manuring will be according to the soil analysis, but during harrowing 6–7 cwt. per acre of basic slag and 2–3 cwt. of potato or beet manure can be worked in profitably.

The seed mixture will vary according to the soil but should, in any case, include such deep-rooting, palatable herbs as yarrow, burnett, chicory and ribwort plantain and have a clover/grasses ratio of about 30 to 70. By ploughing and re-seeding a poor pasture can be converted to a first-class sward in *one* year.

It is possible to alter the constituent growth of poor land by a process of grazing with sheep, so as to remove the matted grasses and allow soil aeration, and by constant deep harrowing and applications of lime, phosphates and potash, together with supplies of nitrogen, but the process of conversion may take anything between five to eight years.

Moderate grassland will be improved by resting, harrowing and manurial treatment, whilst good grass will only remain so if subjected to the same treatment.

Rotational Systems

In order to carry out cultivation and fertilising and to give pasture adequate rest periods for the making of new growth it is obvious that the available area must be divided either by permanent or electric fencing, so that animals graze one part whilst the others are being rested or treated.

How this rotational system of preparation, rest, growth and grazing periods is arranged depends on the number of animals, the quality of the grass, the acreage available and the individual circumstances.

It is, however, essential that such a rotational system is carried out if the best results, and the most economical ones, are to be obtained from the land available. An arrangement should, therefore, be made to ensure a maximum amount of grass being available throughout the growing season from spring to autumn. Ideally horses should have large acreages to graze over, but unless we are possessed of a 200 acre park this will not be possible, and the land at our disposal will have to be divided into small units, varying from say six acres at the outside to a minimum of one, or even half, acre strips, depending upon the acreage and the number of horses involved. Land required for spring grazing or for haymaking must be left free from the previous autumn.

Fertilising
Liming, best done in November, can then be carried out at a rate of from ½ to 2 tons per acre at an interval of five years on lime deficient land. The rains will then have ample time to wash in the dressing.

Periodical dressings of basic slag (a phosphatic fertiliser) are necessary for maximum grass production. These are applied in the autumn, at intervals of between three and five years, at a rate of 8 cwt. per acre. Phosphates stimulate clover growth and being slow acting remain active for a long period.

Clovers, apart from being highly nutritious, attract nitrogen from the air and so assist the root development and growth of the surrounding grasses.

Land which is notably deficient in potash (sandy soils are particularly affected in this respect) require occasional dressings of potash salts, which are applied at a rate of between ½ to 1 cwt. per acre.

Just as important as these fertilisers, however, is the provision of humus, containing nitrogen, in the form of honest muck. Autumn is again the best time for applying stable manure, but land so treated must be kept for haymaking, as it will not be fit for grazing until after haymaking time in June.

Nitrogen, in the form of nitro-chalk or sulphate of ammonia, if spread on pasture land in February (2 cwt. per acre) greatly assists growth and will produce a pasture suitable for grazing considerably earlier in the spring.

Because certain grasses come into growth earlier than others it is unwise to carry out a rigid rotational plan always using the same paddock or strip for early grazing, or hay, as the case may be. Unless the plan is varied from year to year the result will be for certain grasses to disappear entirely, thus altering the balanced composition.

Harrowing

The remaining partner in grassland management is cultivation achieved by harrowing, which should be carried out when the field has been grazed thoroughly.

The object of harrowing is firstly soil aeration, achieved by opening the soil up and removing the old growths, mosses, etc., which choke it and prevent the access of air and nitrogen to the root systems. Harrowing also spreads the droppings which, if allowed to remain in heaps, soon sour the ground and encourage tufty growth which horses will not eat. Moreover, heaps of dung breed parasites and are the principal vehicle, apart from the animal itself, in the red-worm cycle.

Harrowing operations should be carried out when the land is just damp, and never during or after a frost when great damage could be done. Harrowing should be drastic and carried out in both directions, the more the sward resembles a ploughed field at the finish the more effective is the operation.

Rolling

The other form of cultivation, of almost equal importance, is rolling. The winter frosts and heavy rains loosen the topsoil, which is not a condition conducive to vigorous plant growth, which needs firm ground if it is to thrive. Rolling makes the topsoil firm and supplies the necessary growth conditions.

Inter-Grazing

Whilst the treatment of pastures advocated will undoubtedly produce excellent grazing it is, unfortunately, true that the horse's eating habits are not helpful in achieving ideal swards without the assistance of other animals.

Horses are selective grazers, leaving whole patches completely untouched and grazing others entirely bare. These left-over patches soon become coarse and tufty and the only satisfactory way of achieving level grazing and preventing horse-sick pastures is by alternating bullocks with horses.

Unfortunately, the vast majority of horse-keepers do not have bullocks, and most of them will find it difficult to make an arrangement with someone who does. Be that as it may, if it is at all possible every effort should be made to inter-graze cattle with horses.

Cattle and horses appear to be complementary in their grazing habits, the one eating what the other leaves and vice versa. Each will graze over the droppings of the other, whilst refusing to do so over its own. Cattle, too, combat red-worm infestation, the worm being eliminated when taken into the body of any host other than its natural one.

Horses graze on shorter grasses (four to five inches is ideal) by biting, whereas cattle prefer longer growths, which they pull off with their tongues.

As a result a field in which horses have little grazing, will, if it has tufty high grasses in it untouched by them, provide a feeding ground for bullocks. Conversely a field grazed by bullocks, who are unable to cope with the shorter growth so effectively, will offer adequate feed for horses, and when grazed by both, alternately, will be level.

No field should be grazed bare, whether bullocks are employed or not, otherwise there will be no covering left to retain moisture and the recovery period will be protracted. Once the field or strip has been used, the harrows should be put on to aerate the soil and spread the droppings, if these have not already been removed by hand.

For many people the problem of harrowing may appear, at first sight, insuperable. How, in fact, to obtain harrows and then, how to drag them across the fields?

A small chain harrow is not, however, very expensive and with a little searching around a second-hand one may be found for very little money.

A tractor is not, perhaps, so easily obtained or borrowed, unless one is engaged in farming, but a Land-Rover, or even a Mini will pull a harrow, and if the fields are not too rough the Mini will not suffer.

A friend of mine, determined to practise good grass management, but too car-proud to risk his immaculate vehicle, has solved the problem by improvising some harness and pressing his hunter into service. Despite one or two occasions when the field was harrowed rather more swiftly than would be considered necessary, neither he nor the hunter seem to have suffered any ill-effects.

140

The Foot & Shoeing

Inevitably no chapter devoted to the horse's foot can omit the old saying, 'No foot—no 'oss'. There are many horsey sayings that amount to nothing more than uninformed nonsense, but this one is clear, shining, gospel truth.

The necessity to shoe the horse with rims of iron is a direct result of domestication, the horse in its feral state having a hoof which is sufficiently hard to withstand the wear caused by the distances and the country over which he has to travel.

Working, however, under weight, at speed, and nowadays for a considerable part of the time on roads, the horn would wear too quickly, would break away and the animal would become footsore unless the foot was protected.

As a result of our interference and the shortage of experienced farriers we can land ourselves, or rather our horses, in considerable trouble. It, therefore, behoves us to know something of the construction of the foot and of the simpler principles of shoeing *(Figs. 10, 11 and 12)*.

Structure of the Foot

The foot is a sensitive, vascular structure containing three bones, the 'coffin' or pedal bone, the navicular bone and the lower parts of the coronet bone; together they form the foot, or pedal, joint. These bones are covered by the soft structures which produce the horn of the hoof, are separated by gristle on their bearing surfaces and the whole joint is surrounded in 'joint oil' to assist its working. To these bones are also attached cartilages, ligaments and the tendons from the muscles of the forearm. The whole is contained in an outer protective case, consisting of the wall, a horny substance which grows down from the coronet and can be likened to our toe or finger-nails (the forefoot of the horse would seem in fact to correspond to the human finger, whilst the hock corresponds to our ankle, so that he proceeds, as it were, on

141

Fig 10 Section of the foot
A Long or great pastern bone (os
   suffraginis)
B Short pastern bone (os coronae)
C Coffin bone (os pedis)
D Navicular bone
E Sensitive frog
F Insensitive frog
G Extensor pedis tendon
H Coronary band
I Crust or wall
J Insensitive laminae
K Sensitive laminae
L Insensitive sole
M Sensitive sole
N Flexor perforans tendon
O Long inferior sesamoid ligament
P Seat of soreness where tendon passes
   over navicular bone

Fig 11 Parts of the foot
A Cushion of heel
B Frog
C Angle of heel
D Cleft of frog
E The bars
F Point of frog
G Wall of foot
H Seat of seedy toe
I White line
J Sole
K Seat of corn
L Seat of thrush

finger tips in front and on toes behind). The wall continues round to
the heels and there turns inwards to form the bars, which rigidly
secure its position.

The underside of the foot embraces the sole and the frog, the
triangular, rubbery substance lying between the angles of the heels.

The outside of this protective case is insensitive, but the inside of the
case, surrounding the pedal bone and running back to the heels, is
fleshy and, therefore, sensitive.

142

If we look at the sole of a scrubbed, unshod foot we shall see what is termed the 'white line' running round the inside of the hard wall. This line divides the outer, insensitive area from the commencement of the inner, sensitive one. As the shoe is fitted to the horny, insensitive wall there is, therefore, very little room for mistake on the part of the farrier when driving home his securing nails.

The horn of the wall is thickest at the toe and the heels, but in the 'quarters', the sides, it becomes considerably thinner.

The white line marks the merging point of the hard outside wall with horny, but less insensitive 'leaves', which in turn merge into 'fleshy leaves' of great sensitivity which connect the wall to the inside structures of the foot.

The sole of the foot is similarly constructed, having a hard, insensitive outer covering, which is none too thick, protecting an inner sensitive casing. This latter is known as the fleshy sole and is the source of the life and growth of the horny sole.

A healthy sole is slightly concave in shape to afford a better foothold and to be less prone to bruising. The horny sole, apart from helping the narrow wall of the foot to carry the weight of the horse, fulfils the purpose of protecting the fleshy sole. In order to do this effectively it needs to be as thick as possible. Nature arranges for it to be continually growing and when it is almost three-quarters of an inch thick the old growth shells off from the foot to make way for new horn. This process causes the sole to look ragged and tempts the unknowledgeable horse-shoer to pare it off. This should not be done, otherwise the sole will be weakened irreparably.

The frog is a wedge-shaped piece of rubbery horn, growing from and protecting the fleshy, sensitive frog above it. Its purpose is to assist in bearing the animal's weight and to form a 'pluperfect *prestissimo*' shock absorber and anti-slip device.

The construction of the foot, therefore, is one that places the burden of the horse's weight upon the outer edge of the wall and the bearing surface to which the shoe is fitted. These are assisted in their task by the sole and the frog.

The sole supports the weight through its naturally flat outer edge and, also, from above by means of its central arch, whether or not, according to whether the going is hard or soft, it actually bears on the ground.

The weight-bearing property of the frog will be qualified to a degree on the shod foot, because the thickness of the shoe will prevent the

143

Fig 12 Lower part of the leg

A Epidermis
B Corium
C Lower end of great
   metacarpal bone
D Extensor pedis
   tendon
E Coronary cushion
F Periople
G Sensitive wall
H Horny wall
I Pedal bone
J Sensitive sole
K Part of plantar
   cushion
L Dotted line
   representing
   flexor pedis
   perforans
M Lateral cartilage
N Flexor pedis
   perforans tendon
O Suffraginis bone
P Sesamoid bone
Q Navicular bone

frog, on hard surfaces, from coming into full use. On soft going, however, the frog fulfils its complete function of weight carrier and shock absorber. From this point alone it is easy to see how inadvisable is the practice of using fast paces on hard surfaces.

The Function of the Frog

The importance of the frog in the anti-concussion apparatus of the horse is worth considerable consideration.

In movement the toe of the foot is slightly raised to allow the heel to meet the ground first. Some of the shock is absorbed by the interplay

144

of the pastern and the variation in the angles made by the shoulder bones, but the greater part is sustained by the two springy cartilages, at the back of the foot, and the india-rubber frog, separated from them by a thick, elastic cushion. The frog, as it touches the ground, is pressed forwards and downwards, taking the initial shock and providing a firm, non-slip hold. It and its supporting cushion spread under the weight and then, with the aid of the supporting cartilages, regain their shape as the pressure is removed.

Having appreciated something of the construction and functions of the foot it should be clear that the paramount consideration in its care is the preservation of the protective outer casing, and the ensurance of its complete freedom and natural action when given the additional protection of a shoe.

Preparation of the Foot

To achieve these objectives certain common-sense rules should be observed in the preparation of the foot.

In the regularly shod foot the horn which has grown on the wall (the rate of growth varies between $\frac{1}{4}$ to $\frac{3}{8}$ inch per month and, therefore, necessitates attention every four weeks if it is not to alter the action of the foot) must be removed by rasping after the old shoes are removed. This operation should not in any way alter the absolutely level bearing surface of the foot, nor should the length of toe and heel be affected.

Ragged pieces of frog may be cut off and any obviously removable flakes on the sole pulled away. For the reasons explained *no further paring or cutting* should be allowed on these two parts.

Some smiths attempt to bring the frog closer to the ground, when preparing the foot, by rasping the wall at the heels. This is in any case impossible due to the thickness of the new shoe and only serves to weaken the wall at a very vulnerable point, as well as to throw more strain on the tendons and ligaments by lowering the heel.

A common fault in preparation is the 'dumping' of the foot. This is when the toe is rasped either to shorten it or to make the foot fit the shoe. If the toe is in need of shortening it must be effected by rasping from the ground surface. Rasping the front of the wall removes a part of the already thin layer of insensitive horn and affords a smaller area into which a nail can be safely driven.

The bars of the foot should not be cut away in an effort to make the heels look wider. This practice weakens the heels, causing them to contract and to be unable to fulfil their purpose.

145

Hot and Cold Shoeing

Following the preparation of the foot the shoe can be fixed by either hot-shoeing or cold-shoeing.

Hot-shoeing involves heating the shoe and placing it for a few seconds on the foot, burning a brown rim where it touches. The object is not to provide a more secure seating for the shoe, but to check the fitting and to ensure the whole is in perfect contact, as will be shown by a complete brown rim. An incomplete rim entails further rasping until the surface is level.

Most blacksmiths prefer to shoe hot as it is the surest way of getting a perfect fit but, today, cold-shoeing, where the completed shoe is nailed to the foot without being heated, is becoming increasingly necessary and prevalent. The only disadvantage of hot-shoeing is when a smith makes the shoe too hot and holds it against the hoof too long, thinking he is making a good 'bed' for it. What happens, of course, is that the burnt horn breaks away and the result is just the opposite.

I have, in fact, read an American authority, who condemned hot-shoeing entirely for this reason, advocating cold-shoeing under all circumstances. I cannot agree with him and I have the feeling that his conclusions were probably made out of necessity.

The Well-Made Shoe

The shoe itself must follow the rim of the wall. It must be neither too wide, too long nor too short.

Too wide a shoe encourages brushing, the striking of the opposite leg; too long a shoe, projecting beyond the heels, is liable to be torn off by the hind shoe, whilst a shoe that is too short allows bruising of the heels and the formation of corns.

'Dumping' can also occur in the fitting of the shoe, when the latter is too small. It is a most reprehensible practice.

The number of nails required to secure the shoe should be as few as possible. Each nail weakens the wall and the horn surrounding it becomes brittle, making it more difficult to place the nails at subsequent shoeings. For a hunter four nails on the outside and three on the inside are usually deemed sufficient.

The actual driving home of the nails in the narrow space of insensitive horn available is a matter calling for experience. A nail too close to the fleshy leaves is said to 'press' and causes bruising of the sensitive laminae of the inner wall. One that enters the sensitive wall is said to 'prick' and causes immediate lameness.

146

Nails leaving the wall too high ('high' nailing) or too low ('shallow' nailing) are usually indicative of faulty workmanship, although in cases of brittle or broken feet both may be necessary.

When the nails are driven home the protruding points are wrung off and the shanks turned up to form the securing 'clenches', which are then hammered down.

Rasping the wall of the hoof after the shoe is secured to finish the job off is another foolish practice which removes the natural oils in the wall as well as weakening the structure. The clenches may be rasped briefly, but nothing more is required.

Point of a Well-Shod Foot
The points noticeable in a well-shod foot are:

1 No rasping of the wall
2 No 'dumping' of the wall
3 Shoe fits the foot
4 Clenches are even, no 'high' or 'shallow' nails and none driven into old nail holes
5 No nail heads protruding below the ground surface of the shoe
6 No paring of the sole or frog
7 No cutting of the bars, heels level
8 No interference by the shoe of the frog
9 No uneven bearing between foot and shoe

Types of Shoes
The types of shoes available are very numerous and the skilled smith can assist weak feet or faulty action by employing various types *(Fig. 13)*.

The commonest one, however, is the *fullered* shoe with the centre hollowed out, which, it is claimed, is lighter, gives a better hold and helps the fitting of the nail.

It does not, however, wear so well and the nails are not so secure as in a *plain* shoe with a 'stamped' hole embracing the nail on all four sides. A plain shoe is one in which the ground surface is flat.

A fullered shoe is frequently a *concave* one also. A concave shoe being narrower on its ground surface than on its bearing surface. It is lighter and not so likely to be pulled off.

A *feather-edge* shoe is used on horses that go so close as to 'brush'. The inside edge being made very thin and sloped inwards from the

147

top, necessitating the shoe being nailed on at the toe and the opposite quarter.

A *seated* shoe is one hollowed so that the bearing surface is on the wall alone. Its object is to remove pressure from the sole, which will be necessary in horses having flat, instead of concave, soles. Its disadvantage is that it is very prone to getting pulled off in anything but perfect going.

For show-jumping, to give greater grip and as anti-slip devices, studs can be inserted into shoes. The most common, and those in

Fig 13 Types of shoes

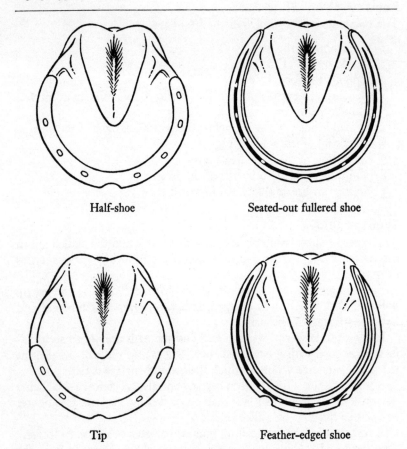

Half-shoe   Seated-out fullered shoe

Tip   Feather-edged shoe

greatest use, is the range of Mordax studs and specially hard-tipped nails.

To insert studs a threaded hole must be made in the heel of the shoe, which needs plugging when the stud is not in actual use, and one is supplied with a 'tap' to clear the thread. Jumping studs are usually used on the outside of the rear heels.

Care at Grass

Unshod feet of horses at grass require just as much attention as those of the horse in work.

Feet should be inspected once every six weeks and the horn growth rasped off and rounded to prevent splitting of the horn.

Toes or heels may have to be lowered to keep the foot in proportion and the animals should be trotted out frequently to check for any signs of lameness or foot-soreness. If an animal is footsore it is better to put shoes on again to allow the feet to grow. Feet which break easily may be protected by shoeing with 'tips', half shoes fitting round the toe only. The best shoes are those handmade for the foot by the smith, but the machine-made shoe is probably more common today.

In addition, of course, there is a serious shortage of trained and skilful farriers outside the established horse centres, such as New-market. In such places there are families, in well-established businesses, whose skill and experience is of a remarkably high order, but this is not the case elsewhere and it is a problem that causes concern to thousands of horse-owners. There are a number of 'horse-shoers' about whose standard of work is often deplorable, and whose knowledge of the horse's foot no more than rudimentary, but these can hardly be regarded as good omens for the future.

The Worshipful Company of Farriers and the Rural Industries Bureau are at present running apprenticeship schemes and doing all in their power to increase the number of skilled farriers, but one is bound to wonder whether their efforts will result in an adequate number of smiths to serve the growing community of horse-keepers.

It seems to me more than possible that the British Horse Society will one day be persuaded to run courses for horse-owners, teaching them how to put theory into practice and to shoe their own horses.

Common Ailments & Their Treatment

It should be understood quite clearly that while it is important for the horse-owner to be able to diagnose and treat the more common ailments and injuries, it is even more important that he or she should know when to call in the veterinary surgeon. Nothing is more dangerous than amateur, unskilled treatment, and the motto of the horse-owner should be 'When in the slightest doubt—call in the vet'.

There are all sorts of horsey remedies, they are as numerous as horsey sayings and often as far removed from the truth. As a well-known vet wrote recently: 'There are no magic cures any more—they have all been put into bottles and tins'. There are, however, certain straightforward, common-sense methods of dealing with the simpler ailments which are within the province of the horse-keeper and with which he should be conversant.

The General Signs of Health and Disease

The horse quickly reveals the state of his health through the appearance of various parts of his body, his excreta, and by means of his temperature, pulse and respiration.

In health the eye is bright and big and the membranes under the lids and those of the nostrils are an even pink in colour. Redness denotes inflamation, white shows debility, a yellow colour is symptomatic of liver disorders and bright purple is indicative of improper blood aeration, as in pneumonia, etc.

The coat lies flat and has a sheen to it, although this will not be apparent in horses wintering out. A staring coat can mean general malnutrition. When the hair is easily pulled from the mane it is as well to look for other general symptoms of ill-health.

The skin is loose and clean. If it is tight it may be due to malnutrition or the onset of some disease. Lice infestation also makes the skin tight, but is more easily discernible than most troubles.

Limbs should feel cool and be free from swelling. Puffiness indicates strains, poor circulation, irritation or possibly a heart condition.

Droppings and urine. The former will vary in colour and consistency, but should be generally well formed, slightly moist and not be strong smelling. The accompaniment of mucus is the result of a deranged digestion. Yellow, strongly smelling droppings may denote disorders of the liver and the presence of red worm.

The water should be almost without colour; thick, highly-coloured urine indicates kidney trouble and bloody water an inflammation of that organ. An excessive urine flow means diabetes, whilst a constant and obviously painful dribble accompanies bladder inflammation.

The normal temperature of the horse is 100°–101·5°F. Above this level gives reason to suspect a general infection.

As horses vary in their normal temperatures, it is wise to take and note the normal temperature when in health for future comparison. Using a clinical thermometer, shaken before use, which has been dipped in glycerine, insert the instrument for some three minutes into the rectum. As the temperature is inclined to rise slightly in the day time it is as well to take two or three readings at different times. After use wash the thermometer in cold water. Clinical thermometers register up to 110° and will burst in water hotter than this.

The normal rate of the pulse is 35–40 beats per minute. An increase in the pulse rate when at rest usually signifies a fever. Up to 50 beats per minute can be taken to mean that the horse is in pain. The pulse is conveniently taken on the inner surface of the lower jaw or just behind the elbow.

Respiration at rest is between eight and twelve breaths per minute. Faster than this indicates pain and an almost certain rise in temperature.

The teeth are in need of attention if food, left in the manger, is wet or balled.

Injuries and Wounds

Wounds fall into one of the following categories: Punctures, Cuts and Tears, Deep Wounds, Bruise Wounds.

The most common form of puncture is that caused by a thorn and, therefore, a painstaking inspection of the legs is necessary after hunting. On locating a thorn, remove it at once. If it cannot be withdrawn expert help is needed to cut it out. Poulticing is rarely effective and can result in a big leg for some time.

Once the thorn is removed, however, a poultice of Epsom salts and glycerine will draw out any residual infection.

Puncture wounds from stakes, nails etc., as well as from thorns, are dangerous if they are near, or likely to affect, a joint and need expert attention; otherwise treat as for thorns.

Punctures of the sole of the foot are also dangerous, as there is a likelihood of the horse coming into contact with material carrying tetanus germs. Regular tetanus injections are advisable, but if these have not been given an immediate injection is necessary. The puncture must be opened to allow drainage and the foot stood in a bucket of salt water for half-an-hour. Then a poultice of wet, unheated, brewer's yeast should be packed into the sole, the foot then wrapped in mackintosh, or something similar, to draw the wound, and the whole secured in a sack.

Yeast has the property of killing infection and should not be used with other antiseptics which will destroy this characteristic. The poultice will need to be changed twice daily for three days, after which a dry dressing of sulphanilamide may be used to prevent excessive formation of healing tissue (proud flesh). Wounds of this nature usually call for veterinary assistance.

Small cuts should be washed well with hot water to which a handful of salt or Epsom salts has been added and then dusted twice daily with sulphanilamide powder.

More serious cuts or tears should be cleansed with a mixture of four parts salt to one part citrate of soda in a solution of one teaspoonful to one pint of boiled water. A lint dressing soaked in the solution and bandaged lightly can then be fixed and left for 24 hours.

Salt induces a flow of lymph and on removing the bandage this will be present as a yellow, sticky substance. This should be swabbed off with the same solution and the wound recovered.

Once tissue (proud flesh) begins to form, a dry, coagulating, dressing (boracic powder) can be applied. A scab will then be made, under which the process of healing will continue.

Deep, large wounds require different treatment. If bleeding is of a venous nature it is easily stopped by copious applications from the hosepipe. The blood in this case is dull red. Arterial blood is bright scarlet and issues in fairly violent spurts from the wound. To control arterial bleeding place a tight bandage or a tourniquet above the wound, nearest to the heart, and bathe continuously with cold water. Arterial bleeding requires veterinary assistance.

Once bleeding has stopped all dirt must be removed from the wound and penicillin applied very freely. A dressing of powdered Epsom salts mixed into a paste with glycerine is then applied on lint, the whole wound covered with oilskin, to promote drawing, and finally bandaged.

Over-reaches are a common form of wound, caused by a blow from the hind shoe lacerating either the bulbs of the heel or the back of a fetlock joint.

Healing in the first case is slow. Any flap of skin and tissue should be removed and the wound cleansed with salt and water. A brewer's yeast poultice, followed by dressings of sulphanilamide powder, should be applied as for a sole puncture.

Should there be excessive proud flesh it can be controlled by dusting with powdered blue-stone. A blow on the joint is far worse as the tendon, or rather its sheath, will almost certainly be damaged, in which case there will be a yellow synovial discharge. Treat as for an over-reach on the heel, but call the vet.

Bruise wounds may be caused by blows or kicks and are not always very conspicuous. They should be treated with cold water to relieve the pain and then gently massaged with a cooling lotion, such as vinegar and water, or a mixture of one part petrol or methylated spirit to ten parts of water. The horse should then be rested and given only gentle exercise.

Kicks in the area inside the second thigh, where the bone is near the surface, are dangerous as they may involve bone damage. A horse suffering a kick of this nature should not be ridden for about a month, but should be rested to give the bone time to heal.

Broken knees, the result of a fall, may vary from a slight graze to a deep wound. In the first case continual bathing with salt and cold water will effect a cure. If, however, the wound is deep and discharging, a poultice of glycerine and Epsom salts smeared on lint and kept in place by a light bandage must be applied twice a day for three or four days. This can be followed by an antiseptic ointment and the wound allowed to make a scab.

Hot applications should *not* be made and bandages never kept on longer than necessary or the specified time.

To encourage the growth of hair on the knees after they have healed there are a number of recipes—most of which have not yet been bottled or tinned. I am assured that melted butter, mixed with the scrapings of burnt cork until the mixture is brown is most efficacious. It should be rubbed in for twenty minutes twice a day, massaging downwards. I have also found a mixture of black sulphur and vaseline to be effective. This mixture must first be melted in order for the constituents to merge.

Girth, Saddle and Bit Galls

These are the result of bad horse management and prevention is better than cure. Rest is the solution and the removal or repair of the offending article of saddlery.

Bit galls can be treated with salt water to harden the skin. In other cases the wounds can be washed with salt water and dusted with sulphanilamide powder.

A more severe injury of the back caused by a badly fitting saddle is when a portion of skin dies due to pressure restricting the blood circulation. This dead portion separates from the living tissue and pus is formed.

A kaolin poultice will help the removal of the core, but it may take time and be so obstinate as to need cutting out. Once the core is removed the wound must be bathed twice daily with salt water and treated with penicillin ointment.

The only way to prevent galls of this sort is to keep saddlery in good repair and properly cleaned, ensuring that it fits the horses. Felt numnahs with holes cut in them to avoid sore places are not an answer, but an admission of incompetence in horse management.

Lameness

In cases of all but obvious lameness the horse must be trotted out to ascertain the source. Lameness in the forelegs can be discerned by watching the head of a horse trotted towards you. If the head appears to rise and fall the lame leg is the one on which the head is raised.

Lameness behind can be seen by watching the highest part of the quarters as the horse trots away. If the horse is lame in either hind leg there will be a definite rise and fall of this point, the affected leg being the one upon which the corresponding hip is raised.

There will possibly be heat in the affected leg or hoof and in extreme cases the horse will stand with an affected foreleg pointed out in front. In slight lameness the pastern of the lame leg is slightly straighter than that of the sound one.

Shoulder lameness is more difficult to detect, but in general the toe of the affected leg is dragged and the whole leg does not reach as far forward as the sound one. At rest the affected limb is held, with the toe on the ground, behind the sound one.

Common Causes of Lameness

Bruised Sole—caused by treading on a sharp stone or something similar. There is usually heat in the foot. The shoe should be removed and the foot poulticed as for punctured soles.

Corns—caused by a bad shoe or one left on too long. The shoe must be removed and the corn pared out.

Thrush—a condition usually found in the hind-feet and caused by standing in dirty stables. The frog sweats and there is a characteristic foul smell and possibly a discharge from the cleft of the frog. The feet should be washed in disinfectant, the affected parts pared away and the cleft dressed *deeply* with Stockholm tar or copper sulphate.

Seedy Toe—an affection where the wall of the foot is separated from the sole at the toe. A soft, mealy horn is formed in the ensuing space. This deposit must be cut away and the cavity packed with three parts bismuth carbonate to one part iodoform mixed into a paste with liquid paraffin. The hole is plugged and the shoe, if possible, replaced. To encourage new growth of the horn Cornucrescine or some similar horn stimulant, such as whale oil and tincture of iodine (seven parts oil to one part iodine), should be applied regularly to the coronet.

Sand Crack—a crack in the hoof wall extending downwards from the coronet. A V burnt by the smith at the base of the crack, or the fixing of a clip, will facilitate healing. A horn stimulant should be applied.

Laminitis—a condition sometimes known as foot-fever. It is an acute form of inflammation within the outer protective casing of the foot, affecting the sensitive laminae *(Fig. 14)*. The outer wall cannot expand so the condition is very painful. The temperature rises, there may be

Fig 14 Appearance of the foot
affected by laminitis

sweating and the animal is unwilling to move or to rise if down.

It is caused by hard work when in unfit condition, too heating a diet with an insufficiency of exercise, galloping on hard ground and, in the case of ponies, who are particularly susceptible, grazing on lush pasture and being overweight.

Cure lies in restricting the diet, feeding laxative foods and cutting back the feet under veterinary supervision. Injections can be given and the animal will have to be forced to walk on hard ground until the circulatory troubles are resolved.

Navicular Disease—the cause is generally considered to be of congenital origin combined with concussion at work. In brief terms it is an ulcer formation of the navicular bone and lameness at first occurs intermittently without apparent cause. The animal points the limb, or each alternately if both are affected, and begins to move on the heels of his forefeet. The disease can be diagnosed by X-ray, but there is no cure.

Ringbone—a condition affecting the pastern bones resulting in a bony enlargement round the top of the hoof (low ring-bone), or round the pastern bones (high ring-bone). If caused by a blow or by undue concussion; rest and blistering may effect a cure. If the condition is hereditary, involving the joint itself, recovery is unlikely.

Sidebone—an ossification of the cartilages on the side of the foot. It is usually restricted to the heavier class of horse. Lameness only occurs in the preliminary stages and once these are passed the horse goes sound again *(Fig. 15)*.

Sesamoiditis—an interference with the ligaments of the foot caused by the sesamoid bones becoming injured or inflamed due to concussion. There is much pain and a *hard* swelling is apparent on the joint. Rest and blistering may effect a cure, but the action is usually 'pottery' after the disease *(Fig. 16)*.

Pedal Ostitis—inflammation of the pedal bone due to concussion. Acute lameness is caused and the foot is sensitive to a tap with a hammer on the sole. Injections of Cortisone in the heel often cure the condition.

Splints—bony enlargements on the cannon bone or splint bones of the fore and hind legs which rarely occur after the age of five years. Caused by jarring, they do not always cause lameness. Initially a swelling and heat can be felt and the horse will then be lame. Once the splint is set lameness disappears and this process can be accelerated by Cortisone treatment *(Fig. 15)*.

Splint

Sidebone

Fig 15 Splint and sidebone   Fig 16 Sesamoiditis

Sore Shins—an inflammation of the cannon bone membrane accompanied by noticeable swelling of the forelimb and considerable tenderness. It is commonly supposed to be caused by the effect of concussion on immature bone and is found in very young animals. The animal should be rested, given laxative food and a kaolin poultice applied for seven days, followed by a mild blister *(Fig. 17)*.

Spavin—inflammation of bones in the hock, giving rise to a bony enlargement on the inside of the joint. Flexion causes pain and movement is restricted, there is a dragging of the toe and the limb is thrown outwards. Lameness tends to decrease with exercise. Rest and firing followed by a blister will usually effect a cure.

Swollen legs—old horses are particularly susceptible to swellings in the fetlock joints due to wear and tear and a consequent blood congestion in the limbs. Upward hand-rubbing of the legs is helpful, and the hosepipe and pressure bandages also relieve the condition.

Sprains—tendon sprains in the flexors of the foreleg are fairly common and a horse experiencing such a sprain is often described as 'broken down'. The causes of such strains are either associated with fast work, umping or sometimes they may be the result of a conformation not

Point of Hock
Curb

Fig 17 Sore shins   Fig 18 Curb

best equipped to meet excessive demands in the way of speed. The
extent of the strain varies between very slight, when heat is present,
and a little swelling but possibly no lameness; to severe, when the
fibres are ruptured and there will be extensive swelling and lameness.
Finally there is the complete breakdown when both the superficial
and deep tendons are ruptured. Swelling is now even more evident,
lameness is acute and much pain is present. In the first two cases
kaolin poultices will bring relief and the horse can be shod so as to throw
more weight on the toe and, therefore, put less strain on the tendon.
Cold water treatment should be used and then a blister applied after
some four or five weeks. The blister must be applied to both legs and
the sound leg must be supported with a bandage as it will be carrying
most of the weight. After a couple of months rest the horse can be given
walking exercise and gradually brought back to ordinary work. Long
rest is not advisable as it permits the formation of permanent adhesions.
In the case of a bad breakdown firing will have to be resorted to after
the first blistering.

158

The suspensory ligament which runs from behind the knee to hold the fetlock joint can be damaged when a rupture of the tendon occurs, but it is usually caused by jarring on hard surfaces. Lameness does not occur, but the stride is shortened. Providing it is not connected with tendon ruptures it can be treated with hot water fomentations and kaolin poultices followed by blistering and a few weeks rest.

A **Curb** is a strain of the ligament joining the hock to the cannon bone and is seen as a swelling immediately under the point of the hock. Slight lameness is the result, but the condition, confined to young horses, disappears with maturity *(Fig. 18)*.

Stringhalt is a peculiar and violent upward action of the hind legs which does not seem to affect a horse's performance. How it occurs, or why, is something of a mystery and there appears to be no remedy.

Bursal enlargements *(Fig. 19)* are exemplified in *thorough-pin*, a soft swelling above the hock on either side; *bog spavin*, in front of the hock; *windgalls* above the fetlock joint; *capped hock*, on the point of hock and *capped elbow*, occurring on the elbow itself and caused by the shoe of the forefoot exerting pressure when the horse is lying down.

A bursa is a sack of fluid acting as a buffer between a ligament, tendon or muscle passing over a bone. If through pressure the sack is stretched it becomes filled with fluid.

Blistering is the usual way of removing these puffy swellings, but they can also be drained and Cortisone injected.

A **capped elbow** is best cured by putting a 'sausage' boot round the fetlock to prevent the foot coming into contact with the elbow.

(Blisters are counter-irritants applied to produce an inflammation. The effect is to draw the blood to the area being treated in order to accelerate the natural process of repair. Hot fomentations should be applied with a thick piece of blanket, which holds the heat for a longer time, and Epsom salts should be added to the hot water to increase its drawing power.)

Digestive Complaints

Colic—a severe stomach-ache to which the horse, by reason of his stomach structure, is particularly susceptible. It can be caused be almost anything to do with his food, from eating too much at ony session to sudden changes in his diet or eating bad food.

Usually the horse displays his uneasiness by looking at his flanks, kicking at them, pawing the ground, getting down and up again, and attempting to pass water. The temperature is not affected, but the

Fig 19 Bursal enlargements

pulse rate may increase and the breathing be laboured. In more acute cases the membranes of the eye may become inflamed and the horse will break out in a sweat.

In relatively mild cases a drench will be effective. This can be one of the proprietary 'colic drinks' (preferably not made with a chlorydyne base, which deadens the pain and consequently the nerves, therefore militating against nerve impulses which would promote bowel action) or a home-made drink consisting of one pint kaolin emulsion, half a pint of water and two tablespoons of sal volatile. Another effective drink is one and a half pints linseed oil, two tablespoons whiskey or brandy and two tablespoons turpentine.

To give a drench you will need an assistant and a drenching bottle. Squash manufacturers now supply their goods in a plastic bottle which is ideal and cannot be broken in the teeth. Stand on the off-side, get the assistant to lift the head up and, standing on a stool, insert the neck of the bottle in the corner of the mouth, over the bars, and trickle a little of the drink in, rubbing the throat to assist it to go down. Each time you have got a quantity down let the horse lower his head and swallow. Stop pouring if he starts to cough. If the horse is difficult and large, a pitchfork, with the prongs protected by large corks, inserted in the noseband of the head collar at one side, a prong each side of the square to which the cheek is attached, will raise the head without too much effort.

After giving the drench, rug the horse up well with the top rug turned inside out to avoid its being soaked with sweat. If the drench has had no effect within an hour a vet must be called.

Walking the horse, to prevent his hurting himself by violent rolling in the box, can be done while a spasm of pain is taking place, but the horse should be allowed to rest between spasms.

A twisted gut—regarded as a form of colic, which can arise from a violent attack of the colic already described, when the horse might throw himself to the ground. It can also be caused by a fall when the bowel is overladen with food or by a very strong purgative causing excessive bowel action. The gut lies in coils along the length of the back, supported by a membrane called the mesentery. Should the mesentery be torn from the gut it revolves on itself causing acute pain. A twisted gut is fatal—nothing can be done except to put the animal down as quickly as possible.

Constipation—usually the fault of the diet and the best cure is to feed grass and bran mashes.

Diarrhoea—the treatment for diarrhoea caused by diet, such as a sudden change to green food, is obvious, but if the condition persists then it is probable that the bowel may be inflamed, either due to heavy worm infestation or to some irritant food. The temperature will be normal in this case; if, however, it is not, then there may be an enteritic infection. It is then as well to call in expert advice rather than to indulge in home doctoring in the form of purges.

Lampas—a condition in which the upper jaw, behind the incisors, becomes swollen *(Fig. 20)*. It is due to a digestional derangement and its cure lies in improving the animal's general condition. A ten-day course of one tablespoon, given night and morning either in the feed or

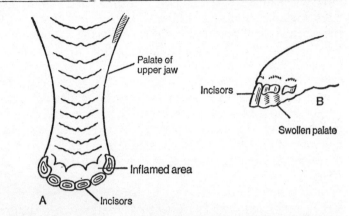

A Palate showing inflamed area   B Side view (cut away) to show swollen area

Fig 20 Lampas

in water, of a mixture of 8 oz. Epsom salts, 4 oz. glucose, 2 oz. bicarbonate of soda, ½ oz. Nitrate of potash will act as a corrective, but the cure is in the conditioning of the animal.

Skin Diseases
These can be divided into those which are contagious and those which are not Principal among the contagious skin affections is *Mange*, of which there are three types, all caused by parasites.
Sarcoptic Mange affects the head, neck, withers, shoulders and some part of the sides. It is characterised by small lumps from which issues a yellow discharge. As the discharge dries the hair falls out and a scaly patch remains. The animal is constantly rubbing and there is intense irritation.
Psoroptic Mange is similar, but affects the base of the mane and tail. Both diseases must be notified under law and outbreaks are controlled by an appointed veterinary surgeon of the Ministry of Agriculture.
Symbiotic Mange is unpleasant, but does not come in the same category. The lower legs, knees and hocks are affected, hair falls out and there is again intense irritation. The hair must be clipped off and the legs washed twice a week with Dermoline, folowed by an antiparasite dressing containing Derris Root. The horse should be isolated, his box disinfected and all his clothing etc., fumigated, disinfected, or

burnt. Clothing worn by the attendant should not come in contact with other animals.

Itchy Mane or Tail. This sort of irritation can be due to a parasite or to a high blood condition. In the former instance treatment is as for mange. In the latter the parts should be washed in Dermoline, or a similar medicated shampoo, and the horse put on laxative foods. Coconut oil, rubbed in gently, is often an additional help.

Ringworm is very contagious and is caused by a fungus. Symptoms are raised circles of hair, on the neck and shoulders initially, from which the hair falls out, leaving grey-white crusts. As the fungus is under the crusts they must first be removed by scrubbing before applying Gentian Violet or Iodine ointment. Isolation and disinfection routine must be carried out to prevent the disease spreading to other horses.

Lice are found on horses in poor condition, but can also be picked up when animals are out at grass. A heavy infestation causes loss of condition due to the blood sucking propensities of the parasite. The coat appears blotched and the horse rubs continually. The lice will be visible to the naked eye. The horse must be clipped and then washed with paraffin, or with a solution of one tablespoon carbolic acid in one pint of water. All clippings, etc., must be burnt and it is best to disinfect the stable.

The non-contagious diseases are:

Mud Fever—this is a skin irritation, derived from mud, which affects the legs and sometimes the belly. Certain soils are more prone to cause the disease than others. The legs are hot and swollen, a thin discharge is noticeable on the hair and cracks form on the skin. The horse moves very stiffly. The horse should be fed a laxative diet with no heating foods. Heat should be applied by means of boracic lint soaked in boiling water and squeezed out in a towel. The lint is then *quickly* applied to the leg, cotton wool put over it and the whole secured with a stable bandage. The effect is to reduce congestion in the blood vessels. The treatment is carried out twice daily until the inflammation is lessened and this is then followed by the application of an antiseptic ointment such as Protocon.

Cracked Heels are similar and caused by mud or neglecting to dry wet heels. The heel becomes chapped and the horse moves with difficulty. The same treatment as for mud fever is effective.

Humour is a pimply skin condition caused by overheated blood and is best treated by a laxative diet and a dose of 4 oz. Epsom salts in one pint water.

Nettlerash or Urticaria is caused by an allergy to something in the diet. Areas of varying size become raised with the hair standing erect. They can be treated with a solution of bicarbonate of soda—two tablespoons to one pint water, and the horse should be given a laxative diet with a dose of Epsom salts.

Warts of the small pointed type occur usually on the nose, lips and ears. They often disappear of their own accord, but may be treated with treacle, castor oil or sump oil. Caustic potash may also be used, but with care.

A cylindrical wart appears on the under surface of the belly and round the sheath. Single warts may be removed by tieing a piece of thread round their necks to cut off the blood supply, when they will eventually drop off. Where these warts occur in large numbers they may need expert surgical attention.

Warbles lay their eggs in the late summer on the horse's skin and the resultant larvae work their way into the back and sides. The following spring a hard lump appears under the skin, which becomes larger until a small hole can be seen at the top. If the lump is squeezed before th e larva is ready to be pushed out, or if the lump is ignored and receives pressure from a saddle, the larva will burst and the ensuing infection will cause a large swelling lasting for some weeks. The lump should, therefore, be softened with hot fomentations and kaolin poultices and squeezed gently each day until the larva is forced out. The hole will then heal and the lump will subside.

Sweet Itch is an allergic complaint caused by some constituent in the spring and summer grass in combination with the sun's rays. It does not, therefore, occur during the autumn and winter. Areas of the mane, neck, withers and tail become irritative and inflamed and the animal rubs continually. A yellowish discharge can be seen and the hair falls out. The only solution is to avoid green foods and keep the animal in during the day to avoid the sun as much as possible.

Kur-Mange applied as a weekly dressing, the contents of one tin being dissolved in a quart of warm water, can be brushed gently on the affected parts and allowed to dry. Applications of Benzyl benzoate every other day are also helpful.

Hidebound is not a disaese, but a sure sign of worms and should be treated accordingly. The skin is dry and dull and the animal is generally in poor condition.

Respiratory Diseases

Horses are particularly prone to contracting coughs and colds, which are usually caused by lack of ventilation and changes in temperature when stabled.

A Simple Cough accompanied by a clear, thin nasal discharge, a slight rise in temperature and swollen throat glands is best treated by allowing plenty of fresh air, a laxative diet and the administration of a cough electuary. The latter is given on a flat stick inserted into the mouth and wiped off on the tongue. A cough, accompanied by a rise in temperature of three or four degrees, a thick discharge and an increased breathing rate is likely to be due to a lung infection. The horse should be kept warm and the vet called to give antibiotic treatment.

A Stomach Cough, caused by the diet, is recognisable as a harsh, dry cough, as opposed to the softer noise heard in the two types of cough already mentioned. It occurs at exercise and in the stable and it is advisable to cut out all hard foods, substituting mashes, grass and hay in their place. In addition a tablespoon of a mixture of ½ lb. Epsom salts, ½ oz. bicarbonate of soda, ½ oz. potassium nitrate, may be given in the water twice a day.

Cold in the Head is similar to that experienced by humans. As in all cases of respiratory conditions the horse should be rested—failure to do so may result in pneumonia. A cold will probably be accompanied by a cough, temperature will rise, the coat will be dull and the discharge from the nose will soon become thick.

A corrective medicine, as for stomach cough, may be given and the horse should be given eucalyptus inhalations. To administer an inhalation two sacks are needed, one inside the other. Put hay into the sack, sprinkle a tablespoon of eucalyptus over it and then add a kettle of boiling water. The sack should then be held over the animal's nostrils. The horse should be kept well rugged, but allowed plenty of fresh air.

Equine Influenza, caused by a virus, is the very infectious condition which swept through this country a few years ago. It is marked by a persistent cough which continues long after the period of active infection. There is now a protective vaccine made to give almost entire immunity.

Emphysema (Broken Wind) is caused by over-distension of the lung vesicles caused by undue strain. It can occur after pneumonia, pleurisy, a chronic cough or similar complaints, and can also be caused by exercising after excessive feeding on bulky foods.

The preliminary stages are marked by a harsh, dry cough, which gets worse with exercise, and a nasal discharge. Later the breathing after any exertion is laboured and there is a distinct alteration in the manner of exhalation. The flanks appear to heave twice as the air is expelled. There is also a radical change in appearance, the flanks falling away and the stomach being distended.

There is little hope of a cure, but relief can be effected by reducing the hay ration drastically and substituting chopped and dampened oat straw.

Raw potatoes, given at the rate of ¾ lb. per day and chopped green gorse (not cut when in flower) mixed with the oat straw and other feed is helpful. Fast work must, of course, be entirely eliminated.

Whistling and Roaring are affections of the wind, but are concerned with the larynx and are the result of a paralysis of one of the main nerves on the left side. Roaring is an exaggerated form of whistling.

Whistling may be due to fast work when the horse is out of condition, or even galloping when at grass, or it is possibly an after effect of some septic infection, such as strangles. Treatment is surgical and if performed early has every hope of success.

Big, heavyweight horses are more prone to these affections than others. Ponies, for instance, very seldom, if ever, suffer from whistling. Thick, bull-necked animals would seem to be more easily affected, particularly when they carry their heads somewhat 'over-bent'.

Other Diseases

Azoturia, commonly known as 'Monday morning disease' occurs in high-fed animals whose exercise has been insufficient to cope with the intake of heating foods. The horse will be attacked with the disease when at exercise. There will be marked stiffening of the loins followed by sweating and general signs of distress. The muscles of the loins and quarters become very hard and painful to the touch. When urine is passed it is a definite coffee colour and smells, of all things, of violets. There will be a rise in temperature. The animal must be got back to his stable, under his own power if the attack is mild, or by horse-box. The vet should be called at once and the horse's loins and back covered with hot blankets.

Once an attack has occurred great attention must be paid to the regulation of diet and exercise.

Strangles This is a contagious disease caused by an organism called the streptococcus of strangles. Young horses are more susceptible and the disease can be caught from mangers, stables, paddocks, etc., carrying the infection.

The most recognisable symptom is the formation of abscesses in the glands behind and under the lower jaw *(Fig. 21)*. These are hot and painful. There is a rise in temperature, the horse is dull and off his feed and a thick, yellow, nasal discharge occurs, together with a cough.

Isolation and disinfection routine must be carried out and the horse kept warm with rugs and bandages. The first objective is the bursting of the abscesses. To this end hot fomentations should be applied. If this is not done the infection spreads to the rest of the body.

Cough electuaries can be given to soothe the throat. Complete cure lies in rest and good food after the attack to restore lost condition.

Tetanus is a disease caused by the entry of the tetanus bacillus into the body through a wound or scratch. It is more prevalent in some parts of the country than others. In general it is a fatal disease. There is a high temperature, a stiffening of the limbs, a setting, or locking, of the jaws and extreme distress. Prevention is better than cure and the house should be immunised by injections of anti-tetanus serum.

Fig 21 Strangles

Affected glands

Where the dose, in cases of proprietary medicines etc., is related to the weight of the horse the weight can be estimated by the following method. Take the measurement round the girth and the length from elbow to point of buttock in inches, then operate this formula:

$$\frac{\text{Girth} \times \text{Length}}{300} = \text{Total Weight in lb.}$$

As will be seen from the causes of many of these complaints, much trouble and expense can be avoided by the exercise of forethought and good horse and stable management. A list of items suggested for a veterinary chest is appended.

VETERINARY CHEST

Anti-parasite dressing
Bicarbonate of soda
Bismuth carbonate
Boracic powder
Clinical thermometer
Colic drink
Cotton wool
Cornucrescine
Cough electuary
Dermoline shampoo
Dettol
Drenching bottle (plastic squash bottle)
Embrocation
Epsom salts
Eucalyptus
Gamgee tissue
Gentian violet
Glucose
Glycerine oil
Iodine
Iodoform powder
Kaolin
Lint
Medicinal linseed oil
Medicinal turpentine
Methylated spirit
Nitrate of potash
Oiled silk
Packet brewer's yeast
Packet citrate of soda
Packet sulphanilamide powder
Penicillin ointment
Protocon ointment
Sal volatile
Stockholm tar
Surgical bandages
Surgical scissors

OVERLEAF:

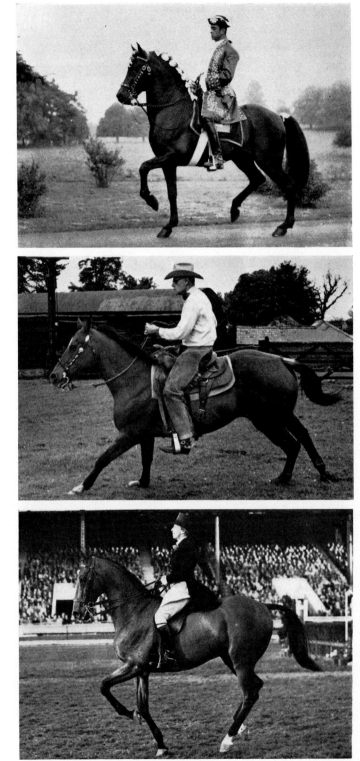

37 Señor Nuno
Oliveira on the
Andalusian stallion,
Ansioso

38 Mr. Gregory
Lougher on one of
his superbly trained
Quarter Horses

39 Mrs. V. D. S.
Williams on her
dressage horse,
Pilgrim

40 OVERLEAF :
The Caprilli system
in Italy, the country
of its origin

41 Supremacy of leg over hand

Riding and Training the Horse

To attain the highest peak of perfection in the art of riding is beyond the aspirations and the capabilities of most people. Perfection is, indeed, a state beyond us all and to reach a stage where it can be even dimly discerned demands of the horseman much hard work, a high degree of dedication and far above average talent.

This is not to say, however, that the average, intelligent person of normal physique cannot obtain great satisfaction from riding, and with a little conscious effort become a competent horseman and horse-master.

To learn to sit on a horse and to be able to exercise a rudimentary control over his actions without falling off is not difficult. We shall, however, obtain greater enjoyment, ride with more consideration for our horses, and with greater safety to ourselves and to other people, if we devote a little time and thought to understanding the horse and increasing our ability in the saddle.

It is an unhappy fact that the number of horses who are mismanaged, badly ridden and generally abused rises in direct ratio to the increasing number of riders and horse owners.

This is not to say that the majority of horses are actively ill-treated, although there are such cases, but rather that there are too many who are abused, and consequently spoilt, through the ignorance and inefficiency of their riders.

Cruelty and Abuse

There is a difference between cruelty and abuse, although it is one which the horse may be unable to appreciate. It is cruelty when a man knowingly continues to ride an exhausted horse, possibly to its death, to satisfy his personal ego. It is abuse when a man does the same thing, but is too ignorant to know that his horse is exhausted. It is cruelty when a rider, in anger, spurs his horse violently and then with equal force tears at his mouth. It is abuse when an incompetent rider kicks his horse in the ribs and then, to preserve his balance, jags his mouth by hanging on to the reins.

Unfortunately the horse cannot differentiate between the two. To him the result is the same.

Security and Control

Although it may not be apparent in the standard of driving seen on the roads, it is a law that no person shall drive a motor-car, unaccompanied, until he or she has passed a test to prove their competence, which involves learning the technique of placing and controlling a vehicle. There is then a further legal requirement incumbent upon the car-owner, enforced for both his own and other people's safety, which is that his car must be in roadworthy condition. Amongst other things this entails having a vehicle that has effective brakes and efficient steering.

It is a pity that similar laws are not practicable in respect of people wishing to ride and own horses, for the need is in some ways as great because a living animal is concerned.

It is of no great consequence if a driver tears the gearbox out of his motor-car as a result of his incompetence or, I suppose, is it mine or anybody else's business if a rider wishes to break his neck on a horse he cannot control, but it is a matter of concern if good horses are spoilt and abused because their owners have not bothered to learn the techniques of security and control.

There are two types of riders the horse could well do without. Those who regard themselves as God's gift to the horse (how salutary it would be to have the horse's opinion on the subject) and those who profess undying love for him in capital letters. In the former case they will not learn because they consider they know it all, and in the second they are too stupid to realise that their love is of the wrong kind and is no substitute for knowledge and ability.

A System of Communication

The foundation of equitation, a term which in its simplest form means sitting or riding a horse, is the establishment of communication between the rider and his partner.

The most primitive and basic communication is for the rider to thump his legs into the horse's ribs, reinforcing the action with a cut from the whip. This means 'go forward', and most horses will get the idea in time. A yank on the sensitive mouth, into which has been inserted a piece of metal, which will vary in the intensity of its action according to its shape, means 'stop'.

Such basic signals, relying for their efficiency on the fear of intense pain, are not, however, anything to do with horsemanship and are unlikely to lead to a *rapport* between horse and rider. Surprisingly there are many riders (again, not horsemen) who do not advance much beyond this stage.

The result is usually a spoilt, unhappy horse and a rider who never appreciates the enormous satisfaction and pleasure to be derived from riding in a civilised manner and in harmony with his horse. This is not to say the rider obtains no pleasure—I think he does, but it is a perverse enjoyment of the 'show him who's boss' variety.

It is not in rough actions, but in the finer shades of meaning, transmitted through the quiet disposition of the body and the infinitely varied pressures of hand and leg, that the horseman establishes complete communication with the horse and obtains his full co-operation.

Before one achieves this happy state, however, it is obviously necessary for the rider to learn the system of signals and for his body to be able to transmit them. Secondly, and of equal importance, it is helpful, indeed essential, that the horse should understand the significance of the signals he receives from the rider. Unless, therefore, the rider knows his job it is unlikely that the horse will learn his.

The well-trained and intelligent rider will, therefore, improve his horse and the range of communication, and consequently the degree of co-operation between the two, will increase. Conversely, the ignorant rider on a horse that has received little education in the system is unlikely to advance very far, and if he obtains a horse that is capable, by virtue of his training, of a high degree of co-operation, his inability to transmit his wishes intelligibly will result in first confusing the horse, and later reducing him to the same level as his master.

Fortunately, the basis of communication is simple and the two signals 'go forward' and 'stop', in varying degrees of intensity, are pretty well universal. It is, of course, possible to build an individual system on these elementary actions which ultimately bear little relationship to the base. One could, for instance, teach a horse to canter by pulling his right ear and to halt when his shoulder was slapped. In time the horse would come to rely on these signals and would not obey the more conventional ones. In fact, it would be possible to devise a system which owed nothing to the accepted signals. To produce horses trained in such a way might be amusing, but few people are likely to appreciate so warped a sense of humour.

The Objective

It is only when a system of communication has been established, on both sides, that the rider can proceed to his objective. To my mind that is gained when one has a horse that is comfortable and safe to ride at all paces, jumps small and varied obstacles willingly and calmly and is obedient to the will of the rider. Many riders will decide that this is the ultimate objective as far as they are concerned. This stage of training will, indeed, be sufficient for the average rider, who has neither the time nor inclination to do more than hacking, hunting and to join in riding club events, and it is fairly easily accomplished.

Others, having completed this elementary training, will be more ambitious and will proceed to further, advanced objectives, which will enable them to enter the more demanding fields of dressage, show-jumping or horse trials.

Which Method?

Exactly how this objective should be achieved will occupy the minds of horsemen for as long as men and horses occupy the same planet. What is certain is that complete agreement is never likely to be reached.

That this state exists need not, however, bother us in the elementary stages, for all the theorists agree, or almost agree, upon at least one fundamental. The rider's legs and (depending upon the school of thought subscribed to) his back and seat provide *forward movement* by activating the horse's source of propulsion, his quarters and hind legs, whilst the hands, acting as a sort of brake and steering wheel, control the forehand, i.e. the part of the horse in front of the saddle.

Without delving into the history of equitation, which is a complex, but fascinating study for the serious horseman, there exist two distinct European methods, as well as many more which borrow a little from both. At the risk of over simplification these two methods can be termed the German and the Italian.

The former is based upon the classical equitation derived from the movements of war horses in the Middle Ages and before, continued and enlarged in the Renaissance period, and having as a later base the example and writings of de la Guérinière, the great French riding master of the 18th century.

Collection Versus Extension

In its purest form it is exemplified in the work of the Spanish Riding School of Vienna, where the so-called High School movements performed, such as *passage* (a lofty, cadenced trot of great energy) and *piaffe* (the same trot executed on the spot without the horse gaining ground) require a very high degree of collection and complete submission on the part of the horse to the indications of the rider. Collection is a shortening of the outline, or the posture, of the horse obtained by compression of the horse towards his centre. That is the hind legs are engaged well beneath the body and the head and neck are held high and withdrawn in accordance with the movement to the rear of the centre of balance. In extreme collection, as in *piaffe*, the forehand will be held high and the croup will be lowered as the hindlegs are increasingly engaged under the belly. Collection results in elevation of the paces and, therefore, a shorter stride. By the rider *influencing* the horse to assume this posture the balance of the horse, with the greater proportion of the body weight resting on the hindlegs, is correspondingly moved to the rear.

Such a system is ideally suited to obtaining the objectives required in High School or dressage riding, but slow, elevated and collected paces are of little use to the horse whose purpose is to jump and to gallop across country. In fact to impose so high a degree of collection on such a horse might well prove disastrous.

In general, however, whilst not asking for advanced High School movements, the 19th century cavalry schools were influenced by the principle of collection to a considerable extent.

It was in opposition to these methods and principles that the Italian system, evolved by Captain Caprilli and known either as the Caprilli system, or the 'forward seat', came into being at the turn of the century. The Caprilli system discarded collection as unnecessary and unnatural and was designed to meet the needs of mobile cavalry *(Plate 37)*. The emphasis was upon cross-country riding and jumping and it encouraged extension (the lengthening of the posture) with the rider *not* imposing a balance upon the horse, but allowing him to adapt his balance to the conditions of the terrain without interference, the rider's body-weight being placed over, or in equilibrium with, the shifting centre of balance of the horse in motion. Contrary to the classical school the Italians did not *sit* in the saddle, but rather *perched* on it.

In extension, as in the gallop, the centre of balance of the horse moves forward as more of the weight is thrown on the forehand. The Italian rider, therefore, moved his body forward, seat out of the saddle, and let his hands follow the extended head and neck of the horse.

The rider in this position was the least possible encumbrance to the horse's movement. There was likewise no interference from the rider over fences. The horse was to position himself, without being 'placed' at the fence by his rider, and the execution of the leap was his affair.

Today the system practised at Vienna is still the greatest influence in the production of the specialised dressage horse. Caprilli's system is, however, rarely practised *in its entirety*. Had not Caprilli died young, as the result of a riding accident in his early forties, it is probable that he would have developed his theories and even altered them. As it is, the pure Italian system, while remaining in its essentials the basis of riding over obstacles, has been adapted to suit the needs and the temperaments of individuals and nations.

The Germans, for instance, adopt the forward seat over fences but do not embrace the theory of non-interference, nor do they discard collection. They ride their horses with great accuracy and precision, the rider being wholly dominant in regard to pace, approach and take-off, demanding and receiving complete obedience. They may not be elegant horsemen, but they are effective. The method suits them and they carry it out with thoroughness and success.

The ideal of the horse moving and jumping in complete freedom, unhindered by the rider, is undoubtedly appealing, but it entails the possession of exceptional horses, expertly trained in the system, for it to be practised successfully.

Although adherents of the pure forward seat will argue, admittedly with some logic, that the seat they advocate has every advantage, the average rider will not find it easy to maintain for anything but short periods, and the exclusion of the back and seat as aids limits the rider's control to a significant degree.

In this country, and indeed elsewhere, we have taken a middle course between the two roads of complete dominance and complete freedom. Whether there is a recognisable British seat is doubtful, but, in general, with our background of the hunting field, we allow our horses to do a little thinking for themselves, and do not encourage them to place complete reliance on the rider. To my mind this is nearer to the ideal of a partnership and more acceptable than complete domination. Even so opinions differ, sometimes considerably, as to the means used to attain the end.

Theory and Practice

It may well be asked why it is necessary to approach the business of riding in such painstaking fashion when there are numbers of men and women (there will be one or two in every hunt) who know nothing of the finer points of equitation and yet whose horses carry them well, and to all intents happily, for many seasons. The answer is that these men and women are brave, natural riders who, by experience, have found for themselves an effective method of crossing a country. How they do it is something of a closed book and, beyond remarking that it is as well to leave his head alone, they are usually hard put to explain their inherent prowess in the saddle.

Books on equitations are rarely perused by such people—there is after all no point in their attempting to change their seat, or to absorb new ideas, when they have evolved a perfectly effective method of their own.

I know of more than one eminent judge whose seat on a horse is an affront to the eyes, and, one would think, to the horse also. Yet I would that horses went as well for me as they do for these gentlemen.

They are, however, the exceptional horsemen—certainly not the average ones, who form the great majority of the riding public. In addition they are dangerous people to copy.

The less talented, among whom I include myself, must work that much harder, absorb a little theory by intelligent application, and then learn how to put it into practice if they are to get as much, and possibly more, satisfaction from their riding. This is particularly the case for those who come to riding a little later in life. I am neither as brave nor as supple as I was 20 years ago, but my horses probably go better, and I ride them more intelligently and considerately than I did in my extreme youth.

The Penalties of Limitation

In those days my ambition was to become a superlative horseman. I never achieved it because I had neither the means nor, in consequence, the time and I was not possessed of the necessary talent.

Once I had accepted my limitations in this latter respect I realised that if I was to be a no more than competent horseman and horse master, anything that I did with horse would be the result of conscious study, planning and execution. Because of my lack of natural talent it is necessary for me first to define a final objective, possible of accomplishment on the part of both myself and the individual horse; secondly, to divide the road to this goal into a series of smaller objectives; and thirdly to formulate, by studying the characteristics of the horse, a method which will achieve each one of them. Finally when the operation is commenced I must never forget to make sure that each minor objective is made secure before I pass on to the next.

Three Factors in Riding and Training

The natural horseman will achieve his ends much quicker than people in my situation, that he may not know how he has done so, or why he carries out certain actions, is of no consequence to him.

The elementary analysis which follows will not help such men to improve themselves, it is given for the benefit of those whose gifts are not so great and then only as a very tentative guide.

The objective I have referred to, that of producing a balanced, obedient horse, is certainly within the scope of any intelligent person willing to make the efforts of the sort I have indicated. The establishment of communication will, however, be made more quickly and more satisfactorily if the rider has an understanding of three factors:

1 The mental make-up and characteristics of the horse
2 The physical structure of the horse as it relates to movement and balance
3 The elementary theory of riding

Obviously, the application of this knowledge will be dependent upon the physical ability of the rider to put it into practise, but even this facility can be acquired without too much difficulty by riders of normal physique who are not entirely without equestrian tact.

INSTINCT AND CHARACTERISTICS

Many of the methods employed in training the horse and reaching a state of communication with him arise from the animal's peculiar mental make-up. It is through our knowledge of these special traits that we are able to use them to our advantage and adapt them to our purpose.

The first quality to recognise in the horse is that of *gregariousness*. He is a herd animal and his instinct is always to remain with, or to return to, his own kind. Although it is an instinct which is overcome when the rider has gained a sufficiently advanced state of obedience (as when a horse leaves his companions to jump in the show-ring on his own, or is turned aside from a line of horses in the hunting field to

176

follow an independent route of his rider's choosing) it is never entirely eliminated.

On the other hand it is an instinct which can be exploited, and explains why a hunter will jump obstacles, which on his own he might well decline, when in the company of other horses or when, having become separated from his fellows, he is asked to return to them.

In a similar way a horse can be encouraged in the early stages of his jumping training by asking him to jump towards his stables and the companions who occupy them.

Complementary to this gregarious instinct is the question of *security* or, perhaps, the lack of security.

The horse in the wild state finds security in the company of his companions in the herd. Removal from the environment, by however many hundreds of years, and re-alignment of his sense of security to his altered circumstances, may well colour his whole outlook, and detract from this basic need. This is particularly the case when a horse is kept singly, and manifestations of insecurity are more likely to occur with such horses than with those in say a racing stable or riding school.

I have already mentioned that in the wild state the majority of horses submit happily enough to the discipline of the dominant stallion, the leader of the herd, and that in domestication it is possible for his human master to assume this function. This responsibility for leadership and security is one that the horse-owner must fulfil before he can hope to achieve communication or co-operation. An insecure horse is rarely a calm horse, and a horse that is not calm is never attentive or receptive.

It is this lack of security which makes a horse in new surroundings unwilling to leave his box or even to nap (i.e. refuse to go the way he is asked) when first ridden by a new owner. Should the rider not recognise this and, instead of encouraging the horse and allaying his fears, set about him, almost irreparable damage will be done to the relationship.

It should also be recognised that the horse associates, or should associate, his stable with security as well, of course, as the place where he is fed, a procedure which influences him not inconsiderably. The effect upon him will be the same as that produced by other horses and he will always go more willingly towards it than away from it. It is as well, therefore, when siting a schooling area to keep it away from the *immediate* proximity of the stable.

The *love of routine*, particularly with regard to feeding times and exercise periods, is closely connected with security and the latter will be affected if a routine is not maintained.

Work does not come naturally to a horse, even after centuries of subservience. By nature he is a *lazy*, tranquil creature and if left to his own devices is quite content to spend the time eating, sleeping and browsing. It is, therefore, quite beyond his comprehension as to why his master should want him to gallop across this field, trot down that lane or jump over a log, when he could more easily walk around it. Fortunately the horse is extremely *co-operative*, far more so than a dog, and is more than ready to fall in with his master's wishes, even to the extent of overcoming his natural instincts, when, and this is the important part, he understands what those wishes are. This is rather remarkable when we consider how *nervous* the horse is. Essentially he is highly strung and very easily frightened, a sudden movement or a strange object on a familiar path will rouse his deepest instincts and his defence is to flee from this potential danger. One of the most important traits to appreciate is the extraordinary *sensitivity* of the horse. He is extremely sensitive to pain or to the threat of pain.

The horse is not equipped to play an aggressive role, his safety lies in his ability to flee from danger and as a result his tolerance of pain is low.

Other four-footed animals of less strength, the dog is one of them, are not nearly so sensitive in this respect and will turn upon an aggressor—not so the horse—his defence is always in flight.

Horses that are said to *fight* the bit are not in fact doing so. The horse pulls against a rider whose uneducated hands act in similar fashion, not in a spirit of opposition, but because he is trying to get away from the pain he experiences. It is this innate sensitivity, combined with his desire to please, that allows us to control the body of the horse by the indications of our legs, as for instance when we apply one leg to move the quarters. In this case the horse, unless physically unable to comply with our request or in a state of high excitement, moves *away* from the pressure.

In the green horse we may have to supplement the pressure of the leg by a tap with the whip and while the horse may not, or should not, consciously associate the tap with the fear of pain, subconsciously he will do so and will move away in consequence.

It is only when the horse is confused, excited, physically incapable of co-operation, or when the stronger instinct of self-preservation or the fear of experiencing greater pain assumes an ascendancy, that he resists the simple indications of his rider.

One of the more frustrating characteristics of the horse is his propensity to become *excited*. Other horses will produce this reaction, the tension of the rider can do so, and it is particularly apparent when he is asked to jump or to do something a little out of his normal routine. This trait is hardly one that is helpful to the rider and, while no amount of training will eradicate it entirely, it should be a prime consideration to keep it within reasonable bounds. In all forms of schooling the aim must be to obtain the necessary responses in a state of calm. An excited horse is never attentive.

It may seem difficult to understand how this timorous, sensitive fellow can also have *courage*. And yet, paradoxically, most horses possess this quality in abundance. The horse will, if ridden by a firm, sensitive horseman, overcome his natural fears, and launch himself over strange obstacles. Tired, and without the stimulus of his fellows, he will battle on in response to the urging of his rider. He will cross marshy ground, although every wild instinct tells him that this is terrain which is dangerous and to be avoided.

It is true that he will do these things if the rider induces in him excitement, bordering on panic. A horse is often, and wrongly, made to jump in this way a fence he has consistently refused, instead of being taken back to jump lower and less difficult obstacles. To use such methods only results, however, in producing a horse that is ultimately so soured that he may become impossible.

Finally, and of great significance, is the *memory* of the horse, which is highly developed and very retentive. Once the animal has associated certain signals with certain movements he does not forget the lesson. Conversely, if he associates a movement or a particular place with discomfort or fear he does not forget this either and will envince excitement and resistance.

It is largely by our understanding this extraordinary capacity to remember and to associate various happenings with the memory of pleasure or discomfort that we are able to train the horse.

Reward and Punishment

As a result of our knowledge, rewards for co-operation will be frequent and punishment for disobedience very rare indeed. Always, in fact, the carrot—rarely the whip.

The 'carrot' need not necessarily be an edible one and, in fact, too many titbits can result in a horse becoming silly and in extreme cases something of a bully.

A horse can just as well be rewarded for good work by an encouraging vocal noise—I say noise because the horse does not understand words—only the tone of voice in which they are uttered. A horse will feel equally rewarded by being called 'a b ... old b ...', providing the tone of voice is of the right sort, as being addressed as 'mummy's pet booflekins'. In the same way a pat on the neck, or being allowed to stretch out his head and neck after a period of work asking for collection, is just as much a reward as one of a more material kind.

The edible reward should certainly be given, and sometimes it will prove to be a useful bribe, but it should be reserved for special occasions.

As an instance of the trouble that can be encountered by the indiscriminate use of titbits, I remember a horse I had who found lateral work (i.e. sidesteps) difficult. Very patiently I eventually obtained a couple of steps, then, without thinking, I took a piece of biscuit from my pocket and gave the horse his reward from the saddle. I found this worked so well that very soon I had obtained four sidesteps—and there it stopped. When the horse had completed just four steps he would halt and turn his head, waiting for his biscuit. I must confess I never had the heart to try and break him of this habit which he had acquired entirely from his master.

To overdo the reward is forgiveable, but to do the same when it comes to punishment is both stupid and inexcusable. In almost every case where the horse resists there is a very good reason for him doing so.

There are, to my mind, three main reasons for resistance: when the horse is asked to do something beyond his physical and mental capacity; when it causes him pain to comply, because of an ill-fitting bit, a rank bad horseman, a strained muscle, an incorrectly made shoe or a painful back condition or when he becomes confused by the inability of the rider to convey his wishes clearly through the medium of the aids. In each of these instances the fault is not that of the horse, but of the rider.

Horses, like humans, however, are not all, or always, angels, even though they may be more fitted for Heaven than their masters. Occasionally we may find a horse who is deliberately disobedient and wilful. He must then be corrected firmly, but without anger. Even in these cases it is usually the fault of some previous owner who has provoked the initial resistance and we should be very wary lest the punishment is too severe in relation to the crime. The majority of horses are extremely susceptible to the voice and in the same way that a reward need not be a real carrot, so punishment is not necessarily the whip. A good growl is often sufficient to produce the required result. If the whip has to be used a slap on the shoulder or a sharp tap to reinforce the leg is usually enough. I would only hit a horse hard if he persisted in running back, which is just too dangerous to be tolerated, and then I would hit him very sharply, once on either side, accompanied by a salutary dig with the spurs.

The important thing to remember is that punishment must be immediate if it is to be effective. This the horse understands and remembers.

To punish him five minutes after the event does no good at all, it only serves to confuse him, as he cannot understand why he is being punished. It is only when he associates immediate punishment with a particular resistance that he understands the cause and effect.

It is, of course, the height of stupidity to punish a horse who is frightened, as for instance when he shys or plays up in traffic. We are then only confirming and adding to the fear in his mind of the particular object which caused the trouble. Our purpose on these occasions is to demand his obedience and distract his attention away from the traffic or the flapping sack on the hedgerow.

Never should the horse be punished through the bit. It is permissible for the more experienced to resist, intermittently, a continued mouth resistance on the part of the horse and even to give a light upwards jerk, but no more than might cause a momentary discomfort. The bit is the most delicate of the lines of communication set up between horse and rider and if it is abused the structure of confidence collapses. It will take months of patient work to rebuild it.

Finally, the intelligent horseman will never allow himself to be put in a position where he is forced to punish the horse.

Does the Horse Think?

Whether this highly strung animal, who has the ability to evoke so great a fascination in us humans, is intelligent or not depends on one's interpretation of intelligence.

Many great horsemen have said he is not intelligent, but is purely governed by his peculiar characteristics which the greater mental capacity of man has turned to his own ends. I would not deny the horse's inability to think in abstract terms, but there are far too many instances which display equine intelligence for me to agree that he is unintelligent. I am sure horses are intelligent, they vary in degree as do humans, and their intelligence is certainly not of the sort we easily

181

recognise, but it is there if we, the masters, can develop it. This is the whole crux of the matter. Intelligence will be governed and developed by environment and by the ability and sensitivity of the human individual concerned.

The mistake is to try to humanise our animals and to endow them with the sort of understanding we would like them to have. Horses are not human, they are animal, in their own right and with their own dignity.

On the whole I find them as intelligent, and often far more attractive, than many of my two-legged acquaintances.

The Physical Structure of a Horse

If it is important for us to understand the mental make-up of the horse it is just as essential that we should understand his physical anatomy as well.

In very simple terms we are confronted with a relatively rigid body mass supported by four pillars. The equilibrium of the mass is then adjusted by the agency of the head and neck acting as a sort of pendulum with a weight—the head—at one end.

The movement of this body mass is on an almost central point which is termed the centre of balance, or the centre of gravity. It is, in fact, rather like a see-saw which pivots on a central support.

In the horse at rest the centre of balance is determined as being at the intersection of two imaginary lines. The first is drawn vertically through the centre of the body, some ten inches behind the withers, and the second, horizontally, through the point of the shoulder to the buttock *(Fig. 22)*.

This can be proved quite conclusively by taking two large scales and persuading the horse to stand with his hind feet on one scale and his forefeet on the other. The exact position of balance will vary slightly according to the conformation of the subject but, all in all, the intersecting point, which has been referred to, will be found to be more or less correct.

It was once assumed that a balanced horse distributed his weight equally over all four limbs. This is, in fact, a fallacy. The horse at rest, standing on all four feet, has a greater weight upon the forelegs than on the hind legs, while in movement the balance of the horse and the distribution of weight shifts according to posture of his body.

At speed the outline, or the posture, of the body is extended and to maintain its equilibrium the head and neck are stretched out. The

Fig 22 The Centre of Balance in the horse at halt

centre of balance, following the extension of head and neck, then moves forward. Conversely if the head and neck are raised, lightening and raising the forehand, the horse, in order to remain balanced, lowers the quarters, engaging the hind legs under the body, and in consequence the centre of his balance moves to the rear in accordance with his altered and shortened posture. Should the horse move laterally the centre of balance is shifted from the centre towards the direction of the movement. Likewise a horse turning sharply at speed shifts his centre of balance inwards in accordance with the turn's direction.

A horse maintains equilibrium in movement by repeatedly losing and regaining his balance. If a leg or legs do not come to earth at precisely the correct moment he will experience a longer period of momentary equilibrium loss and will stumble. If the leg is unable to reach the ground in a certain time he will fall. In either case he will endeavour to maintain his balance by movements of his head and neck, which control the weighting of his limbs and the shifting of his point of equilibrium.

A horse, therefore, rarely distributes his weight evenly over the four pillars supporting his body mass. In extreme extension, as in the gallop of the racehorse, the horse may be balanced, but his weight is carried to a large extent on his forelegs. In extreme collection, as in the dressage horse, the weight is transferred to the hind legs.

Unhampered by any weight upon his back, or by a hand imposing restraint upon the position of his head and neck, the horse can gallop over rough ground, adjusting his centre of balance by means of moving his head and neck, to suit the requirements of the particular terrain he is crossing. He stops and turns gracefully, easily and at will. But this is not the case when he is carrying a burden in the shape of a human being, who may weigh one-fifth of his total body weight. The retention of balance is then made more difficult because not only has he to cope with his own problem, but with an additional shifting body as well, having a centre of balance of its own.

One could quote the instance of a man being asked to run carrying an unevenly weighted knapsack slung from his shoulders, in such a way that it bumped his bottom as he ran, to illustrate the point. It must, however, be obvious that just as the man will be able to run better with an evenly weighted knapsack, strapped securely, as high on his back as possible and, therefore, as near to his centre of balance (the true centre being on top of his head) as the limits of practicability allow, so it will be easier for the horse if his burden is sited over *his* centre of balance, shifting in accordance with his movement and to all intents and purposes fused to his own body.

In riding across country, therefore, the rider, if he is to be the least possible encumbrance to his horse, and is to allow the animal to perform with maximum efficiency, must align his body weight with that of the advancing and retreating centre of balance of his mount.

As the movements of head and neck, by contracting and decontracting and by being raised and lowered, control the equilibrium of the horse it follows that, ideally, the rider should not interfere or impose a head position, but that his hands should follow every movement of the head.

This would be acceptable to the pure, non-interference Caprillists' school and possibly to many more of us if we had horses upon whom we could entirely rely. When, however, obstacles are to be surmounted the horse usually needs some assistance from the senior member of the partnership and we will, in fact, by the actions of our bodies impose a posture on the horse, asking him to shift his centre in accordance with the demands our actions make, although in the actual take off and in the flight over the fence we will revert to the policy of non-interference, positioning our bodies over and in line with the movement of the centre of balance.

Surprisingly, to many, the horse is not by nature very well equipped to carry weight, and it is only by training him that he becomes conditioned to carry a rider and is physically able to answer the indications

42 *A secure, balanced seat*

43 *The hands held naturally and
the correct distance apart*

44 *Working on the lunge without reins*

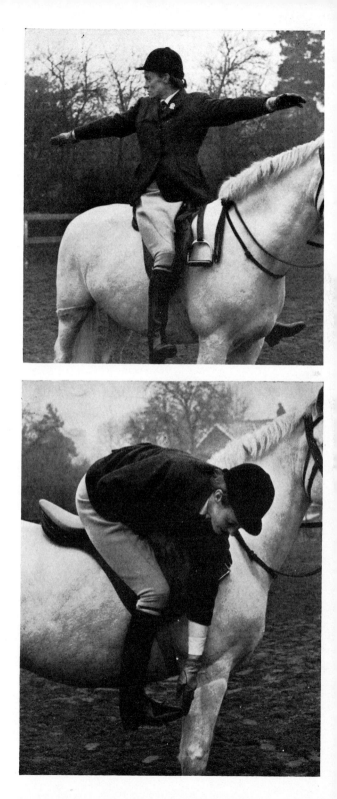

45, 46, 47 and 48 Some suppling exercises which can be carried out by the rider

49 A nicely fitted modern saddle

which ask him to shorten or lengthen his posture, and so to shift his centre of balance to comply with our requirements.

The rider can be said to be in balance with his horse when his body is weighted over the horse's pivoting point, the centre of balance, at all paces. The horse, when ridden, is balanced when his weight distribution is such that he is able to extend or shorten his posture and, therefore, the line of his balance (the line of balance is upwards from rear to front in collection, when the forehand is lightened, and the opposite way round in extension, when the forehand is weighted) either in response to the indications of the rider or, in the absence of those indications, in accordance to the particular circumstances of the moment.

The propulsive power of the horse is, as we have seen and as most people are aware, contained in the quarters and hind legs of the horse. What is perhaps not so readily appreciated is that the power which drives the body mass forwards is the same as that which powers the changes of direction made by the body mass. In the minds of a great many riders, I am sure, is the mistaken idea that the propulsive power, the engine of the horse, is connected from the pelvic structure, via the backbone, to the horse's head. This, of course, is not so. The quarters are connected to the *shoulders*, but the head and neck, as will be seen from a glance at the diagram of a skeleton, are free, flexible, and not influenced or connected to the movement of the quarters. Unless this is understood clearly we shall, and many people do, continue to ride thinking that the position of head and neck, when bent laterally to one side or the other, governs the directional movement of body mass. We will, in fact, think that where the head is pointed the body will automatically follow.

Very often, of course, this is exactly what does happen, because the horse associates the bending of his head to the left or right as an indication from the rider that that is the way he wishes to go. The green horse, or one that has decided that to turn left is not in accordance with his wishes, is quite able to turn to the right even though his head points in the opposite direction. In fact the more the head in these circumstances is inclined to the left the easier it becomes for the horse to move to the right.

The horse pushes his body round a corner by engaging the inside hind leg more strongly and further beneath his body. That is, in a turn to the left it is the left hindleg which is employed and vice versa. It is rather like a skater who in a similar fashion turns on his inside leg.

The change of direction is, therefore, initiated from the rear and it is the positioning of the shoulders, connected to the propelling force by the spine, which completes the turn. In the trained horse, accustomed to move under weight, the slight inclination of the head and neck in the direction of the turn acts in accordance with the movement of his centre of balance and follows the inclination of the shoulder. The movement then is from rear to front, not the opposite way about.

Most of us will have seen the recalcitrant pony with his nose pulled round almost to his rider's toe, persisting in moving in the opposite direction, despite the thumping legs and exhortations of his rider.

Apart from his obvious wilful intent, the extreme position of his head is placing his body in a situation where he can best accomplish his disobedience. The inside shoulder is so completely restricted as to make movement in that direction impossible and, in addition, his *outside* hind leg will be engaged so far under him that it contributes materially to his intention to do the opposite to what is required by his rider.

The disposition of the head can be clearly seen when working a young horse on the lunge, particularly at the canter, where he will very often hold his head outside the circle rather than following a correct line. He is then using the head and neck as a balancer to counteract the inward movement of his gravitational centre, and freeing his inside shoulder to more easily cope with the movement. As his body becomes more supple and his balance improves he will not find it necessary to use his head and neck in this way, although when turning sharply at speed he may do so. Indeed, an experienced and skilful show-jumping rider may be seen to incline his horse's head outside the direction of the movement, in order to prevent the horse 'falling in' towards the centre of the turn, when he is moving at speed in a restricted space.

A further misconception concerns the flexibility of the spine and the back. We are often told, by eminent authorities, that the horse 'bends round the rider's inside leg'. The impression given is of the spine being bent rather like a bow, the greatest extent of the bend being at its centre. This, in fact, does not and cannot happen. The spine is virtually rigid, except in the lumbar vertebrae near the croup where a small degree of flexion is possible.

It is because of the inflexibility of the spine combined, in the untrained horse, with stiff muscles on either side of the backbone and with the natural over-development of one side, that the horse experiences difficulty in making a true circle, i.e. one in which the track of the forelegs is exactly followed by that of the hind legs.

186

The one-sided development of the horse, which is rather like human beings being either right or left-handed, is usually on the right or off-side. It commences with the curved position taken by the embryo within the womb, and is further encouraged by our handling young stock from the nearside.

As a result untrained or partially trained animals will usually turn more easily to the left than to the right. Early training is, therefore, aimed at the encouragement of *equal* muscular development and spinal flexion; until this has been achieved the horse will ride 'one-sided'.

In the trained, supple and developed horse, working on a circle, a little flexion takes place in the lumbar area, the head and neck are inclined on to the line of direction, the rib cage on the outside of the circle assumes a prominence, while that on the inside flattens, and the outside shoulder is pushed outwards and slightly in advance of the inside one. The appearance is then that of the horse being bent round the rider's inside leg.

The Mouth and Bitting

As the majority of riders are so greatly concerned, often to the point of obsession, with the horse's head and particularly his mouth, it seems reasonable that before inflicting various pieces of ironmongery upon this most sensitive part of the animal's anatomy we should understand something of its construction. Indeed, unless we inspect a horse's mouth and have a knowledge of the action of the various bits which are available I cannot see how a correct selection for a particular horse can be made.

Benjamin Latchford, the greatest of the 19th century loriners, once said that there was 'a key to every horse's mouth'. He also said that of every twenty bits he made 'nineteen are for men's heads and one for the horse's'; be that as it may, it is surely advisable to have a look at the lock before selecting a key.

As we have already seen, each jaw in a full mouth contains six incisor and twelve molar teeth. We have also noted that the upper jaw is larger than the lower and that the upper molars grow down and outwards, while the lower ones behave in opposite fashion. It is not difficult to see that because of this arrangement the outside of the top molars and the inside of the lower ones will receive little wear. Unless, therefore, the teeth receive regular attention the enamel on these sides will become sharp and the cheeks or tongue, or both, will be in danger of laceration. Obviously there will be no key to a mouth in this condition.

It may appear to be elementary to urge regular, daily inspection of the mouth and yet I wonder how frequently many horse-keepers do inspect their charges' mouths in the course of a year. Not very often I suspect.

An inspection of the mouth will reveal the *bars*, an area of gum between the incisor and molar teeth and the *tongue*. We shall also be able to see how thinly protected are the *corners of the mouth*.

In general the bars will be more or less sharply defined and shaped like an inverted V, or they will be broad, flat and fleshy. The former are more usually found in Thoroughbred horses and the latter in those of more common descent. *Both in their virgin state are sensitive*, the first being more so than the second. Occasionally, and may we be forgiven, we shall see bars that are heavily callused and even deformed by severe bitting and heavy hands.

It follows, therefore, that a mouth with sharply defined, thinly protected bars, will require the lightest (in reality the least severe) of bits and the most sensitive of hands if the horse is not to become demented by pain. Conversely, in extreme cases where the bars are unduly flat and heavily covered, it may be necessary to use a slightly sharper bit if we are to communicate our wishes satisfactorily.

All mouths are sensitive to a greater or lesser degree, but there are no hard-mouthed horses, only hard-handed riders.

In the same way there are no horses with one-sided mouths. It is possible, I suppose, for a horse's mouth to become less sensitive upon one side or the other if his rider persists in using one rein to the virtual exclusion of the other. The real trouble, though, in the one-sided horse is not in his mouth, but in the one-sided muscular development of his back and the flexibility of his spine.

The tongue, too, can cause bitting troubles. Often, particularly in Thoroughbred horses, it appears almost too big for the mouth. As a result the organ tends to spread over the bars and so obstruct the direct action of the bit upon those parts and upon the lower jaw.

There is then the difference in the actual shape of the mouth, a blood horse usually having a long, thin structure and a common horse the reverse. The structure of the mouth in this respect is, therefore, a determining factor in the choice of bits other than those of the snaffle group. A Pelham bit, for instance, is just not suitable for a long mouth. If the mouthpiece is correctly adjusted to touch the corners of the lips the curb chain cannot fit into the curb groove, but will ride too high on the unprotected jaw bones, causing chafing, even ossification, and certainly unnecessary pain and discomfort. In some cases this can be partially overcome by using a vulcanite mouthpiece which, being as thick again as a metal one, allows the chain to take up a lower position.

On the other hand a Pelham bit may well suit a short mouth, which just will not comfortably accommodate a Weymouth bit and bradoon.

A cursory examination of the jaw bones will show how important it is for the curb chain to fit correctly. The curb groove at the base of the jaw bones is fairly heavily protected with gristle, but above this point the bones are covered only with skin and, therefore, are easily susceptible to injury.

Whatever the bit selected it should never be one of the pencil-thin variety. The bars and the corners of the mouth, upon which the bit acts, are composed of millions of sensory nerves. The narrower the bit the more confined is the area upon which it exerts pressure and the more quickly will that area become numb and insensitive. A broad bit, with a large, flat mouthpiece, is softer in its action as it spreads the pressure over a correspondingly larger area and affords greater comfort to the horse.

Horses, as we have seen, pull *against* pain in order to get away from it, and control is never attained by its infliction.

The Five Bitting Groups and Their Action

Having gone so far this is probably an opportune time to study the action of bits and the various types which are commonly employed.

I have dealt with this subject in more detail in the book *Saddlery* (Country Life Limited, 1963, 25s.), but as it is clearly necessary for the horseman to understand what the piece of metal at the end of his reins is doing it will be as well to recapitulate the main points.

Briefly, the object of the bit is to *assist* us in obtaining direction and regulating the pace. If we wish to enlarge that basic definition, we might say it is the means whereby we suggest a desirable head position, which makes it easy for the horse to co-operate with our indications in regard to pace and direction. Please note the inference that the bit is not a means of domination, nor is it a peremptory command, but rather *an invitation to co-operate*.

The principle involved is as follows: there are five main groups of bits, all of which, sometimes strengthened by the aid of auxiliaries such as nosebands and martingales, act upon one or more of seven parts of the horse's head. The parts involved are the *bars*, the *corners of the*

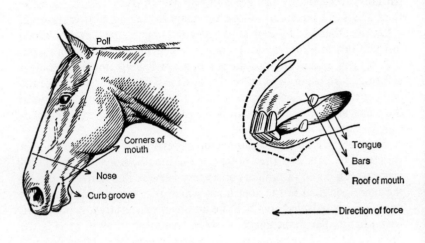

Poll

Corners of
mouth

Nose

Curb groove

Tongue

Bars

Roof of mouth

Direction of force

Fig 23 Parts of the head affected by the action of various bit groups

lips, the *tongue*, the *curb groove*, the *poll*, sometimes the *nose* and occasionally the *roof of the mouth* (*Fig. 23*).

The five bit groups are the *Snaffle*, the *Weymouth bit and bradoon*, the *Pelham*, the *Gag*, and the *Bitless* bridle, which may assume a variety of shapes, as indeed may some of the other groups.

The snaffle *(Fig. 24)* acts upwards on the corners of the lips when the head is held low, as might be the case with a young, green horse, or to the rear when the head is held higher, so that the bit acts across the lower jaw, involving an increased contact on the bars and rather less on the corners of the lips. The snaffle may be either jointed or have a mullen or half-moon shaped mouthpiece. The last named is the milder and becomes even more so when constructed not of metal, but of flexible rubber.

The bradoon part of the Weymouth combination *(Fig. 25)* acts in the same way as the snaffle, although, when used in conjunction with the curb, its function is more towards raising the head. The curb bit is vastly more complicated and acts upon a number of the specified parts of the head. It consists of a mouthpiece with a hump in the middle,

190

known as the *tongue port*, to which are fitted cheeks of varying length, to the eye of which is fastened a curb chain.

The purpose of the port (the German word is *züngfreiheit*, meaning tongue freedom) is to allow the tongue to be accommodated within its shape and so prevent it from lying over the bars and obstructing the action of the mouthpiece's bearing surfaces. Upon the size and shape of the port depends the degree of accommodation for the tongue.

The mouthpiece, when the cheeks of the bit assume an angle of 45 degrees or more in response to rein pressure, exerts a downward influence, and one which operates slightly to the rear, on the bars.

This downward movement is further accentuated by the forward movement of the eye, to which the cheek pieces of the bridle are attached. When the cheek is inclined at an angle out of the vertical it follows that the eye, by means of its attachment to the bridle cheek pieces, exerts a downward pressure on the poll.

There is then the additional restraint of the tightening curb chain

Fig 24 A good type of snaffle

on the curb groove encouraging the horse to give, or flex the lower jaw.

Only in bits with a tongue port of excessive height is pressure imposed upon the roof of the mouth. Such bits are not within the realm of civilised horsemanship.

The severity, or otherwise, of the bit depends upon the length of

Port

Eye

Cheek

Fig 25 A Weymouth bit and bradoon

the cheek, greater leverage being obtained with a long cheek than with a short one.

Upon the length of cheek below the mouthpiece depends the pressure on the bars, whilst the length of cheek above the mouthpiece dictates the degree of pressure imposed upon the poll.

The action of the Weymouth, therefore, is highly sophisticated, allowing the rider to suggest a head position with great accuracy.

The Pelham *(Fig. 26)* which, admittedly, suits some mouths, is a hybrid attempting the impossible. It seeks to combine the action of snaffle and curb in one mouthpiece, an aim which cannot wholly succeed.

When the snaffle rein predominates the action is that of the snaffle, when the curb predominates that of the curb bit. With very skilful rein control it is just possible that some sort of combination of the two is possible, but it is rarely achieved.

Usually the mouthpiece does not have a port, but is of the half-moon variety, and when this is the case greater pressure is brought on the tongue and there is a less definite action on the bars.

The Gag snaffle *(Fig. 27)*, by passing the bridle cheek through holes in the bit rings, becomes an accentuation of the ordinary snaffle in its action. It can be regarded as raising the head by severe upward pressure against the corners of the mouth, although, in fact, it exerts an equal, if not so painful, pressure downwards on the poll.

Fig 26 A Pelham

Unless carefully handled it can result in an inflexible head carriage and restrict extension of the head and neck.

The last of the bit groups, the bitless bridle, operates purely on the nose, just above the base of the nasal bone. It can be used to restore the confidence of horses with badly bruised mouths and in its simplest form is the basis of training used on the Western horse (*Fig. 28*).

I use it consistently in the schooling of young horses before the gradual introduction of a bit, and always when teaching jumping. I only wish more people would appreciate its efficacy.

The nose is also employed when a drop noseband is used with a snaffle. The noseband is useful in preventing evasions, such as sliding the bit across the mouth and out of its central position, evasion by excessive opening of the mouth and in restraining an over-impetuous animal by inducing him to lower his head and accept the action of the bit.

Martingales, never an end in themselves, reinforce or assist the bit action by restricting the upward movement of the head. I once used them extensively, appreciating the extra control they afforded and for the sake of the life-line provided in the shape of the neck strap. Nowadays, I consider them largely unnecessary, but retain the neck strap to preserve my seat and dignity in unforeseen eventualities.

No bit can possibly be effective unless properly fitted. The snaffle may project half an inch either side of the mouth, and should touch the

193

Fig 27 A gag snaffle

Fig 28 Two bitless bridles

corners of the lips. When a curb bit is used, as in the Weymouth, it should rest about halfway along the bars. Curb chains should not be used without lipstraps, which prevent their rising out of the curb groove.

When a drop noseband is fitted it must lie some three inches above the nostrils, which entails the *drop* part (i.e. the rear strap which fastens under the mouthpiece of the bit) being long enough to allow the nosepiece to assume this position.

There are hundreds of bits made in every form that man can devise, all of which are aimed at controlling the horse. Most of them can be ignored, and some should be condemned as monuments to ignorance. A competent horseman, given a horse that has not been entirely ruined, should need no more than a snaffle, possibly a drop-noseband, and a Weymouth bit and bradoon. If he is so inclined I commend, in addition, the acquisition of some form of bitless bridle.

ELEMENTARY THEORY

Having absorbed this much it is now necessary to consider a little fundamental theory. This is not difficult in itself, the problem is putting it into practice, which requires a little more time, but is made easier if we know what we are trying to achieve.

The key to good riding is supremacy of leg over hand *(Plate 41)* and it is, therefore, unfortunate that a fundamental requirement when teaching or learning to ride is that the beginner should have a leg on either side of the horse and sit facing the front end. The instinct of self-preservation is the strongest of all, and when the would-be horseman is placed on what is to him an insecure base it is not surprising that he should regard the reins placed in his hands as convenient lifelines.

Once he achieves a degree of security he may not be quite so reliant on the reins to preserve his balance, but he is still facing the front and is physically in connection with the horse's head, which he can see. He also knows that most horses will turn, after a fashion, if he pulls the necessary rein, and that if he pulls both simultaneously the horse may stop, again, after a fashion.

Many riders go no further than this and for the rest of their days ride their horses with their hands alone. They have become obsessed with the front end, by which means they seek to control and position their unfortunate animals. They may even decide to go in for a little dressage and will fly to the nearest saddler's shop for a Weymouth bit and bradoon, by which means they fondly imagine they will achieve 'collection'.

Oh! that they could all be turned round to face the horse's tail and become, if not obsessed, at least aware of the engine, the driving force, which is behind the saddle, and upon the proper control of which depends the posture and balance of the horse.

The Aid Combination

In equitation we have at our disposal certain aids, that is we communicate with the horse by using our voice and the various parts of our body. These are known as natural aids. Artificial, supplementary or auxiliary aids are the whip and the spurs.

I term these signals the Aid Combination and it is best explained by a diagram which, for obvious reasons, I call the Wheel of Equitation *(Fig. 29)*. The wheel has a central hub—the strong, supple and

Fig 29 Wheel of Equitation

independent seat. It then has four spokes—the legs, the trunk, which includes the seat, the back and the disposition of the weight, the hands and the head.

If one of these spokes is weak it cannot perform its function and the wheel collapses. If the wheel has no hub to which the spokes are connected we have no wheel at all.

First then, the independent seat, which can be defined as one having no dependence upon the reins for its security, and in which the limbs and body weight are in a state of physical freedom and are able to influence the horse according to the rider's wishes, while the rider remains *in balance* with the horse.

Upon this seat, the hub of the equitational wheel, depends the effectiveness of the aids. Without it the limbs are restricted in their movement, being more concerned with staying on than in communicating with the horse.

Similarly, each spoke is dependent upon its fellows and the aids they represent are only effective when used in combination, which does not mean they are necessarily used *simultaneously*.

We have already recognised as a fundamental fact that the horse is propelled forward by the engagement of his quarters and hind legs, the source of his forward movement, and that his posture and balance is similarly controlled. We ride, therefore, from rear to front, the legs initiating movement and the hands directing, in part, and controlling the power created.

What then are the functions of the aids within the combination? Let us take first the head aid, as it is the first link in the chain. Without thought any subsequent action is likely to be abortive.

Before asking the horse to perform a movement, think first. This may sound so elementary as to be ludicrous, but unless one can ride intelligently, always asking of the horse a little less, rather than a little more, than he is capable of performing, the result can hardly be successful.

In very simple terms the function of the legs and trunk is to create energy behind the saddle. The horsey term is *impulsion*. In answer to the action of these aids the horse's quarters and hind legs are brought under him to supply the necessary thrust for forward movement. The energy thus created is then either released or contained by the action of the hands connected by the rein to the bit.

The easiest way to understand this is to think of a horse as a length of spiral spring (a simile used by Lt.-Col. Jack Talbot-Ponsonby, which

I acknowledge with thanks). When the legs and trunk push from the back and the hands restrain at the front then the spring is contained in compressed, or shortened, form between the two points. If the legs and trunk continue to push and the hands instead of restraining, open, then the spring will be elongated, or extended.

The hand controls the degree of compression created by the legs, but without the push from behind its actions are negated. In riding true forward movement is impossible without the action of the aids creating the necessary thrust. The hand is, therefore, dependent upon the actions of the legs and trunk and can only operate on the horse effectively and correctly if energy behind the saddle has first been created and then maintained.

This is why the true art of horsemanship rests on the phrase, supremacy of leg over hand.

Remember, always, THOUGHT before ACTION, LEG before HAND.

When impulsion is created and maintained and the hand restrains, we shall, in the trained horse, achieve *collection*. That is a shortening of the outline of the horse by strong engagement of the hind legs beneath the body, a withdrawal, raising and lightening of the forehand and a corresponding movement to the rear of the centre of balance. The stride then becomes shorter and more elevated and the pace slower.

Conversely, when the hands release the energy (the impulsion is never, in fact, entirely expended, the hands always retaining a portion) there will be a lengthening of the outline, which is *extension*. The head and neck will be lowered and stretched, the point of balance will move forward and the stride will be longer and lower and the pace faster.

The ability to extend and shorten the horse at will is necessary to achieve a balanced, obedient and supple horse. To a certain point it is fairly easily accomplished, but the extremes of collection require great skill on the part of the rider if the horse is not to lose the ability to extend. Extreme collection is unnecessary in the average riding horse. It is sufficient to be able to vary the speed of the pace and to be able to obtain very brief periods of compression. I have said that the legs and the trunk create the power and the hands control the output, but it is clear how necessary it is for the aids to be used in combination.

The legs not only create power, but they also control the positioning of the quarters, while the hands, used in combination with the former, control the forehand.

Each leg and each hand is used in conjunction with its partner, the one directing, the other supporting. In almost every case the action of the legs precedes that of the hands.

The Function of the Aids

The three prime and elementary essentials of control are to go forward, to stop, or to go slower, and to turn to either right or left. While the application of the aids to produce certain movements is dealt with later in this section the principles involved in their use should be understood.

Pressure by both legs applied slightly to the rear of the girth induces the horse to move forward.

The application of one leg, a little further back, supported by a lighter application of the other, causes the horse to move his quarters away from the stronger leg. The function of the supporting leg is then to control the degree of movement. The rider's leg also controls the corresponding hind leg of the horse, i.e. the rider's left leg controls the horse's near hind and vice versa. Therefore, when riding a circle, when the horse is being *pushed* round the corner by his *inside* hind-leg, it is the rider's inside leg, activating the corresponding hind-leg, which provides the impulsion. The rider's outside leg, held a little behind the girth, is in support and controls the bend of the quarters, preventing them from moving outside the line of the circle.

The seat and back of a rider sitting as it were with open, spread seat bones and not on the tensed muscles of the buttocks, which would raise him out of the saddle and out of contact with the horse, are a powerful aid to forward movement and the energetic engagement of the hindquarters. Used in concert with the hands and the legs they assist in obtaining either extension or collection. The effect of a back braced and a seat driving *forward*, not *downwards*, when used with the legs and a hand that restrains, is to achieve a shortening of the posture —a compression of the spring.

Under the same circumstances, but with the hand releasing, the effect is to urge the horse into extension.

In collection the trunk, by inclining slightly to the rear, alters the weight distribution and induces the horse to further alter his posture by *imposing* upon him the necessity to move his centre of gravity to the rear in order to conform with the altered weight distribution of the rider. In lateral movements the weight of the rider, to remain in balance with his horse, will be placed correspondingly on the side towards which the horse is moving.

While, in general, the rule is for the rider to position his weight over the centre of gravity of the horse, there are occasions when the experienced rider can deliberately use the weight aid to assist the movement he asks of the horse, and to place the horse in a position where it is he who must alter his centre of gravity to conform with his rider's weight distribution.

With the application of the hand aids, the pattern of the aid combination is almost complete. The ideal to aim for is the elastic fingers and forearm connected to a rubber elbow joint. The action taken by the hand on a schooled horse, or on the horse that is being trained, is a closing of the fingers, possibly accompanied by a slight flexion of the wrist to restrain, and an opening of the fingers accompanied, possibly, by a forward pushing movement to release and induce extension. The hand may close, it may open, it may move forward, sideways, upwards or downwards, but never back. If it moves back it pulls, and it is pulling that provokes pulling on the part of the horse. The pulling hand not only encourages the horse to pull, but it also restricts the stride *and the essential forward movement*.

The demands made by the hand are always intermittent, never must they descend to a dead, maintained pressure. The hand asks and almost immediately yields. If the required reaction is not obtained it acts again and yields immediately it receives a response. It is the dead, unyielding pressure which causes a similar reaction in the horse.

To move forward the hand follows the indication of the legs by opening slightly. In movement it is the legs which *push* the horse into accepting contact with the hand. The hand must never be allowed to make contact by withdrawing or pulling. *Always it is the last link in the chain, never the first.*

At the halt the horse is *pushed* up by the legs to a hand which closes. The hand is in fact a sort of door which is opened to allow the horse to pass through, and closed, in varying degrees, to decrease the pace and to halt. It is unfortunate that we speak of 'pulling up' a horse, which is what many of us, in fact, do, rather than *pushing up* to a halt. It is equally unfortunate that while we are told to 'close the legs and feel the reins' when halting, we are not always told that there is a time to release the legs. Far too often the instruction is interpreted as a clamping of the legs on the horse coupled with a fairly hefty tug on the reins.

This is a total misconception. The action of the legs is to send the horse into contact with the hand, the moment this is accomplished the

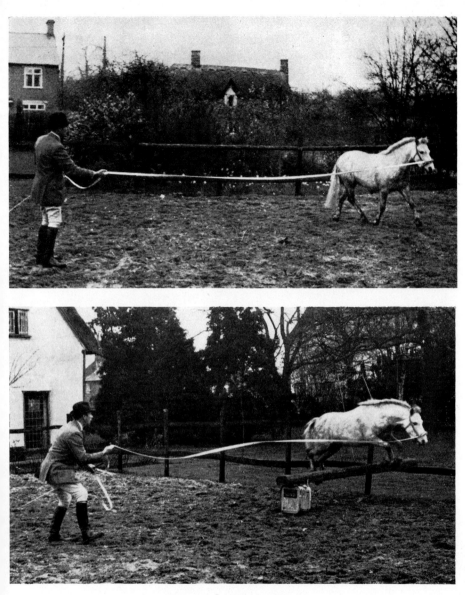

50 ABOVE: *Lungeing at the trot*

51 BELOW: *The pony jumping freely on the lunge*

52 ABOVE *A magnificent shot of a free-jumping horse on the lunge*

53 BELOW: *Miss Sylvia Stanier working a horse on the long reins*

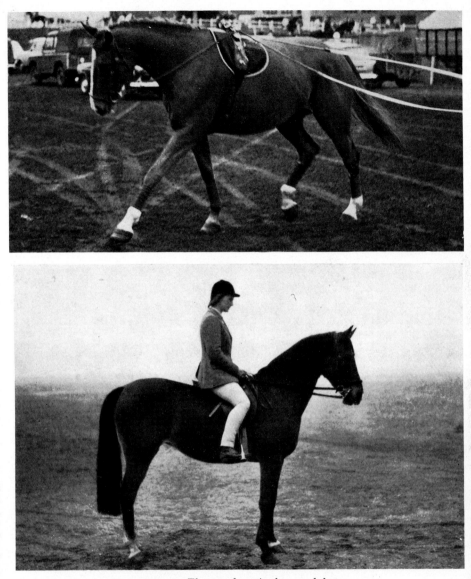

54 ABOVE: *The same horse in the extended trot*

55 BELOW: *A balanced halt*

56 ABOVE: *A nice free ordinary trot*

57 BELOW: *A collected trot*

hand closes. The leg has now done its work and is then relaxed, and for a moment the hand predominates, while the legs are held in readiness to ensure that the quarters remain straight.

By my book and on my horses, if you go on pushing into a closed hand you are asking the horse to stand up on end.

In changing direction the two hands act in conjunction, just as the legs do. The inside hand indicates the direction, leading the horse through the bend, while the outside hand supports, preventing the horse falling in towards the centre.

The elementary way to turn a corner is by the use of what is called the direct rein. In turning to the left, the inside, left hand is turned finger nails uppermost, thumb pointing in the direction of the movement, and is carried slightly outwards.

The right hand, still having contact with the mouth and supporting its opposite number, moves slightly forward to allow the horse's head and neck to bend to the left. If this is not immediately effective the direct rein can be further strengthened by the supporting hand, held slightly forward, but pressing intermittently against the withers to push the shoulder in the required direction. The rein acts in the turn a split second following the increased pressure of the leg.

Later in the horse's training it will be sufficient, providing there is absolutely equal tension on both reins, to slightly release the tension on the outside rein, i.e. the right rein when turning to the left and vice versa.

Finally, when the horse is supple, balanced and very responsive, the inside hand will ask, by a brief squeeze of the rein, for a slight relaxation, a giving, of the inside jaw. In time the slight movement of the hands in the required direction will be sufficient to obtain the turn and an automatic relaxation. In all movement, with the exception of the trot where the centre of balance is relatively static, the hands follow the motion of the head. Failure of the hands to follow the motions made by the balancing agents results in restriction of the movement.

In all cases, however, the efficiency of the hand depends on the impulsion created by the legs and follows their action.

Without this impulsion, the horse becomes like a becalmed boat. You may then turn the rudder as much as you like, but without the boat being in motion, moving forward, it will remain becalmed and will turn neither to left nor right. The rider must therefore make the fullest use of his legs and very little of his hands.

Where resistance to the hand is met it can be countered by first using the legs, and possibly the back and seat, with even more energy and in certain cases by rather more active and sometimes seemingly unorthodox rein aids.

The use, for instance, of what is called by some people the *intermediate* rein, is invaluable in obtaining a decrease of pace and a checking of over-enthusiastic impulsion should the horse resist the intermittent, direct action. The right hand, supported by a slightly raised left hand, is moved above the withers where it resists. The effect is to push the weight of the horse's body directly on to the line of this resisting rein. The position of the hand, either hand can be used, can be varied according to the variation in the direction of the thrust it seeks to oppose.

By experience, we shall find other uses of the rein to counteract resistances or to assist us in positioning. Benoist-Gironière, the French author and horseman, holds, for instance, that if we study the reaction of the horse to the action of the rider, we will often do what at first may seem to have quite the opposite effect on the horse. If, for instance, the horse persists in raising his head unduly we only increase his resistance by dropping the hands. The answer is to raise the hands, whereupon the horse reacts by dropping his head; the opposite is the case when the horse refuses to raise his head.

This may at first sound anything but logical, but it does work if employed with tact by a skilled horseman. In much the same way it does not take one long when training a young horse to discover that the quick application of the opposite aids will often achieve the result wanted without provoking resistance to the point where we must enter into a battle.

The last of the natural aids is the voice, the use of which in certain circles is regarded with disfavour, which is a pity, as it can be so effective. As I teach obedience to the voice in the early stages of lungeing, I see no reason why I should not continue to use it in mounted training to reinforce, or to let the horse more easily understand, the application of the other aids. If I give the horse the aids to halt and he does not at first respond, what is more easy, or effective, with a horse who is already accustomed to obeying the voice, than to say 'whoa'. If he then stops I have achieved my object without upsetting him and in a little while he will obey the aids without the addition of my 'whoa'.

A horse is so easily soothed or encouraged by the voice that I see no reason why he should be deprived of something which he enjoys and to which he responds.

The artificial aids of the whip and spurs are used purely to reinforce

202

the leg. The former can be tapped behind the rider's leg if no response is received when the leg is applied, and the latter, far from being cruel, allows the experienced horseman to make even finer and lighter indications of his wishes.

These then are the aids, the means of communication, but as we have seen they cannot be put to use unless the rider has first obtained a secure seat. It is only out of security that we are able to achieve control.

The Rider's Seat

First let us consider how the rider should sit and secondly, how he can maintain this seat when the horse is in motion.

Clearly, as we are all different in make and shape, it is impossible to lay down a fixed position which will suit us all. What we must do is to adapt our conformation so that the seat employed is the one in which we can most efficiently remain in balance with the horse and apply the aids freely and effectively *(Plate 42)*.

To remain in balance it will be necessary for us to sit in the deepest part of the saddle. The leathers can then be adjusted to suit our length of leg, neither too short, which would have a tendency to push our seats towards the cantle and reduce its effectiveness, nor too long, which would affect our security and leave our feet continually reaching for the irons. The lower leg is then drawn back with the heel lowered and the toe raised. In this position the thigh and half way down the calf is in contact with the barrel of the horse and readily available to apply the aids. The knee is then flat on the saddle flap and pointed to the front. If then, with the iron on the ball of the foot, the toe is inclined slightly outwards, the heel pushed even further down and the weight placed more on the inside of the iron, so that the outside of the boot sole is raised, the knee and thigh are pressed even closer into the saddle. It may not be necessary in the slower paces to adopt this locking position of the leg, but it gives greater security at the faster paces and when crossing a country, when the seat is raised from the saddle.

The mistake made by beginners is to grip—grip is only necessary in emergencies and is achieved by pushing the heel down as described.

Continual efforts to grip only raise the rider from the saddle, instead of encouraging him to sit with an open seat pushing the flesh of the buttocks behind him and sitting on the seat bones.

The trunk and head are held erect, but not stiff. The head is important, if it is allowed to drop down it effects not only the back, which rounds, but also the security of the seat.

203

The arms are held naturally at the side. Keep your elbows in by all means, but don't clamp them to your body. The hand is held, following the line of the forearm, slightly curved, with the thumb uppermost. The rein should form a straight line between bit and elbow, which precludes this wretched habit of fixing the hands on the withers. Most important is that the two hands should be held the width of the bit apart *(Plate 43)*. Hands clasped together and held in the pit of the stomach are useless. For some reason I cannot explain, the horse, as it were, passes up into contact with the bit through the hands and if these are held together the passing up process stops there. Never carry the hands as though on the handle-bars of a bicycle. They become immediately inflexible and insensitive.

The length of the rein is largely dictated by the conformation of the horse and the position of his head. Too long reins cause the hands to move back in order to effect control. Reins held too short disturb the weight positioning of the rider and are usually too tight. The rein, therefore, should be only as long as is practicable—and this is a few inches longer than most of us think. In this position the rider has virtually anchored the lower half of his body, but without conscious effort and without rigidity.

In the full seat, that is when sitting in the saddle at either walk, trot or canter, the body remains upright, the spine undulating with the movement. When the half seat is employed, the rider maintains the same anchoring leg position, but inclines his trunk forward without rounding the back, and raises his buttocks out of the saddle while maintaining a slight contact with his fork. The weight is then taken on the pivot of his knee and upon the heel. To post at the trot a slight forward inclination of the trunk is all that is necessary, and the seat bones need only rise an inch or two from the saddle.

If the knee and the lower leg maintain their position the rider, with some practice, will not find it difficult to remain in balance. Once, however, the knee straightens, and the lower leg goes forward in advance of the vertical line formed by head, knee and toe, balance is lost and the rider is behind the movement of the horse.

The problem, of course, is to be able to maintain this seat and the only way is to practise on a horse, preferably on the lunge, without reins and with an instructor correcting the position *(Plate 44)*.

There are numerous exercises which are helpful, some of which are illustrated, but the real answer to the development of this deep seat is work on the lunge *(Plates 45–48)*.

It is well worthwhile going to a good instructor to develop this basis of equitation. Practising on your own is all very well, but you cannot see your own faults and you are likely to get into bad habits which will be almost impossible to eradicate later on.

Work on the lunge on a schooled horse is, I am convinced, essential. Certainly the work should be carried out without reins but not, without irons for too long a period. We normally ride with irons so I see no point, and a number of dangers, in working without them.

At a later stage, jumping without reins over low fences in an enclosed lane is an excellent exercise for balance and security. Again there is no need to dispense with the irons, nor do I believe in pupils being made to fold their arms, stretch their arms over their heads or thumb their noses. One does not perform these antics when jumping with reins, so why do them when the reins are removed? It is not helpful to the balance and it is, therefore, much better to encourage the pupil to push his arms forward on either side of the withers in a line with the horse's mouth. This at least is something like following the movement of the head, whereas I can think of no occasion when it would be necessary to jump a fence with the reins held in arms outstretched above the head.

For the young and agile any sort of activity work, such as vaulting, jumping facing the tail or anything else you like, is good for balance and confidence.

The Saddle
Finally, although a properly designed saddle will not teach anyone to ride, it goes a long way to helping the rider sit correctly.

The modern all-purpose or general-purpose saddle is made so that the rider, with the minimum of effort and the maximum comfort and security, is placed over the centre of the horse's balance. It achieves this object by having, amongst other features, a dipped seat and the stirrup bars positioned forward. At the same time it allows the rider to sit in the closest contact with his horse and in no way hinders the application of the aids *(Plate 49)*.

Some of the more old-fashioned saddles, of pre-war vintage, seem to have been made in deliberate defiance of present day equestrian practice. The seats were flat, the head or pommel stood rather higher than the cantle, the waist was so wide as to spread the thighs and the bars were positioned so far to the rear as to ensure that the rider could only sit behind the movement. In addition, they were uncomfortable.

The modern saddle is a real help to the rider and an essential part of his equipment. As Lt.-Col. Frank Weldon wrote in the foreword to my book, *Saddlery*, 'not only does it put the rider willy-nilly into the most convenient position for the horse to bear his weight and understand his signals, but it is infinitely more comfortable to sit in, and above all, almost impossible to fall out of. I would no more dream of using a conventional hunting saddle in preference to a modern general purpose one for hacking, hunting or cross-country riding than I would pick a kitchen stool rather than a well-upholstered armchair for a Sunday afternoon nap'.

I agree with every word—or almost. There are some of us who could fall out of anything.

Preparing the Horse

Before proceeding to the various ridden movements I have included this section on lungeing, loose schooling and the use of long reins.

Lungeing, in particular, is a subject which appears to be neglected or misunderstood by far too many horse-keepers. There are even people who look upon it as a sort of equine treadmill and label it as a cruel practice. In cases where a horse is chased round in a small circle the condemnation may be justified, but this sort of thing is very far removed from the proper purpose of the exercise.

All horses and ponies young or old, benefit from work on the lunge.

Lungeing, in its simplest form, is getting the horse to work round the trainer in a circle to either hand, the horse being controlled by means of a line from the trainer's hand to a cavesson (a special type of head-collar), by the voice and by the trainer's long whip.

There is no *mystique* connected with the exercise; anybody, even a child, can acquire the simple technique and its value is inestimable.

The objects of lungeing are these:

1 To teach a young horse to go forward freely
2 To improve the balance of all horses
3 To build up and make supple the muscles naturally, without their being formed in opposition to the rider's weight
4 To flex the spine, as far as this is possible
5 To encourage equal muscle development on both sides of the horse
6 To condition young or weak animals before subjecting them to the rider's weight
7 To exercise animals who for one reason or another cannot be ridden
8 To make calm an over-fresh horse before riding him
9 To accustom the horse to this work so that he can be safely ridden

on the lunge, without reins, for the purpose of developing the strength and security of the rider's seat

10 To teach the horse acceptance of discipline, and the habit of obedience

11 As a means of introducing the horse to jumping

A number of these objectives may need little further explanation, but it is as well to consider the principal ones in more detail.

The natural balance is improved, and consequently the quality of the individual paces, by this work on circles, which encourages the horse to use his hind legs. As we have seen, in order for the horse to turn correctly and easily, he brings his inside hind leg further under him so as to push himself round the corner. Properly worked on the lunge the hind-legs are constantly engaged, and in the latter stages of the exercise we shall discern a marked improvement in the head carriage as a result of the lightened forehand induced by the activity of the hind-legs under the horse.

Because the backbone is capable of very little flexion the horse finds difficulty in making a true circle: a difficulty which is increased by stiff muscles on either side of the spine and by the natural over-development of one side.

This natural disposition to one-sidedness is further encouraged by our handling horses almost entirely from the near side. It is, for instance, particularly noticeable when young stock are led out in hand. In early training not only does the horse prefer to go on a certain rein, generally the left one, but the trainer finds it easier as well, and if he is unwise tends to give too little work, instead of rather more, on the opposite rein.

The result is for the horse to avoid working on the rein which causes him physical discomfort and on which he has difficulty in adjusting his centre of balance. Very often he is then dubbed as having a one-sided mouth. By this time he may have, but the primary reason for his resistance is not that his mouth is insensitive, but that his bodily development is unequal. Without equality of development he will be unable to engage, on a circle, the inside hind leg and will be driven into making a resistance.

Finally, on the lunge, there will be no restriction in the development of the back muscles, which might well occur under saddle when the immature muscle structure may stiffen in opposition to the weight.

It should be clear from the foregoing how necessary it is to condition the horse before riding him. Nothing is more dangerous than to ride a young or weak horse before his back muscles are strong enough to take the weight. At best the horse will hollow the back to avoid discomfort, and it is more than likely that he will become sour and un-cooperative. In addition it is possible to do lasting damage to the spine. Horses with sore backs (quite unforgiveable in any stable) can be exercised on the lunge and parents will find it useful in conditioning ponies before their riders return for the holidays.

It is not just a question of discretion being the better part of valour that prompts me to advise the lungeing of over-fresh horses before they are ridden. It is just sound common sense.

There is really no point is getting up on a mad fresh horse bursting with oats and *joie-de-vivre*. It may please you to 'master' him, that is if you don't finish up flat on your back, but in the process there has probably been a certain amount of rough handling and the whole procedure is hardly conducive to a sympathetic partnership. It is far better that the horse should expend his high spirits, quite harmlessly, on the end of a lunge and be ridden when he has regained a calm and receptive frame of mind.

Lastly, the great value of the lunge is in teaching obedience and discipline. These habits once implanted greatly facilitate future training. Their inculcation is, in fact, the basis of training.

Of equal importance is the opportunity given by the exercise in developing of the trainer's sympathy with his pupil and enlarging his understanding of the horse's mental and physical capacities. It is indeed quite surprising how the mental affinity between horse and rider can grow under the conditions that pertain during lungeing. Our own Welsh pony is a remarkable example of the partnership that can be attained and besides carrying out transitions both on the lunge and loose can be controlled, if only for a matter of minutes, by my 'thinking' commands at him. I do not claim that this is in any way thought transference, because it is possible that he perceives involuntary movements on my part, but it shows to what extent a mutual understanding can be achieved.

While lungeing is easy to understand and is enjoyable for the horse who, in general, likes to be under discipline and takes pleasure in co-operating, it is fairly hard physical work, particularly in the early stages. Ten or fifteen minutes are quite enough for the early lessons and forty minutes are the very maximum for a fit, trained animal. Periods of twenty to thirty minutes are usually as much as the average horse can manage without losing his concentration. Long periods on the lunge for young or older animals will impose far too great a strain on the body structure.

Facilities and Equipment

These items are neither complicated, nor difficult to obtain.

Ideally an enclosed flat *manège* is the most suitable, and for the later training a piece of undulating ground which can be roped-off, or otherwise enclosed, is very useful. The purpose of lungeing over an uneven surface is to improve further the balance of the horse by accustoming him to make more frequent adjustments to his centre of gravity.

Any patch of ground, a corner of a field is convenient, will do in the absence of a school and a temporary enclosure is easily made with stakes and a few lengths of rope. It is, however, important that the area should be enclosed in some way, as in the open a horse has too much to distract his attention from the job in hand.

The essential equipment required comprises a lunge cavesson, that is, a stout sort of head collar which has a padded nosepiece which fits snugly and which is equipped with three rings, set on swivels; one in the centre and one on either side. In addition one needs a lunge rein and a long whip.

I also like to have two further dees set at the rear of the cavesson nosepiece, on either side, for fitting side-reins when the time comes. When buying a cavesson choose one of light, modern design, not the enormous, over-weighted, pre-war variety.

The lunge rein is usually of web, which has the advantage of not burning the hand should the pupil become playful. It again should be as light as possible and can fasten to the cavesson ring by either a swivel mounted hook, or a strap and buckle set on a swivel mounting. Without these swivels, which, incidentally need to be kept well-greased, the rein very quickly gets twisted and tangled.

The whip, equipped with a long thong and lash, is useless if it is not properly balanced and light. I use one made entirely of nylon, which is as near perfect as I require.

I have termed these three items 'essential', which in essence they are, but much can be done with a headcollar, a piece of rope and a long switch from the hedge.

Side-reins are an additional item of equipment which are not always entirely necessary. I do use them, but only for short periods, or perhaps with a young horse. The type to buy are those fitted with clips and a buckle to give plenty of adjustment. Some years ago I advocated the use of side-reins in which a piece of elastic or a rubber ring was inserted. I now believe this to be wrong as the elastic, although it gives to the movement of the head, exerts too constant a restraint, which the horse avoids by withdrawing his head and possibly becoming overbent. My side-reins are, therefore, now made of plain leather about half an inch wide.

Young horses, or horses unaccustomed to the exercise, are prone to knocking their legs about when working on a circle and, therefore, polo boots or exercise bandages over cotton wool are a necessary protection.

The fitting of the cavesson is very important; the nosepiece should fit fairly tightly, well above the nostrils, and the jowl strap will need to be reasonably tight if the headpiece is not to pull forward over the outside eye.

I usually fasten the lunge rein to the central nose ring where it gives more control, but others attach it to the inside ring. I have occasionally had horses who threw their heads about when the lunge was fixed in the first fashion but went well when it was fastened on the inside ring. In much the same way I have found horses carrying their heads too much towards the centre when the inside ring was used, and who went better with it on the nose. It, therefore, depends upon the individual.

I should say that the late Henry Wynmalen, for whom I had the highest regard, advocated the lunge being attached to a ring at the back of the cavesson, behind the jaw bones. I have never tried this method, but I would not presume to disagree with so great an authority.

Method

The first stage in teaching the exercise requires an assistant to lead the horse round the trainer. I like my assistant on the outside of the animal, not on the inside. My reason for this is that I find the horse is more likely to come into the centre (which he must not do) when the assistant, placed on the inside, eventually moves away from him than otherwise. In addition, I want the horse to concentrate his attention upon me, and this is more difficult for him to do if I am shielded by the body of the assistant.

The trainer stands in the centre with the rein in the leading hand, that is the left hand when the horse circles on the left rein and vice versa, the spare end of the rein is passed across the body and held in loops in the other hand. It is important not to have the rein hanging round one's feet—it is only too easy to become upended should the horse try to get away. The whip is held, point to the rear and resting on the ground, by the trainer's free hand, i.e. the right hand for the left rein and the opposite for the right.

At this stage the trainer should position himself in what I term the 'Triangle of Control'.

He places his body facing, and slightly to the rear of, the animal's hip, he is then *behind* the horse and able to encourage him forward, if necessary with a slight movement of the whip.

Should the trainer position himself in advance of this position, nearer or opposite the horse's shoulder, the horse will endeavour to turn away from him, or even turn round, and control will be lost. Correct positioning is almost the whole secret of successful lungeing.

To commence with the pony is led round the trainer by the assistant until he accepts the situation calmly and goes quietly on both reins, carrying the weight on the lunge line, which should be rather less than taut.

Once this is achieved the first of the words of command can be taught. This is the halt from the walk. Again it is not what you say, but the way that you say it. I use the word 'whoa' and the tone should be low and drawn out, as in all commands asking for a decrease in pace. For those asking for upward transitions, i.e. walk to trot, trot to canter, the command is divided into a preparatory drawn out note and a sharp executive snap, as in 'CAANN–TER!' The voice need not be loud, but it should be clear and incisive and the tone and words used always remain the same.

On the trainer giving the command 'whoa' (I introduce a personal and entirely irrelevant *tremolo* into the word) he will immediately follow the command with a tightening of the fingers on the rein. The assistant, who has been holding the cavesson very lightly, now brings the horse to a halt, immediately making him stand squarely on all four legs.

The trainer then walks *out* to the horse and rewards him. Don't let the assistant perform this task—the relationship that is being built is between horse and trainer and nothing must obtrude upon it.

I always go out to the horse to reward, *never* do I ask him to come in to me. If he is encouraged to come in at this or any other stage he will continue to do so, and you will never get a proper halt.

The horse will very quickly understand the meaning of 'whoa' and will associate it with being rewarded. It will not be long before one can

212

dispense with both the tightening of the rein and the assistant's help in obtaining a halt.

I continue to use an assistant until the horse has learnt the transitions from halt to trot and from trot to halt, and obeys my voice at once. This may take three or four lessons and during this time I accustom the animal to accepting the movement of the whip when he is asked to go forward; this is a sweeping movement with the point still resting on the ground. He is also taught to move away from the whip when it is pointed at his shoulder as an indication that he should move outwards and not fall in towards the centre.

By the fourth lesson, sometimes earlier, I have the assistant walking on the outside of the horse some six feet from his head, and in the following lesson dispense with his services altogether.

Now I must concentrate on maintaining my triangle of control, keeping always behind the animal and urging him forward. It is at this stage that one encounters the occasional disobedience.

The horse, if he has never been brought to the centre, will not usually try to come in to the trainer, but if he does one must alter one's position to get in line with his hip and drive him forward. A flip on the lunge rein, and the resultant smack as the ripple finishes on the nose, will usually be sufficient to make him stay out. He may, too, try to make off. Under no circumstances should the trainer then dig his heels in and pull the horse round on his forehand. This is most dangerous and can cause serious strains. The way to cope with the predicament is to go with the horse, checking him by intermittent jerks on the rein. The same thing can happen if the trainer urges the horse forward too strongly, but in this case even greater tact is required. The fault in this instance is that of the trainer, whose urgings the horse has obeyed. The horse must not, therefore, be punished. The trainer must go with him and restrain him very gently.

In these early lessons I am more concerned with the horse going forward than his making a perfect circle and I, therefore, move about fairly freely on something resembling a circle within the track made by the horse. I concentrate on keeping the rein not quite taut and, of course, I change the rein, i.e. the direction, very frequently, giving rather more work on the stiff side than on the other *(Plate 50)*.

There is a school of thought which insists that the trainer pivots on his heel and forces the horse to accept the circle. I am not in favour of this method as it encourages the horse to hang against the rein and to take his quarters outside the track of the forefeet.

To change the rein I again use a simple method which I find more satisfactory than threatening the poor animal with the whip and chasing him round on the opposite rein. I halt the horse, walk out to him and lead him across the school, where I halt him facing the opposite direction. I then move away from him, having reversed whip and rein in my hands, and ask him to walk-on or trot as the case may be.

If the horse bucks or plunges on the rein I allow him to do so until I think he has done enough, when a sharp word will bring him back to the job in hand.

The next stage is to insist, gradually, on a proper circle. When this is established I teach, by judicious slackening and tightening of the rein, which will in time give way to my voice alone, the variations in pace at walk and trot. I ask, and receive very quickly, a free extended walk and trot and the same paces in something of a more collected fashion with a more energetic engagement of the hind legs.

Throughout this initial training it is essential to teach one lesson at a time, recapitulating at the beginning of the next session to make sure the lesson has been properly learnt.

The whip is used only to indicate the trainer's wishes, a week or two's work is lost if the animal is struck with it and learns to regard it as something to be feared instead of respected.

Once I have established the trot, with no straining at the rein, I urge the horse into the canter. If after a circle or two (the first ones may be a little exuberant) I find he is pulling on the rein I have started too early and must go back to more work on the trot. Circling at the canter is difficult and hard work for the horse. It should not, therefore, be overdone. Should the horse strike off with the wrong leg (i.e. he should lead with his left fore on a circle to the left and vice versa) bring him back to halt and start again. Continue this until he automatically strikes off correctly on the word of command.

The final stage in this work on the flat is reached when the horse goes through the upward and downward transitions, including the variations, such as canter from halt, halt from canter, etc., and is able to vary the pace of each gait at word of command. By this time the head will have been persuaded to follow the track and not be held to the outside of it. The horse will have been worked over rough ground as well as on the flat surface of the school and will have become pretty well balanced.

Use of the Side-Reins

If I think the head carriage could be improved I might attach a pair of

214

side-reins from a roller to the rear rings of the cavesson. I attach them so that they are of equal length each side, and loose enough so that they hang slack when the head is withdrawn and raised.

The only other time I might be tempted to use them is on a very unruly subject. Improperly and tightly adjusted side-reins, particularly if attached to the bit rings, can cause the horse to withdraw the head to too great an extent or to practise other forms of evasions. The result will be stiffness in the neck and possibly in the back.

Jumping on the Lunge

Following this the horse can be introduced to jumping, first by walking, and then trotting, over spaced poles along the side of the school *(Plate 51 and 52)*. The trainer should by this time experience little difficulty in positioning himself to allow the animal to negotiate the poles in a straight line. These poles, once the horse accepts them calmly, are later replaced by low cavalletti, over which the horse is asked to trot.

Any tendency to rush is checked with the voice and the trainer concentrates on getting the horse to drop his head, round his back, and pick up all four feet energetically and with rhythm.

Following this, the same procedure, starting with the poles, can be carried out on a circle. This is much more difficult and takes a little time to perform correctly. Later the horse, now quite accustomed to jumping and full of confidence, can be lunged over a variety of low fences at trot and at canter, the approach being controlled by the voice.

Under no circumstances should the horse ever be lunged off the bit. The risk of damaging the mouth, and the confidence of the horse in the trainer, is too great.

Loose Schooling

As the ultimate test of obedience I remove the lunge rein and work the horse in the school loose. I do, however, leave the cavesson on. It is probably unnecessary, but the horse associates the wearing of it with work and discipline and so it remains. I carry out all the movements described, including jumping, purely on the word of command, assisted by the strategic positioning of my body a little to the rear of the horse.

Once again there is no *mystique*, and this stage of training and obedience is easily taught by a person of average sensitivity, intelligence and competence.

Should the horse be disobedient when loose, particularly regarding the halt, it is best to ignore him and urge him on. He will soon settle and be glad to stop when asked. It is possible, and is sometimes recommended, that a horse who will not stop on the lunge or loose, should be driven against the corner of the school. I have no doubt it is effective, but it won't exactly cement the understanding we are trying to achieve. If the training is carried out on the lines indicated the matter should never arise, or at any rate assume such proportions as to warrant a rather drastic remedy.

Initially one may have to do rather more walking about when the horse is loose to keep him on the outside track, but never having been brought into the centre he will soon stay out of his own accord.

There are people who disapprove of loose jumping and attribute all sorts of evils to the practice. To my mind there is no better way of teaching jumping. The horse, completely free, works out the approach and judges the distance for himself, and if he is not overfaced rarely makes a mistake. It is also an excellent study for the rider, who observes at close quarters the exact movements of the horse when jumping, and is made to realise the importance of the animal being completely unrestricted in his execution of the leap.

Most loose jumping is carried out in an enclosed jumping lane. I do not possess one, and so have to make do with solidly erected fences in my small outdoor school, in reality a not too well-drained sand ring. I may have to work harder, but my animals jump fences without wings, low but solid, and as yet have no idea of running out.

Any horse, of any age, benefits from schooling of this sort and it lays a very firm foundation for future mounted work, as well as creating close bonds of understanding and trust between pupil and master.

Long Reins

Long reining is primarily a part of the young horse's education, used to improve balance and to teach him the movements he will be asked to make under the saddle, from the ground.

Generally speaking long reining in this country, with notable exceptions, is a rather primitive proceeding. It can, however, be an art when it is performed by a skilled trainer such as Miss Sylvia Stanier, who gave a fascinating display of advanced movements on the long reins at the 1966 Horse of the Year Show. Miss Stanier, using the Danish system, taught to her by Mr. Schmit-Jensen, showed how the horse, without the burden of the rider, could display great freedom and correct movement *(Plates 53 and 54)*.

For myself I have always been something of an anti-long reiner, persuading myself that the simpler mounted movements which I required could be better taught from the saddle. I say 'persuaded', but I suspect the truth is really that I am not very expert at the exercise.

I do not long rein horses, but I do find it a helpful exercise, after lungeing, when dealing with ponies, many of whom in these days are very badly made and have had little or no schooling.

The English method, apart from the horse often being trussed up like a chicken, involves the use of the outside rein round the quarters. As much of the work involves circling it is then possible for the horse to lean his whole weight on this outside rein and consequently upon his mouth.

The method used by Miss Stanier employs the reins in a different fashion. They pass from the bit through the terrets (upright brass rings) of an ordinary harness driving pad, and thence directly to the trainer's hand.

One of my principle objections is that the weight of the reins (which can be considerable) is borne directly on the mouth. If, however, they are used in the fashion described and, in addition, are as light as possible (light plough lines are very good) this disadvantage is largely overcome.

As in lungeing, the position of the trainer is vitally important, but in addition, as he is driving off the mouth, his hands must be extra-sensitive and must follow the motions of the head in rhythm with the movement. The exercise is also much harder work for the trainer, who has to be very active and nimble if he is not to get left behind.

The trainer positions himself in line with the hip and slightly to the rear, about six or seven feet away from the pony. He holds a rein in either hand and in the one nearest the pony he carries the whip. For the purpose of the exercise a lunge whip, which has a long thong, is altogether too difficult to manage. The ideal is a long schooling whip between four and five feet long. It is held by the butt, with the point behind the trainer.

The pony is then asked to walk forward, which he should do quite calmly and freely. It is possible that he will, at first, become excited and a little frightened of the trainer behind him, and he may also be reluctant to go forward freely. Bear with him in this and do not frighten him further by sudden movements of either yourself or the whip.

If he becomes over-excited and there is a danger of both trainer and pony getting into a tangle, release the outside rein, take a couple of strides sideways and have him circle you as he would do on the lunge.

When he is calm commence the walk again round the school. As he becomes used to this move him, on a necessary tighter turn, across the school but on the same rein.

After a lesson or two the trainer will be able to place himself directly behind the pony and when he wishes to change the rein has only to raise his hands, so that the reins clear the back, and move himself a couple of strides in the required direction, changing his whip as he goes.

Changes of direction at the walk are not difficult, but at trot and canter require some dexterity. It is as well, therefore, to master these changes thoroughly before attempting them at the faster paces. I find that when starting the changes of direction it is possible to get the rein caught up in the tail. It shouldn't happen, but it can do, and it is a reasonable precaution to bandage the tail up short in polo fashion.

There is always a tendency for the beginner to hang on to the reins, which must be avoided at all costs. Hold the reins naturally, as one would a bridle rein, and use the fingers supported by a flexible wrist. The action of the fingers is the same as when riding, they close and squeeze, but never pull. In the same way the inside rein leads the horse round the turn and the outside one, moving forward to allow for the bend of head and neck, is in support to prevent any falling in of the forehand towards the centre.

Once the pony is able to carry out circles of varying size to either hand at the walk and is quite calm I begin a little mouthing education. I bring him to the halt, which if he has been properly schooled on the lunge, will be a correct one, and then stand myself directly behind him and as close to him as I can get. I do not recommend that this should be done with anything but an animal you know well, but if a proper relationship exists he will not kick you. Holding the reins in line with his mouth and with an equal and very light tension, I then vibrate, very gently, one rein, rather in the manner of a violinist. With patience, and some tact, I then get a decontraction of the lower jaw on that side, with the head slightly bent in the direction of the hand. I work equally on both sides of the mouth and eventually with both reins until the pony will bridle, flex, relax, whatever you like, in response to the lightest movements of the fingers.

I then carry out the same exercises at the walk, and now ask for both an extended free walk and also a more shortened and collected one.

The same procedure is followed at the trot, and when this pace is

218

established in the same way, the canter is introduced. Always, after a *short* period of collection the horse must be rewarded by being allowed to extend his head and neck.

In both these paces the trainer is required to do a certain amount of moving about and one tends to move inside the pony and do rather more work on the circle to save one's legs and wind.

It is possible for the very skilled to execute a flying change of leg at the canter and, indeed, alternate changes on a straight line. I am not nearly so expert and content myself with a figure of eight at the canter, changing the leading leg in the centre after coming back to four or so steps at the trot.

If the lungeing programme has been carried out properly the horse or pony will automatically strike off with the inside foreleg leading at the canter on either rein. This is an important lesson to have taught, for the animal when positioned for the canter under saddle, that is when his body is slightly bent towards the inside, will strike off correctly on the inside leg quite naturally.

One could go further on the long reins, teaching side-steps and so on, but as I only long rein ponies I do not go so far, lest the animal becomes confused when ridden by an inexpert child.

I do, however, teach the rein-back, the turn on the quarters and the turn on the forehand from the ground. Possibly because I am not a naturally talented horseman I have always regarded the rein-back as a most difficult movement, and yet it is something that is almost expected of every Pony Club member. I must say that most rein-backs when practised in show classes by *either* children or adults are pretty painful to behold.

The movement cannot be contemplated until the horse can manage a balanced halt with the quarters well under him and passes freely up to the bit in response to his rider's leg action.

The rein-back is *not* a walk in reverse. The walk is a pace of four distinct beats. If the horse starts the movement with the right hind leg the sequence is as follows: right hind, right fore, left hind, left fore.

The walk is propelled from rear to front, whereas the rein-back is from front to rear and is a pace of two beats, the legs moving in diagonal pairs.

I teach the movement in a corner of the school placing the pony alongside one fence and facing the other. I then stand close to him in line with his hip. I make sure he is standing collectedly and then close and open each hand alternately, urging him first to move the forelegs and then, diagonally, the hind legs to the rear. I ask only for one step to start with and am content when I get four clear steps. The rails on one side and my body on the other keep the pony straight, and the fence in front prevents his going forward.

If with these aids he still does not understand I have an assistant tap his foreleg or even tread on his toe.

The moment he has performed the required number of steps he is asked to go forward again. Teaching a horse or pony to go back always has an element of danger, lest he should discover that by continuing his backward progress he can put his rider at a disadvantage; for this reason he must always, and immediately, go forward following steps to the rear.

Gradually I dispense with the corner of the school, halting further and further away from the facing fence, until I can eventually get the movement in the open.

I teach the turn on the forehand not only for its practical application, it is so useful when opening a gate, but also to teach the pony obedience to the leg.

Once again I use a corner of the school, but this time I place myself between the pony and the fence alongside him, while he, as before, has a fence in front of him preventing him from moving forward. I stand fairly close to the pony, my whip in the hand nearest to him, and slightly in advance of his hip.

If I wish to make a turn to the left I am on his left side. I then bend his head slightly to the left and tap him with my whip just behind the girth on his left side. He is then obliged to move his quarters away from me and to pivot round his forehand or, strictly speaking, round his left foreleg. As before one or two steps to start with are quite sufficient. Obviously the turn on the forehand is only made from the halt; to attempt it in movement would not only be pointless, but dangerous.

The turn on the quarters, in which the horse pivots on the inside hind leg, is rather more difficult, as it involves moving the shoulder. If I wish to make the turn to the right I place the pony in the corner of the school and position myself close up and behind the right buttock. From this position I can prevent his going backwards, the fence in front stops any forward inclination and the fence alongside bars any movement of the quarters to the left. I then incline the head to the right and lead the forehand round the quarters. If I have any difficulty I remove the right rein from the terret so that I can 'open' it to a greater extent to lead the horse round.

220

I am still not wholly convinced of the value of long-reining for the horse, but I am sure it is very useful for children's ponies who cannot be schooled from the saddle by an adult.

I would not discourage anyone from long-reining their horse, but I would suggest they start on a pony. The native ones, in particular, are very co-operative, more biddable, and much quicker on the uptake than the average horse.

Teaching Paces, Movements & Jumping

Facilities

In order to improve the paces and obedience of the horse under saddle we require similar facilities as we need for lungeing him, viz. an enclosed space. Few of us will be able to afford the luxury of a covered school, but an outside ring on level ground, perhaps in the corner of a paddock with the unfenced sides either railed or roped off, is almost as good, if not so comfortable. The surface must, however, be suitable and the going good.

Ground having a subsoil of gravel, chalk or sand provides the best surface because it will be naturally well drained. Clay land is not nearly so good, either in summer or winter.

If one has the space, and is prepared to expend a little money, a very good outdoor ring can be constructed by removing the topsoil to a depth of from six to eight inches, levelling the surface and then laying four inches of broken brick rubble well rolled in with a heavy roller. On top of this a further three inches of small clinker can be laid and rolled in. A two or three inch deep top dressing of rough sand, or a mixture of tan and sawdust, laid on top, then gives a good rideable surface in all weathers.

The size of the school depends on the area you have available, ideally it would be approximately 180 feet × 60 feet, but one can manage quite well in smaller spaces.

We shall also need half a dozen stout poles and at least three cavalletti. The dimensions of a cavalletto are given later in this section (p. 243) and they are not difficult to construct from straight pine poles. They can, of course, be obtained ready-made from a number of firms specialising in the making of jump equipment.

Fences, for jumping schooling, can be improvised very satisfactorily with straw bales, petrol cans, brush and gorse, railway sleepers, etc. At the present time there a number of sleepers available for comparatively little money and they make excellent, if immoveable, solid fences.

Objectives

Overall objectives will naturally differ according to the needs and ambitions of the individual and depend very much upon the latter's conception of an ideal, or even suitable, riding horse.

Indeed, if one has never ridden anything but a riding school horse round the same interminable lanes it is unlikely that one will have the slightest idea of the pleasure to be obtained from riding a schooled horse. On the other hand there are numerous hunting people, owning potentially good horses, who are not much wiser.

The extent to which a horse can be improved by training depends to a considerable degree upon his conformation, but whatever his shape he will certainly be a better, more comfortable and more valuable horse for a little intelligent and simple schooling.

To own an unschooled horse and to make no effort to improve him is rather like owning a boat fitted with a motor, and then to spend all your time rowing the thing.

For the average horseman, owning a horse with no major deficiencies of conformation, it is not difficult to produce a balanced, responsive animal obedient to the indications of leg and hand. Such a horse, in my view, should be smooth to ride at all paces, able to vary the speed within the gaits, capable of moving backwards and sideways for a few steps, of turning on his forehand and quarters and jumping reasonable obstacles calmly and safely.

This is surely not expecting too much. One cannot, of course, hope to have a horse who is always one hundred per cent obedient and responsive. He would be a very dull fellow if he was. He is after all an animal and, like us, he will have his off days, times when he is non co-operative and occasions when he will depart from the straight and narrow path to assert himself as an individual, or just to give rein to his sense of humour.

In order, however, to produce this near-paragon it is necessary to spend a little time on the consideration of ways and means, and rather more time putting them into effect.

One of the objectives in lungeing the horse was the improvement in fluid balance and the greater part of his subsequent schooling is directed to furthering this end.

No horse can be pleasant to ride or be handy in his movements unless he is capable of impulsion. We have already seen that it is impossible to achieve any degree of extension, collection or even forward movement without this quality. Impulsion is the bedrock of riding and impulsion is only obtained from balance. Upon the improvement and the perfection of balance depends the successful outcome of schooling.

Before, however, we can begin schooling from the saddle the horse must be sufficiently muscled to be capable of the work he has to do. If the lungeing programme has been carried out properly and has been alternated with gentle, straightforward hacking much of the groundwork will have been completed, and the horse will be physically and mentally equipped to proceed to work in the school. The rider, too, must be in reasonable physical shape and must prepare himself for the role of instructor.

Good teachers spend more time preparing their lessons than giving them—indeed preparation is the secret of instruction and each lesson should be planned well before riding into the school. This is not to say that one's programme must be inflexible. It must, in fact, be very flexible. Some days everything will go well, on others you will seem to have achieved nothing.

However it goes, the one *inflexible* rule is never to teach a movement before the previous one has been completely assimilated. If the horse finds a lesson difficult and you are not getting anywhere, go back to the previous, and easier, lesson, and then think, when he is put back in his box, in no way upset or confused, whether it was not your fault. In most cases you will find it probably was, so you must work out another line of approach.

Never put a horse into his stable in other than a happy frame of mind. If you do he broods and goes sulky. Never try to teach anything if your temper is becoming frayed. None of us is infallible and we all get agitated, tense or just plain angry sometimes. In this state we can teach nothing. The answer is to get off the horse, walk round the school, smoke a cigarette or recite the longest poem you know by heart, until your temper is very well under control. Then carry out a simple movement which the horse enjoys doing, reward him and finish the lesson there.

The Four Gaits
Before considering the exercises and movements which can be practised in the school we should look at the way in which the horse moves at the various gaits. The four natural gaits of the horse are: Walk, Trot, Canter and Gallop.

The walk is a pace of four separate beats marked by the successive placing of each lateral pair. The sequence of the footfalls when the

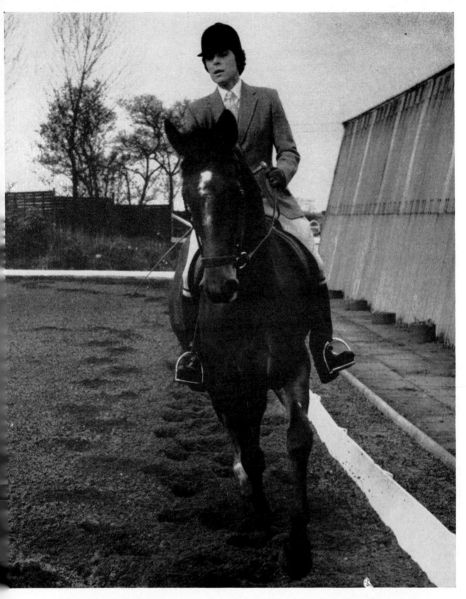

58 The correct positioning of the horse before commencing the actual turn

59 Miss Vera Holden demonstrating the crossing of poles on the ground

60 The turn

walk starts on the left leg is: left hind, left fore, right hind, right fore.

The trot is a pace of two beats, the horse placing one pair of diagonal legs on the ground and springing, following a moment of suspension, on to the other diagonal. One beat is heard as the left hind and the right fore touch the ground simultaneously and one, after the briefest interval as the opposite diagonal touches the ground.

In the canter three beats can, or should, be heard if the horse is cantering correctly. The horse may canter either with the right fore leading (the right lead), or with the left fore (the left lead). In fact, of course, the leading leg is not the first in the sequence of the beats, but the last. On the right lead the sequence is left hind leg, then, simultaneously, the left diagonal, left fore and right hind, and lastly the leading leg, the right fore, then a period of suspension before the next stride is taken.

The canter in the school or on a circle is correct when the right lead is employed on a right-handed circle and left lead on a circle on the left rein. It is a false lead, known as cantering on the wrong leg, when the left lead is used on the right rein and vice versa. It is, however, easy for the rider to feel when he is on the incorrect leg as he receives a fairly violent jolt under the outside of his seat and his outside shoulder will be thrown forward.

The gallop, the fastest pace, which is not used in school work, becomes a four beat pace (i.e. with off-fore leading, near hind, off-hind, near-fore, off-fore, followed by a moment of suspension), but has considerable variation in the sequence of movements according to the speed.

With conscious effort and attention the rider should be able not only to hear the footfalls, but to feel which foot is coming to the ground. When he does he will find, particularly in the canter, how much more effectively and precisely he can apply the aids.

To start the school work first commit to memory the various school figures which are illustrated. These are designed to improve suppleness and balance by asking for continual directional changes and consequently changes in the shifting centre of balance.

Starting the Exercises

Commence work, for short periods only, at the walk round the school, crossing the arena diagonally when you wish to change the rein. At this early stage do not bother about the head position, but concentrate on riding into each corner with active legs, the inside one pushing the horse forward, the outside one preventing the quarters swinging out.

As a second stage pick up the reins and push the horse forward until you feel him making contact with the bit. Now you can commence the smaller circles, more frequent changes of direction and some curves and serpentines. Check the efficiency of your leg aids by riding the *inside* track occasionally, i.e. about nine feet from the wall or rail of the school. Very often you will find your horse tends to go to pieces when divorced from the guiding wall *(Fig. 30)*.

Check, too, the strength of the aids. After a very few lessons it should be possible by a very slight movement of the legs to obtain a turn. If the horse does not immediately respond, reinforce the aid with a tap from a long whip, held in the inside hand, just behind the girth. With a long whip there is no need to remove the hands from the rein and this tap will be sufficient to send the horse on.

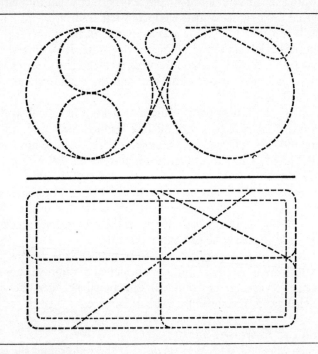

Fig 30 School figures

(*Top*) The variety of school circles and changes of hand. The largest circle is called a volte. (*Bottom*) The various changes of hand possible in the school. The inside dotted line indicates the inside track

226

Under no circumstances strengthen the leg aid or let it degenerate into a kick, otherwise all the future aids asking for greater impulsion will have to be correspondingly stronger in comparison.

In all movements concentrate on keeping the horse straight and only allowing the quarters to follow the track of the forehand.

The Walk

There are three kinds of walk we can attempt in the riding school, the *ordinary* walk, the *collected* and the *extended*. We shall practise the first and last frequently, the second we shall certainly ask for to a certain degree, but not nearly so often.

The *ordinary* walk is when the horse advances freely forward with relaxed long strides, maintaining a light contact with the bit. The *collected* walk is when the rider increases the power of the driving aids; the seat and the back now pushing with each stride, while the legs act intermittently—they are never applied in a dead, continuous, clamping motion. The result is a greater engagement of the hind legs under the body— impulsion in fact. Now, if the hands close slightly on the reins the effect will be to contain the energy generated within the framework of legs and hands. The horse's head will be raised, his balance will shift slightly to the rear and the stride will shorten. In the *extended* walk the horse strides forward on a released, swinging rein, head and neck stretched out and with a free and extended stride activated by the driving aids.

To start with our efforts at collection or shortening will be hardly perceptible and once we feel the horse shortening we should reward him by letting him go into the extended walk, which is so much less demanding of him.

This stage will not, however, be reached for some time and should not be attempted until the work at the trot is becoming established. If in the early lessons we can obtain a good free ordinary walk alternating with an energetic free or extended walk this is sufficient.

Moving Off and The Halt

We can, however, perfect the move-off and the halt, and we can begin asking for those relaxations of the lower jaw mentioned under the heading of long reining.

No horse will move off alertly and in balanced fashion unless he is first brought to attention.

Start by mounting the horse, insisting on his remaining still while you do so. If he moves off before you are ready, place him in a corner of the school facing the wall or fence and spend ten minutes getting up and down. If he moves as you are half way up, come down again and make a fresh start.

Most horses get into the habit of moving off as soon as the rider puts a toe in the iron because they are well aware that the same toe will, within seconds, be dug into their ribs. If you cannot mount from the ground unassisted have some one give you a leg up or use a mounting block. It is more dignified, less exhausting and does not exasperate the horse by pulling him off balance and subjecting him to the discomfort of a shifted saddle.

Pause a moment, to settle yourself in the saddle, before picking up the reins. Pick them up quietly and gently to give the horse no opportunity to anticipate the command to move off. Now bring him to attention by a momentary, and very slight, application of both legs pushing him up to hands which, again momentarily, squeeze the reins. Now apply the legs again and open the hand slightly to allow the horse to move forward.

In a similar way the horse must be given warning of your intention to halt and he must be in contact with the hand before he can do so. The aids to halt commence with a stretching of the back, and loins (but not a leaning back of the trunk, which would impose greater weight on the quarters and encourage the horse to lean on the bit), increased pressure from the seat bones and a slightly increased drive from the legs sending the horse up to a hand which closes. Initially we may have to repeat the hand aid before the horse understands, but the moment he obeys the hand must yield. Once the legs have acted, and the horse has shortened his posture to conform with the closing hand, the legs must revert to a passive state, being held ready to control any deviation of the quarter from the straight line. Within a short time the horse will stop immediately from the walk, but at first he may need to take a step or two before he can halt entirely *(Plate 55)*.

Relaxation
At the halt, practise immobility for a few seconds before moving off again and when this is easily obtained ask for the relaxation of the lower jaw. The hand works in the same way as on the long reins, the fingers vibrating gently on the required side, the other hand supporting.

It is possible that you will find the horse relaxes the jaw quite easily on one side, but resists on the other, for reasons already explained.

Usually it will be the right side to which he objects and we can overcome this, getting him to lower his head and relax the jaw, by walking him off on the left rein with the fingers closing slightly on this side as we proceed down the long side of the school. We will then vibrate the fingers on the right rein, at the same time using the right leg rather more strongly to push him up to the right rein, while maintaining the light contact on the left one. Gradually we shall get the required relaxation at walk and trot and also at the halt. Once this is achieved equally on both sides, a simultaneous action of the two hands will produce a full and equal relaxation of the jaw and a slight lowering of the head.

The Trot

Now we can introduce the same school figures at the trot, which is the most valuable of the schooling paces.

The trot, like the walk, varies in its form and is obtained by a slightly stronger action of both legs, first from the walk and later from the halt. In this last named case the horse is helped to differentiate between the two pressures involved by the rider applying the trot aid from the halt a little further to the rear than the momentary squeeze asking for walk from halt.

The usual pace will be the *ordinary* trot *(Plate 56)*, which is used when we are hacking. The horse moves forward without restraint, in light contact with the bit, with the hind feet covering the imprint of the fore feet. It is not a fast pace, about eight miles per hour, but it should be energetic and the drive from the quarters apparent. We then have the *collected* and *extended* trots. In the former *(Plate 57)* the head and neck will be raised in accordance with the greater engagement of the horse's hocks under his body and the subsequent movements to the rear of his centre of balance. The stride becomes shorter and higher, but displays great vigour. The horse becomes lighter in front as the line of balance takes an upward tilt from rear to front.

Such collection is, however, unnecessary in the sort of horse we wish to produce and again, as in the walk, if is sufficient if we can obtain a slight shortening from the ordinary trot.

The *extended* trot is the fastest variation within the trotting gait. From the ordinary trot the rider increases the driving force of his legs and, therefore, of the horse's quarters, and allows his hands to follow the forward and lengthening motion of the horse's head. A light contact is maintained, but the horse will seek stronger support from the bit. The overall result will be a lengthening of the stride from the shoulders, covering more ground but without elevation of the action. Neither a shortening of the horse nor his extension should be asked other than for short periods.

As far as the rider is concerned there are two variants of his position within the gait. He may either execute a *rising*, or posting, trot, that is he raises his seat *slightly* out of the saddle, using the knees as a pivot, so that he rests in the saddle on alternate beats only, or he may maintain a 'full seat', *sitting* trot, throughout the movement.

In the sitting trot the rider sits, as it were, with an open, relaxed seat absorbing the shock through a supple and erect back which *undulates* with the movement of the horse.

This is what should happen, that it rarely does is because the sitting trot is used too soon in the horse's training. It is easy enough to sit in balance, i.e. with the rider's weight over the centre of balance of the horse, when the horse is sufficiently balanced and his back muscles are properly developed. Until, however, this is achieved, and it will only be so when the horse is capable of a certain degree of collection within the pace, more harm than good will be done.

If the horse is not well-balanced the effect of the sitting trot will be to over-burden the quarters, as the rider moves *behind* the centre of balance, which will hinder impulsion and the engagement of the hind legs. The very opposite to what we are trying to achieve. If, in addition, the rider's hands are asking for a retraction of the head, the horse's back will hollow and his head will be pulled upwards to a degree where he will become 'over the bit', that is, where the nose is carried upwards and the neck bends upwards from its lower third.

The sitting trot is used in the *collected* pace as a further inducement to full engagement of the quarters and because it is the only position in which the rider can be *in balance* when the horse assumes this posture; if it is consistently employed, before the horse is ready, the result will be to produce a rough uneven pace and resistance throughout.

For short periods it is permissible to use this seat, which greatly facilitates the action of the legs, when we are asking for a shortening of the stride or for any transition in pace, but each short period must be followed by a longer one permitting complete relaxation.

I am quite convinced that much of the criticism levelled at horses and riders when executing even the simplest tests of training, or dressage if you like, has its roots in too great a use of the hand and too early an employment of the sitting trot.

There then remains the question of the diagonal when rising at the trot when executing a circle.

As might be expected there are three schools of thought. One says the rider should rise on the inside fore leg, and consequently the outside hind leg; that is, he is sitting as the inside hind leg advances and is therefore better positioned to use his own leg to drive this hind leg further forward i.e. on a circle to the right he rides the left diagonal and vice versa, a second says the opposite and a third could not care less which diagonal you use.

The first argument would seem to be more logical and is the one I endeavour to practise, but the important thing is to change the diagonal when the rein changes.

(Where the terms left rein and right rein are used they mean a circle to the left and right respectively. The use of 'inside' and 'outside', whether applied to the limbs of either horse or rider, or to the reins, means that limb or rein on the inside or the outside of the circle.)

Poles on the Ground

It is during the work at walk and trot that poles laid on the ground, followed later by cavalletti proper at the trot pace, can be introduced.

The poles, spaced at about four to five feet apart, according to the length of the individual animal's stride, and about six in number, are first laid out on the long side of the school. The horse is first asked to walk over these and later, when he accepts them as commonplace, to trot over them *(Plate 59)*.

He should be allowed to cross the poles with a free head and neck, but without losing the rhythm of his stride. Never allow him to go too fast or to rush at them, much less to attempt to jump them. The object is to help the horse in becoming supple, to improve his balance, to teach him to pick his feet up, which he will do once he has hit a pole or two, and to lay a sound foundation for jumping.

At the trot the rider can best assist the horse by following and encouraging the outward stretching of the head and neck with the hands and by leaning slightly forward with the seat a fraction off the saddle.

As the horse becomes proficient the poles can be laid around the circumference of a twenty metre circle, when the rider must insist upon the horse following the correct track, so that the poles are negotiated at the proper distance apart. The centre of the poles should lie on the required track and the work done equally on either rein. The use of the cavalletti in detail is dealt with later in this section.

The Canter

The canter is the most difficult pace for the horse to perform correctly and should not be attempted in the school until the work at walk and trot is established and the horse's balance at those paces is controlled and fluid.

As in the other paces the variation is between *ordinary*, *extended* and *collected*, but there is the additional complication of teaching the horse to strike off on the correct leg, i.e. inside foreleg leading.

The horse will have already learnt on the lunge, and perhaps in the long reins, how to canter on a circle on the correct lead, but without the burden of the rider to upset his balance. Now he must learn to canter a circle under the rider and to vary the speed, with the consequent shortening and lengthening of his body and the shifting of his centre of balance that this will demand.

He will have been prepared for the work during his ordinary hacking, first by being urged into a canter from a trot, to get him used to the pace, and then by the rider positioning him and applying the aids in such a way as to get him to lead off with one leg or the other.

Positioning the horse previous to a movement is all important in the canter, just as it is when we give notice to him of our intention to make a transition from one pace to the other.

The horse is best able to make the transition from trot to canter when he is slightly bent towards the direction of the movement. If, therefore, we want him to lead with the right foreleg, i.e. to circle to the right, the transition is best taught, initially, at a corner of a field. As the horse approaches the corner at the ordinary trot, on the right rein, the rider sits in the saddle, which he will always do when asking for any transition from one pace to another, and brings the horse to attention by pushing him up to the hands.

He then bends the head slightly to the right, to a point where the eye can just be seen, maintaining support on the left rein to prevent any deviation from the track. At the same time he sits slightly more strongly on the right seat bone and applies his right leg on the girth and the left leg behind the girth.

The supporting rein, apart from maintaining the track, when combined with the push from the rider's seat, prevents the horse altering the rhythm and accelerating.

The alteration in the distribution of the rider's weight is in accordance with the shift of the centre of balance towards the inside, caused by the flexion of the horse's body, and is practised in all circles or turns.

232

The degree to which the rider displaces his weight is dependent upon the degree of flexion of the horse and to some extent upon the speed, when the action of centrifugal force is involved. In time the rider will be able to feel the extent to which the aid should be used as he becomes more finely attuned to the horse's movements.

The seatbone on either side is weighted *not* by collapsing the inside hip, or by pushing forward the corresponding shoulder. The rider leans the upper part of his body sideways very slightly and *stretches* his inside leg. The most common fault is to exaggerate the sideways inclination, to the point of bending at the waist. When this occurs the rider will upset the balance of the horse, provoking a natural, defensive resistance in the opposite direction.

In the canter to the right, the inside, right, leg will be the stronger, as its purpose is to drive forward, and underneath the horse, the right hind leg. The other leg, in its supporting role, controls the bend and will prevent the outward movement of the quarters as well as assisting the movement forward.

How strong these aids should be, and how much stronger the inside than the outside leg, depends on the stage of training. As before, the lighter the aid the better. Should the horse lose his quarters to the outside, or have them moved too much to the inside, the movement is lost, and the fault lies with either too little or too much pressure from the outside leg.

The last factor in the canter aid sequence is the immediate yielding of the hands to allow the horse's head and neck to extent forward as he enters the first canter stride.

When we first commence the exercise in the open we shall, however, be content if the horse strikes off correctly, and we will not bother him by insisting on a perfection of movement which at present he is not capable of performing.

Beyond asking him to go calmly, occasionally to extend in response to the legs, seat and advancing hand, and to come back to the hand when it seeks to check the pace, we need not concern ourself in these early days with more advanced niceties.

If the horse, despite the aids, strikes off incorrectly, stop him and start again. If he displays excitement and attempts to go faster and faster, bring him to a halt, trot one or two small circles on either hand asking for variations in the pace and for one or two relaxations of the lower jaw to either rein, before trying once more. This has the effect of reminding him that obedience is expected and imposing a little discipline.

If, of course, the horse is fresh and mad keen for a gallop it is best to let him get the itch out of his heels, after which he will be in a more co-operative frame of mind.

In the more confined area of the school the horse is positioned in exactly the same way, but it is best to ask for only a few canter strides to start with and then to bring the horse back to the trot.

Once the horse strikes off easily on either rein and is able to canter round the school, varying the pace as he is asked, we can make the rectangle smaller by riding the inside track, which will also remove his reliance on the wall, and then attempt smaller circles, using half the school (i.e. a volte). If the horse finds these small circles difficult you have gone too fast and must do more suppling work at trot and in larger circles at the canter.

Gradually we can ask for the canter stride at increasing distances away from the supporting corner, until we can obtain the correct strike off in the centre of the long side of the school, or in the middle of the arena on either leg.

Quite early in the training at canter in the school the horse can be taught the canter from the walk, which is, in fact, easier for him, as the pattern of footfalls at the walk is more closely related to those of the canter than the footfalls of the trot.

Later he will be able to canter from halt, which is an excellent balancing exercise and should be practised as soon as the work at canter is performed smoothly, without loss of rhythm and with good balance.

The Half-Halt

The *half-halt*, within any gait, is generally understood to be a means of producing a downward transition, i.e. from canter to trot, trot to walk, or for checking the rhythm of a particular gait by shortening the horse. At the canter, particularly, it is also a balancing exercise asking for immediate displacement of the centre of balance to the rear.

In trot or canter the half-halt, used as a balancing exercise, is achieved by the rider sitting firmly in the saddle, using both legs actively behind the girth, to further engage the quarters, while effecting an immediate closing and raising of both hands.

The result is an immediate compression of the horse towards his centre without breaking the gait.

This, however, is not quite the case in the canter pace, when we ask for a transition to trot or walk, or for the full halt from canter.

234

These movements are more easily accomplished if the closing of the inside hand (i.e. right at the canter on the right lead and vice versa) fractionally precedes that of the outside hand, the former closing as the inside fore leg comes to the ground. These actions interrupt the sequence of the foot-falls and the moment of suspension is lost. The outside rein is in fact operating as the outside hind leg touches the ground when the halt will be easily achieved.

To shorten the stride at canter, checking the impulsion, the use of the inside hand, inclining the head towards the leading leg, will slightly close the inside shoulder thus restricting the extent of the stride. Conversely, the use of the outside hand to straighten the head gives greater freedom to the leading shoulder and extends the pace.

Change of Leg at the Canter

Figures of eight, serpentines, etc., will call for the horse to change the leading leg in accordance with the change of direction, and while the skilled horseman will in time obtain a flying change (i.e. a change of lead in the air—the rider changes the canter position at the moment immediately prior to suspension) the average rider will not find this movement necessary.

It will be sufficient, by means of the half-halt, to bring the horse back to trot for a few strides at the centre of the figure of eight, to reposition him and then to strike off with the opposite leg.

Should the horse be reluctant to strike into the canter stride within the school at the commencement of the schooling at this pace he will be encouraged to do so by using a cavalletto at its lowest height. The horse will at this stage be conversant with the poles on the ground and work over cavalletti. If three poles are laid out some six feet apart, followed after an interval of nine or ten feet by a cavalletto at the approach to the corner the horse will usually go into canter to jump the last obstacle.

While the turns and circles involved in school work assist in the improvement of balance and increase the suppleness of the horse their value is lost if they are not performed correctly (*Plates 58 and 60–62*). On the turns the horse's quarters must follow the track made by the forelegs, the horse giving the appearance of being flexed around the rider's inside leg, and being straightened by leg and hand when the turn is completed. Any falling in towards the centre at the turn must be opposed by the supporting leg, hand and weight aids, applied momentarily as the horse attempts to shorten the corner (*Fig. 31*).

235

Fig 31 Bend of the horse when moving on a true circle

The circles, too, must be absolutely true ones, obliging the horse to maintain a sustained bend with increased activity and engagement of the inside hind leg. A common fault is for the horse to slow down on entering the turn, which must be combated by increasingly active leg aids.

Turns at the Halt

The two turns from the halt are those executed on the forehand, when the quarters are moved round the pivot of the inside foreleg, and those on the quarters, when the forehand moves round the pivot of the inside hind leg. Both can either encompass a full turn (180 degrees), a half turn (90 degrees), or for practical purposes even less (*Figs. 32 and 33*).

The turn on the forehand teaches the horse obedience to the lateral action of the leg, after he has learnt the forward and retarding actions, and is usefully employed when opening a gate.

The turn is best taught, at first, in a corner of the school and in a turn to the right the horse would have the wall or fence upon his right side with the joining fence in front of him. In a turn to the right it is the head which moves in that direction, while the body goes to the left. The opposite being the case in a turn to the left.

The aids are simple, and when used in conjunction with the corner of the school are usually easily understood.

First the horse is brought to a balanced halt. The head is then inclined to the right to a point where half the eye can be seen by the rider. It is important that the horse should be pushed well up to his bit as this movement takes place, but not so much that he moves forward.

236

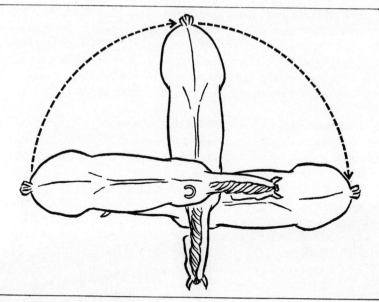

Fig 32 Turn on the forehand

Fig 33 Turn on the quarters

The right leg now acts a good hand's breadth behind the girth, if necessary reinforced by a tap from the long whip held in the right hand, to move the quarters, a step at a time, to the left. The left leg, behind the girth, controls the steps. The left rein supports the right, preventing any outward movement of the shoulder. One or two steps is enough to start with, and they can be increased in number as the horse gets the idea.

The horse is easily prepared for this turn by its being practised in the box, when the trainer, standing to the front of the horse, inclines his head with one hand and taps his flank with the whip in the other. The turn is never attempted while in movement.

The turn on the quarters is just as useful, as it is the prelude to the horse taking side steps (it, too, is used in opening a gate, or rather when moving away from it when it has been opened and closed).

Again the rider for a turn to the right inclines the horse's head in that direction, but at the same time he now weights his right seat-bone. The rein, supported by its companion, is now beginning the movement, while the left leg, a hand's width behind the girth, prevents the quarters moving outwards and controls the turn step by step. The right leg remains in support to prevent the movement of the inside hind which forms the pivot of the turn.

Again a corner of the school can be used with advantage and a tap on the shoulder with the whip, held in the left hand, can be helpful. In both cases the opposite aids apply for turns to the left.

The Rein-Back

I have always regarded this as an advanced movement, only capable of execution by a balanced, trained horse and a rider who has acquired a deep sympathy and understanding of the aids. It is, however, asked for at various riding club tests. I recently judged one where the horse was asked to rein-back between bales of straw which involved at least ten steps, and I have even seen it attempted at Pony Club rallies.

Not surprisingly these efforts, not understood by either horse or rider, result in a complete travesty of the movement and considerable discomfort for the horse.

The rein-back is a pace of two time with the impulsion initiated by the forelegs, and the legs are moved in diagonal pairs *(Plate 63)*.

As in all movements success depends upon correct pre-positioning of the horse. The rider must obtain, before asking for the rein-back, a balanced halt, with the horse in a shortened attitude, by pushing forward from back, seat and legs into the restraining hands. In theory, and in practise also, if the rider continues to apply these aids properly after the halt has been obtained the horse must move backwards, although an improper use of the aids with too great a pressure from leg and hand, might well result in the horse rearing.

However, the horse will better understand this if the rider urges him back through alternate closing pressures on either rein, persuading the corresponding foreleg and then the diagonal hind leg to move to the rear.

Just prior to the rein action the legs can become passive, being held in readiness to counteract any swinging off a straight line by the quarters, or any tendency to take more than one step at a time and run backwards.

Two steps are quite sufficient and three or four, clearly defined, are as much as will ever be required.

Side-Steps

For most riders this work appears to have no immediate practical purpose beyond developing the horse, making him supple and flexible and increasing the rider's sense of the aids. The side-steps, however, teach increased obedience to the leg and give to the rider a far greater degree of control over his horse. As such they are valuable and worth persevering with.

In its very advanced form perfection in work on two tracks is not easily achieved, but it is possible to obtain simple side-steps without too much difficulty.

In lateral movements the horse is bent in the direction of movement with the forehand always in advance of the quarters, the fore- and hind-legs always moving on two distinct tracks. The two principal movements are the *half-pass* and the *full-pass*. In the former the horse moves sideways and forwards, in the latter he moves sideways without advancing to his front. In both cases the outside legs are crossed over and pass in front of the inside ones with the horse's head flexed in the direction he is going.

The turns at the halt will have already prepared the animal for side-steps and we can go a stage further by teaching him, for very short periods only, the suppling movement known as *shoulder-in (Fig. 34)*.

This is best started in the trot pace, immediately after leaving a corner of the school, before the horse has quite straightened out of the turn. The right rein (if on a circle to the right) directs the head,

Fig 34 Shoulder-in

asking for a flexion on that side and in that direction, and is supported by the left hand. Too much rein at this stage closes the shoulder and obviates the movement.

The hand has now moved the forehand over towards the inside track of the school and the right leg, behind the girth, urges the horse forward and engages the right hind leg. The outside rein, however, must support this action, otherwise the horse just goes into another turn. Equally important is the action of the left leg, behind the girth, which encourages and controls the apparent bend of the horse round its opposite number. If impulsion begins to fail the outside leg must move forward on to the girth to assist its partner and provoke increased forward movement. The rider slightly stretches his inside leg to place a little more weight on the inside seat bone.

The horse should now be bent away from the direction in which he is going, and the forehand should describe a track inside that of the quarters.

This is a difficult exercise for the horse and, again, one or two steps are enough on either rein and should be immediately followed by allowing the horse to move on in a straight line, freely and vigorously.

The half-pass itself is most easily introduced away from the school when riding along a quiet road or track. If one is on the left side and wishes to move to the right, the head is again inclined in that direction very slightly, the right seat bone is weighted, the left leg, a hand's width behind the girth pushes the quarters across, while the right limits their movement and maintains the impulsion if necessary. The supporting left hand can assist further by being pressed against the wither intermittently to encourage the lateral movement of the shoulder.

240

61 Riding a circle with the horse correctly bent in the direction of the movement

62 Miss Marie Stokes executing a turn to the right on the quarters

63 The rein back in two time

This is easily achieved under these circumstances and leads to obtaining the same steps, and possibly one or two at the full pass later on if they are required.

The practical application of the side steps, apart from the obvious advantages, can be exploited when riding in traffic or when asking the horse to pass some unusual and frightening object.

Being able to position the horse and to obtain the attention necessary for one or two steps at the shoulder-in is an ideal way of imposing a little discipline and of distracting his mind from the object in question.

Bits Used in Schooling

All the work described can be carried out in a snaffle, with or without the assistance of a drop-noseband, but the change from snaffle to bit and bradoon should not be unduly delayed.

The more sophisticated bridle can be introduced once the school movements can be executed at a canter. Not only does the bit and bradoon assist the flexions, but it encourages a raising of the head and is less likely to have the horse hanging on it, as can happen with the snaffle alone.

The majority of horses go very kindly in this combination, provided that the rider is sufficiently skilled to use it judiciously.

I do not advise the intermediate use of a Pelham, or its use at all, unless the horse's mouth is so constructed as to make the double bridle a permanent impossibility.

The Use of the Cavalletti

Throughout the horse's training use will have to made of poles and cavalletti and it is as well to study the value of the latter in some detail.

The principle benefits of cavalletti are directed towards the training of horse and rider for jumping, which requires a horse to be balanced, supple, calm and obedient and their use is, therefore, complementary at all points in the schooling programme and for all purposes. It can, therefore, be introduced at an early stage.

Once the horse has been lunged over obstacles and accepts jumping as part of his ordinary routine he progresses, under the saddle, to the crossing of spaced poles on the ground, which can then be followed by the cavalletti.

The cavalletti are first laid out at their lowest height between four and a half and five feet (which can later be increased to six feet) apart and the horse is made to approach at the trot out of a large circle. He should cross the cavalletti maintaining impulsion and rhythm, rounding his back and being allowed to stretch out the head and neck.

If one can run to five cavalletti, three should be used initially and then increased to five when the horse negotiates them calmly on either rein *(Plates 64, 65 and 66)*.

A diagram *(Fig. 35)* is given of the suggested dimensions of a cavalletto and it is important that all five should be of the same length and have the same height variations so that by placing them together, or on top of each other, a variety of fences and spreads can be made. The horse is now ready for the introduction of a small jump, which is made by moving cavalletto four up to cavaletto five.

You may now, exactly as before, trot over the first three and still in the same pace jump the last element.

If one has a sufficiency of cavalletti numerous variations in the distance can be made, but it is important not to exceed the lowest height at the trot, otherwise a hop develops which obviates the benefit of the exercise.

Cavalletti work can also be carried out at the canter, starting again with poles, but now spaced twenty feet apart, so that the horse is not tempted to jump two in one stride. Once this is established cavalletti can be substituted at the ten inch height, which can be gradually raised to first fifteen inches, and then to nineteen inches, and the distance apart reduced to ten feet.

Balance is further improved by altering the distances, in multiples of ten between the cavalletti and introducing cavalletti at different heights and spreads.

Finally, and I am indebted to Lt.-Col. J. D. Crawford, F.B.H.S., Director of the Porlock Vale School, for this more advanced exercise, cavalletti can be used on a twenty metre circle after the horse has became accustomed to poles on the ground on a circle of the same diameter. *(Fig. 35* shows the correct distances at trot and canter.)

The canter sequence of cavalletti should be approached on the arc of the circle at the trot with the horse correctly bent, quarters following the track of the forehand, and going into the first stride of the canter to jump the first cavalletto. Still maintaining the bend he should complete the remainder at canter and then quietly be brought back to trot.

Should the horse become excited at any stage always go back to lower cavalletti at a slower pace.

During all work on the circle the rider must insist on the correct bend being kept and the track being maintained.

Fig 35 Construction and arrangement of cavalletti

(*a*) Dimensions
(*b*) The first arrangement of cavalletti so that the final element becomes a jump
(*c*) A further variation in the arrangement of cavalletti
(*d*) (*Left*) The disposition of cavalletti on a 20 metre circle for the trot pace
  (*Right*) for the canter stride

These exercises are of enormous value but, as in all things, progress must be gradual, the horse never being hurried into a more advanced lesson until he has fully assimilated the previous ones.

Jumping

Success at jumping comes from work on the flat, which produces a calm, obedient, supple and balanced horse. If the work described so far has been carried out properly the jumping of small obstacles will be a natural progression of the training, which the horse will accept with confidence and equanimity.

Show-jumping is a specialist art, demanding a horse of exceptional talent, but any reasonably schooled horse should have no difficulty in jumping fences of up to four feet.

Initially the fences in the jumping area should be very low, not more than two feet six inches in height or four feet in width. They should, however, be numerous and varied; this does not mean the outlay of large sums of expensive fences, but rather an outlay of ingenuity and powers of improvisation.

Poles, some of them coloured, sheep hurdles, straw bales, oil drums, brush and railway sleepers can all be pressed into service to make jumps posing different problems of approach and execution. Spread fences are necessary, pyramids, staircases and, if possible, some sort of bank and ditch that involves jumping from one level to another, as well as an in and out *(Plates 67 and 68)*.

Practise jumping these fences, altering their layout as often as possible, until the horse can pop over from any angle without excitement.

Gradually the height and spread can be increased and also the distances between fences. As a general rule, allowing for the horse's stride varying between eight and twenty feet, the following distances are applicable between individual fences:

1 stride	22 feet
2 stride	35 feet
3 stride	47 feet
4 stride	59 feet
5 stride	71 feet and so on

Fences, however, should not be placed at these distances before the horse and rider have accumulated a little experience. Proper education on the flat, whereby the horse can be shortened and lengthened at will and jumps out of a state of balance will, however, go a long way towards solving problems of distance and approach.

244

Allow always at least two feet more space between fences for upright jumps and shorten the distances in front of inclined fences.

However confidently the horse jumps at home he needs outside experience (when to start with he may not go so freely) at small shows, club hunter trials etc., and the more he has the better and the safer jumper he will become.

The Horse Jumping

If we have observed the horse jumping loose we will have noted three main phases, *the take-off, the flight* and *the landing* and we will have realised that his centre of balance alters considerably during the jump.

In the *take-off*, depending in extent upon the height of the fence and the speed at which it is approached, the hind legs are brought under the body, the horse then pushes his forehand off the ground with the forelegs and raises his head and neck; the quarters, hind legs and the back then thrust upwards suddenly, and as the horse enters the *flight* phase he stretches out his head and neck. He then folds the legs and describes an arc over the obstacle with rounded back and with head and neck outstretched.

As he comes in to make the *landing* the horse stretches out his forelegs, placing first one and then the other on the ground. In order at this moment to adjust his balance and decrease the weight carried by the forehand, he then raises head and neck. Then the hind legs come to the ground, behind the forefeet, the head is accordingly lowered and the horse enters into the canter stride.

We shall also see that an upright obstacle is approached at a relatively slow speed and in this case the quarters are very strongly engaged, whereas the forehand is not so much so. The opposite is the case when the obstacle is low and wide. The speed is greater and it is the forehand which is used to a greater extent.

Individual horses, according to their conformation, will also have discovered at which speed they jump best and it is a wise rider who takes mental note of this characteristic.

Position of the Rider

From the foregoing it will be seen that the rider, if he is to allow his horse to jump to the best advantage, should understand the motions made by the horse if he is to remain in balance throughout the jump, and if he is not to interfere with its effectiveness by disturbing the important balancing motions of the head.

To do so his approach to the fence will be made in his jumping position, i.e. body inclined forward, seat clear of the saddle, legs drawn slightly back in a driving position and heels well down to secure the lower half of the body. On a free jumping horse, the position over a low fence remains the same throughout the three phases of the jump, the rider's hands only moving forward to follow the movement of the head.

Should the horse not be going forward freely then the rider will have to use the addional power of his back and seat to drive him on and must then sit in the saddle, timing the forward inclination of his body with the exact moment of take-off, which is not quite so easy at first. It becomes even more difficult when the fence has to be approached slowly. The usual mistake is for the rider to be left behind the movement, when one can but slip the reins and grasp a neckstrap, or even the mane to avoid making matters worse by denying the horse freedom of his head. It is possible to get in advance of the movement, when the upward thrust of the forehand will be correspondingly overweighted and the success of the whole jump will be in jeopardy.

Practise, however, makes perfect, or nearly so, and if the rider jumps as many low fences as possible he will very quickly get the feel of the jump and be able to adjust his balance accordingly. To overjump the horse would, of course, be foolish, but if the fences are *low* there is no reason why twenty to thirty should not be jumped in the course of an hour or more's schooling.

During the jump, as we have seen, non-interference by the hand is of paramount importance. This will not be achieved unless the rider holds his hands the width of the bit apart and moves them forward, below the withers, to follow the motion of the head. Initially, it is better to push the hands too far forward and lose contact, rather than to risk interference with the mouth. If contact is lost it should be replaced as soon as possible, as the horse uses the rein for additional support on landing *(Plates 69 and 70)*.

Work on the lunge over low fences with the rider concentrating on the jumping position, head straight and looking beyond the obstacle, back straight, knees pointed and low, lower leg flat and heel down, is the best basis for a jumping seat.

During the landing, particularly over fences involving a steep descent, the rider will find that to remain in balance his trunk must incline more to the vertical and will be less forward. The landing shock, however, will be absorbed and the rider able to resume his jumping seat if the knee remains bent and the leg position unaltered.

246

While schooling, either on the flat or over fences, is a fascinating occupation it has the same effect upon horses as an overdose of work had upon Jack, who, as will be remembered, became a dull boy.

It is a means to an end—not an end in itself. If we are to keep the horse interested and happy he requires periods of relaxation between the times spent on school work.

Allow him days when he does nothing more than hack gently through the countryside. Take him out to rallies, enter him in hunter trials and take him hunting as much as you can. After all, these are things that are the reason for schooling, and he will learn more during a day's hunting than during a week in the school.

CHILDREN'S PONIES

The training of ponies and their riders presents a far larger problem than can be explained adequately here, but in general, will follow the same principles, even if it does not encompass the same movements.

Once the pony is obedient on the lunge, and paces have been established and the pony is jumping freely, one has an opportunity of strengthening and correcting the rider's seat by working in this medium, and it will be easy to teach both pony and rider the aids.

The aids can be explained to the child and then she can be asked to apply them at a certain point in the school. If the pony is slow to react, or does not understand, the child's aid is reinforced with the spoken, and already learnt, command, *trot, canter* or *whoa*, as it may be. Very quickly the pony will learn what the action of his rider's legs and hands mean and will obey them without the additional incentive of the voice.

Jumping starts again over poles on the ground and progresses to cavalletti and finally, to small, wingless fences of every possible variety.

If the child begins jumping in the school, and on the lunge, reins can be dispensed with, a neck-strap being provided as a help to balance. The pony, who has learnt to jump freely without the rider, will not have his confidence impaired by the fear of having his mouth hurt.

Later the child can jump with reins fastened to the rear rings of the cavesson and, finally, when the seat is secure, with reins to the bit. If the pony has been properly educated on the lunge and a little further simple schooling has been done on long reins the child should experience little difficulty in learning control.

Progressive training of the pony obviates the senseless leg thumping, stick whacking and mouth pulling which weakens the rider's security and is too often seen. Badly schooled ponies only encourage rough handling by the child and can hardly contribute to his or her enjoyment.

It is unlikely that one will ever find what current advertisements term a 'bomb-proof' pony, but certainly something approaching this description is conducive to peace of mind. For this reason the introduction into school work of the 'nuisance game' is both useful and great fun for everybody.

I start by walking with the pony down the drive or round the yard while numerous small helpers bounce balls, under supervision, at a respectable distance. Gradually larger balls are used and the bouncers come nearer to the pony until eventually balls and running children are ignored. The same thing is done with flapping towels, handkerchiefs and newspapers. Finally the pony will work loose in the school to the accompaniment of transistor radios and clapping children, whilst balls can be bounced off his back and flags waved round his head without his batting an eyelid.

Ponies, and horses too, often have an aversion to water and nothing is more annoying, or for a child more unseating, than the animal who dances round every puddle in the road.

The aversion is easily enough overcome by standing the pony, securely tethered, in a yard with a hay net to keep him occupied. A hosepipe can then be turned on at the other end of the yard and left running. Eventually, and inevitably, the pony will be standing in a pool of water which has crept up on him so gradually that he will have hardly noticed it. Water can then be splashed on his legs and it will not be long before he permits with equanimity the hosepipe to be played over his limbs without raising objections.

Traffic is, of course, a major concern in these days and again it pays to walk a pony round farm machinery and to accustom him to moving vehicles in his own surroundings. Once he accepts these he can be taken out on the roads on the inside of a steady horse until he is ready to face traffic on his own. In this regard it is better, and safer, to let the pony face traffic on his own when going back to his stable. He is far less likely to play up at this stage of the ride than when going out.

It should not be too difficult to teach children road sense when riding and to demand their ponies' attention in much the same manner as that already described. Similarly, it is not too much to expect parents to teach, by precept and example, ordinary good manners. The majority of car and lorry-drivers will slow down on meeting a pony or horse. Their courtesy should be acknowledged.

Ponies and children soon become bored and too much serious school

248

64 ABOVE: *Trotting over low cavalletti in line*

65 BELOW: *Trotting over cavalletti set on a 20 metre circle*

66 Cantering over a cavalletti placed on a circle

67 Jumping in an easily constructed jumping-lane

68 Jumping from one height to another

69 A perfect position of horse and rider over a small spread fence

70 The same excellent position over a higher fence

work does them no good. School work is best absorbed when disguised as a game. Bending poles are useful in this respect as are the various Pony Club mounted games. In addition let the pony and child go hacking for the fun of it as much as possible, without worrying about head positions, heels down, elbows in and all the rest of it.

If one has a suitable horse to accompany the child work out a little cross-country jolly involving the jumping of a low log, a small ditch and other little obstacles.

A gallop across a field of stubble, particularly if it is at all undulating, does more for balance and confidence than a month of school exercises.

Lastly, a warning. It is all too easy for a situation to arise where a pony becomes over-reliant on its adult trainer and as a result plays the fool when removed from his immediate control.

The adult should be a background 'father figure'. His job is to start the pony on the right lines, then teach the child how to continue with the training. Once he has laid the foundations of a successful partnership he must then relegate himself to the role of adviser to both sides.

List of Suggested Reading

Chamberlin, H. D., *Training Hunters, Jumpers and Hacks*, Van Nostrand Reinhold Co. Ltd.

Codrington, W. S., *Know Your Horse*, J. A. Allen & Co. Ltd.

Hartley Edwards, E., *Saddlery*, J. A. Allen & Co. Ltd.

Holyoake, J., *Improving Your Pony*, Faber & Faber Ltd.

Holyoake, J., *Improving Your Riding*, Faber & Faber Ltd.

Hope, C. E. G., *Tackle Riding This Way*, Stanley Paul & Co. Ltd.

Hope, C. E. G., and Harris, C., *Riding Techniques in Pictures*, J. A. Allen & Co. Ltd.

Littauer, V. S., *Development of Modern Riding*, J. A. Allen & Co. Ltd.

Sophian, T. J., *Horses and the Law*, J. A. Allen & Co. Ltd.

Talbot-Ponsonby, J. A., *Harmony in Horsemanship*, J. A. Allen & Co. Ltd.

Wynmalen, H., *Equitation*, J. A. Allen & Co. Ltd.

Wynmalen, H., *Dressage*, Museum Press Ltd.

Wynmalen, H., *Horse Breeding and Stud Management*, J. A. Allen & Co. Ltd.

Acknowledgments

My acknowledgment and very grateful thanks are due to: Raymond Brooks-Ward for his kindness in writing the foreword to this book; John Nestle for his help in taking and supplying photographs and for generously placing his extensive library of negatives at my disposal; R. H. Smythe for passages quoted; Daphne Poupart who interpreted, typed and collated my manuscript and my wife and Phyllis Hinton for their constant help and encouragement.

Index